MONTH-BY-MONTH GARDENING

NEW YORK & NEW JERSEY

Quarto is the authority on a wide range of topics.
Quarto educates, entertains and enriches the lives of our readers—enthusiasts and lovers of hands-on living.
www.quartoknows.com

First published in 2016 by Cool Springs Press, an imprint of Quarto Publishing Group USA Inc.,
400 First Avenue North, Suite 400, Minneapolis, MN 55401 USA.
Telephone: (612) 344-8100 Fax: (612) 344-8692

quartoknows.com
Visit our blogs at quartoknows.com

Cool Springs Press titles are also available at discounts in bulk quantity for industrial or sales-promotional use. For details contact the Special Sales Manager at Quarto Publishing Group USA Inc., 400 First Avenue North, Suite 400, Minneapolis, MN 55401 USA.

10 9 8 7 6 5 4 3 2 1

ISBN: 978-1-59186-657-2

Library of Congress Cataloging-in-Publication Data
Names: Copsey, Kate, author.
Title: New York & New Jersey month-by-month gardening : what to do each month to have a beautiful garden all year / Kate Copsey.
Description: Minneapolis, MN : Cool Springs Press, 2016. | Includes index.
Identifiers: LCCN 2016002530 | ISBN 9781591866572 (sc)
Subjects: LCSH: Gardening--New York (State) | Gardening--New Jersey.
Classification: LCC SB453.2.N7 C67 2016 | DDC 635.09747--dc23
LC record available at http://lccn.loc.gov/2016002530

Acquiring Editor: Billie Brownell
Project Manager: Alyssa Bluhm
Art Director: Cindy Samargia Laun
Layout: Danielle Smith-Boldt

Printed in China

MONTH-BY-MONTH GARDENING

NEW YORK & NEW JERSEY

What to Do Each Month to Have a Beautiful Garden All Year

KATE COPSEY

Cool Springs Press
Home and Garden Experts™

MINNEAPOLIS, MINNESOTA

Dedication

To my husband, Clive, who made this book possible. I couldn't do this without your support!

Acknowledgments

Books take many hours to write and involve many people along the way, without whom we would never cross the finish line. My thanks go to all those who shared their thoughts, talents, and expertise along the way.

Thanks to all the Extension Offices in both New York State and New Jersey that happily answered my questions, and to the Master Gardeners in both states who were happy to chat and give advice regarding conditions in their area. Questions were also answered by many of the gardeners who tend the magnificent public gardens in our states.

Thanks as well to all the gardeners and garden writers who were enthusiastic about this project and spurred me on when I needed it. I want to particularly thank Beth Botts and Jo Ellen Meyers Sharp, who have both written similar books.

I also want to acknowledge my husband, Clive, who tended to the practical side of keeping our garden neat and cared for while I was busy writing. His employment is also responsible for me being able to appreciate the gardening conditions in Buffalo and Albany, New York, as well our current New Jersey location.

I am especially grateful to Billie Brownell, who is a great editor to work with, and to the people at Cool Springs Press who coordinated the project.

Contents

Introduction

Realtors talk about curb appeal, a large part of which comes from a beautiful combination of neatly trimmed lawns, well-trimmed shrubs, and healthy containers with colorful annuals. Homeowners are aware of how important the landscape is but often are not sure what to do about it. Doing things at the right time and planning how to deal with upcoming problems—or preferably, heading off those issues—is what this book is about.

Gardeners in New York and New Jersey deal with cold, wet winters and warm, often wet summers. We deal with droughts and hot weather, not to mention hurricanes and blizzards that rearrange the landscape in just a few hours. There are some short-season summer gardeners and some seaside gardeners, but most of us garden in the moderate Zones of 5, 6, or 7, which give us a *huge* plant palette from which to choose.

The gardeners in New York bordering the Great Lakes are well aware of the effect that the lakes have on climate. Cold arctic air that picks up moisture from Lake Erie dumps it right on the Buffalo region, producing huge snowfalls that often break tree limbs; but that same snow also helps protect the perennials from cold air.

Coastal areas of Long Island and the Jersey Shore also have to deal with water issues, as storms heading up the eastern seaboard have the Atlantic Ocean to provide moisture for snowfall totals. The good news is that most coastal air masses that come from the south are warmer, so rain is more frequent than snow. Less snowpack, however, creates colder conditions for near-the-surface crowns of perennials, which bear the brunt of cold air temperatures.

So from the Atlantic Coast to the Great Lakes, we gardeners have challenges, but every gardener I have come across in this region is happy, enthusiastic, and always optimistic about the next season. We all learn from our gardening neighbors, who are always happy to share tips on getting plants to survive. Gardening and caring for your landscape should be fun, so relax and enjoy the time that you spend in the garden.

OUR GEOGRAPHY

Geographically, our area includes the mountain ranges of the Appalachian, Adirondack, and Blue Ridge Mountains, which dominate both states on the east end, while Lakes Erie and Ontario dominate the western and northern counties. Coastal southern areas of New Jersey are part of the lowlands that extend from the mountain ranges to the Atlantic Coast. Northern counties of New York State that extend from the mountains down to the St. Lawrence Seaway are renowned for their heavy winter snows.

Both New Jersey's and New York's growing conditions vary from coastal sands on the eastern side of both states to the very rocky Appalachian Mountain range, where growing is close to impossible. A few western and northern areas of New York State have to deal with remnant lake clay that is often underlaid with layers of yellow- or red-tinted soils that indicate higher levels of aluminum and iron.

The mountains, lakes, and ocean all play major roles in this region's climate. In general, the high mountain areas get much colder than lowland areas while coastal lowlands are slightly warmer than interior areas. The western Great Lakes areas are known for long, heavy winter snow, sometimes starting as early as October, and like many coastal areas, they are slow to warm up in spring. The area gets plenty of moisture in winter and spring, while summers are warm and often dry.

Looking at the zone maps for New Jersey and New York, you will note that the high mountain areas of northern New York are Zone 3 or 4, while coastal areas are a much milder Zone 7 or even 8.

IT STARTS WITH SOIL

Not only can soils be different in our different regions, but soils in your specific garden may change from place to place. Soils have two components: chemical and physical.

CHEMICAL COMPONENTS OF SOIL

One of the key elements to successful growing is soil pH. A soil's pH is measured on a range from 0 (the most acidic) to 14 (alkaline) with 7 as neutral. Most plants like a slightly acidic soil ranging between 5.5 and 6.5 and require a specific pH in order to be able to absorb nutrients. Soil that is too acidic or too alkaline results in poor growth and failing plants. For example, azaleas, rhododendrons, and blueberries like the soil to be slightly more acidic, while lavender prefers a slightly "sweeter" soil, which is more alkaline. Grasses prefer a pH that is close to neutral (7.0). A soil test will let you know your soil's pH and indicate if the reading is within tolerance for the plants you want to grow. See Plan in March.

TO CORRECT SOIL PH

To raise pH on lawns, lime is usually applied in the form of calcium carbonate. Dolomite or dolomitic lime is calcium-magnesium carbonate. Typically, dolomitic fertilizers have about 40 to 60 percent lime and 10 to 20 percent magnesium. Magnesium is rarely missing from soils, but if your soil test indicates a low magnesium level (most common in sandy soils) then use the dolomitic lime preparation. As with all chemicals, an excess of magnesium causes as many problems as a deficit, so don't opt for dolomitic fertilizers unless you know that your magnesium is low. Use a granular or hydrated form rather than a ground or liquid form, which can "burn" plants by excess nitrogen. Wood ashes can be used, as they too contain a high calcium component. Lime is routinely applied to lawns across our area, but if the pH is close to neutral it can do more harm than good. Always make sure you do a soil test on the lawn to establish exactly how much, if any, lime you need to use.

To lower pH, sulfur is most commonly used, although many peat mosses are also acidic and thus can help lower the pH. It is not common on the East Coast to have a soil that is too alkaline, so lowering the pH is usually reserved for specific plants and can be done with commercial products such as those formulated for azaleas and blueberries.

PHYSICAL COMPONENTS OF SOIL

Soils are created from rocks that have been subjected to weathering by waves, water, and environmental actions over millennia. The resulting medium is composed of three types of particles that range from clay, through silt, to sand and rocks. At the **clay** end, tiny particles form an almost solid mass that holds water above it.

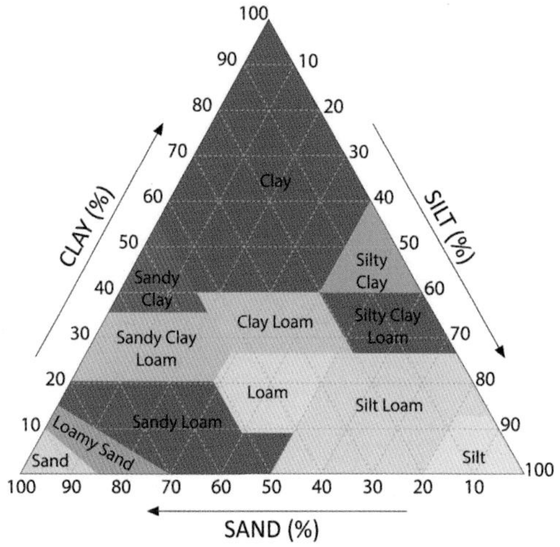

Each side of the soil triangle represents a different soil particle. Find the percentage of each present in your soil. The point inside the triangle where all three percentages intersect is the texture of your soil.

At the other end of the scale is **beach sand**, which is made of large, angular particles that allow water and nutrients to drain through almost immediately.

Silt, which is in the middle of the spectrum, is able to hold nutrients but also drains well.

Loam, which is a good mix of about 45 percent silt, 45 percent sand, and a small amount of clay, is regarded as perfect garden soil. Very few gardens have a perfect loam, but terms like sandy loam or clay loam indicate that the overall soils are fine for growing plants.

Both these conditions, and all soil mixtures along the spectrum, can be helped by adding organic matter such as mulch and compost. Organic matter breaks apart the clay into smaller particles and helps bind sand particles together. The only soil that organic matter cannot help is rocky soil. Here, raised beds are probably the best solution.

WHEN IS THE SOIL READY TO PLANT

March and April are transition months when weather, not the calendar, dictates what can be done in the garden. Warm spring breezes and plants arriving in the stores are likely to bring on an attack of spring fever everywhere, but experienced gardeners learn to take their cue from what is flowering outdoors, in nature, rather than what is flowering in the nursery.

Cool, damp springs are not conducive to warming the soil in the garden; neither is melting snow ponding on top of still-frozen subsoil. Waiting for the right time to get started in the garden makes a big difference to the survival of newly planted shrubs and perennials.

A quick test is to take a small handful of soil and roll it with your hands into a ball. If you can make a perfect ball with the soil, then it is probably still too wet to plant. If it falls apart when you open your hand, then it is dry enough.

Soil temperature is equally important. If you felt a real chill when you picked up some soil, then it is too cold to plant. Summer vegetables need not just unfrozen soil, but *warm* soil, which does not usually arrive until about two weeks after our average last frost date.

WAYS TO HASTEN THE PLANTING PROCESS

A *short-summer garden* is a term used in regions where the frost extends past the end of May and fall frosts start as early as September. In these areas, gardeners are at risk in some years of not being able to get tomatoes into the ground early enough to harvest ripe fruit before the end of August. Try any of these methods if you want to hurry the process.

1. A black plastic sheet over a planting bed helps to magnify the heat of an early spring sun and warms the bed sooner.

If your soil is wet enough to hold its shape when you roll it into a ball, it's too wet to plant.

HERE'S HOW

TO FIND PERCENTAGES OF SOIL COMPONENTS

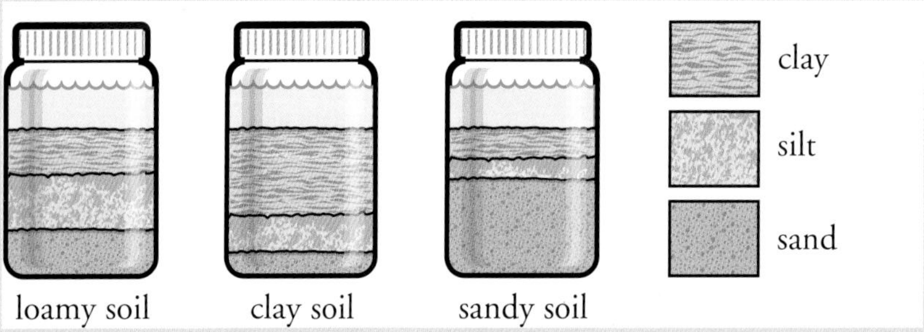

The ideal soil texture is loam, which contains balanced amounts of clay, silt, and sand particles.

To determine the percentages you have of each soil type, conduct a little test. What you'll have at the end of the experiment is a range of particles in layers—fine clay particles on top of heavier, angular sands, and pebbles at the bottom. Organic matter will be seen as a thin layer of black at the top. Soils are divided into four groups according to what you see: sand, sandy loam, silty loam, and clay. A loam is the optimum result. Your goal as a gardener is to increase the organic matter in all your garden beds. With knowledge of your soil type and pH you can correct any issues and *then* think about planting. Here's how to test:

1. Take a clear glass jar, such as a pickle jar, jelly jar, or preserves jar.
2. Dig into the garden bed's soil and take about a cupful of soil from the site.
3. Add water to the jar so that it reaches about an inch above the surface of the soil.
4. Cover the jar with a lid.
5. Shake vigorously for several minutes to make a slurry of soil and water.
6. Place the jar on a flat surface and leave for several hours, even overnight.

You will see that the garden soil has settled into several distinct layers: the heavy grains of sand will be at the bottom, gray or red silts in the middle, and a pale layer of clay on top. Dark brown materials at the top or in the mix are an indication of biological levels—usually small insects, compost, or decaying roots. Ideally, the middle section should be the largest area, with very little clay on the surface.

2. Frost cloths (such as Reemay or other brands) keep cold breezes off plants, which allows them to be planted a little earlier.

3. Using raised beds or building "hills" in the soil allows raised areas to drain quickly and warm up quicker. The idea is that the sun strikes the sides of the "hill" and thus warms the soil in this small raised area faster.

4. Using a cloche (usually glass) over a row of young plants helps keep them warm on cool but sunny days. A single cloche helps individual pepper or tomato plants stay warmer, particularly overnight. A less formal and less expensive option is the little "walls of water" system that has a circle of hollow tubes that are filled with water and help retain heat overnight.

5. Planting grafted vegetables is another option. The vigorous roots on the grafted plant promote rapid growth and earlier fruit set on tomatoes and other summer crops. Rootstocks may also be more resistant to virus problems.

Leave plant tags in the soil to help you remember what you planted and how to treat it.

Getting the right plant for the right place creates an easy-to-care-for landscape and healthy plants. Apart from good soil, plants need light and water. All landscape plans should incorporate soil preparation as well as correct plant choices.

PLAN

Sun patterns around a house vary with the seasons, but a general guide is to consider the north side of the home to be full shade, where hostas and shade-loving plants would grow, and the east side of a home gets morning sun until about noon, and is considered part sun. It is not sufficiently strong to support sun-loving plants. The south side of a house gets afternoon sun, plants that enjoy full-sun conditions are happiest here. Finally, the west side has mid-afternoon to evening sun and can usually support full-sun conditions for plants too. A general guide is that full-sun plants need more than six hours of direct sunlight *not* including anything before 10 a.m. A part-sun condition is between four to six hours of sunlight after 10 a.m. Shade plants enjoy up to about two hours of direct sun, and they will be happy on a few hours of morning sun too. Remember that the height of your house will affect the depth of north-side shade, and that deciduous trees create unique, filtered shade that some plants like, especially in spring.

Keep in mind that the borderline plants that we grow in Zone 7, such as crape myrtles, reflect how-to-grow information that is often written by Southern universities in areas where the afternoon sun is very intense and hot. Those instructions suggest that full *or* part-sun conditions are perfect for these plants. However, we get less heat from the sun, so plant crape myrtles in full sun. Conversely, plants such as Little Honey hydrangeas that have pale yellow leaves, which burn horribly in the southern afternoon sun, can tolerate a lot more northern sun and can be looked at as full or part-sun plants for most of us.

When you plan a new garden, whether the whole landscape or a little mailbox garden, getting the right plants is important. Research plants and shrubs to see how large they get and how much sun they require. At the nursery or home-improvement center, this information should all be noted on the plant tag. Increasingly, you will find a QR code on the tag. Use your smartphone to "decode" the QR code.

For shrubs and trees, the tag should inform you about the plant's mature height, width, and speed of growth. Keep these dimensions in mind when you site the plant in the landscape. An American holly, destined to grow to about 20 feet high and planted under the eave of a home just inches away from the exterior wall, will ultimately fail.

BASIC DESIGN TRICKS

As with anything artistic, landscape design is a reflection of the homeowner's tastes. But here are a few things that make a landscape appealing:

- Perennials look great in masses of similar plants and coordinating colors. Use the color wheel to see which colors work well together. Red next to pink is not the best combination, but pink and blue work well together.
- On long borders, vary the height of the perennials or put a few shrubs into the border to create interest.
- Bulbs look better in groups than as singles planted in a row (the "soldier" effect).
- Balance taller shrubs and trees on one side of the landscape with several shorter ones on the other side.

A well-planned border incorporates plants of different colors and sizes for a more dramatic visual effect.

PLANT

A well-planted tree, shrub, or perennial lasts a lot longer than a poorly planted one. Whether you are planting an annual, perennial, shrub, or tree, the first rule is to have the right-sized hole. Most plants are sold in a container with their roots underneath the soil. The level that a plant will sit in your garden should be the same as the level it sits in this nursery container. When planting grafted items, the graft should be just *above* the soil level.

The latest recommendation is to dig a hole to about the same size as the container, then upend the plant so that you can figure out its final size. If there is a bunch of loose soil and roots at the bottom of the container, it means your hole doesn't need to be quite as deep.

Plants that are in containers that decompose, including balled-and-burlapped shrubs and trees, are subject to the same size hole as described above. Some annuals in peat containers sit lower than the top of their pots, so you need to tear the top of the peat pot down when planted. (An exposed container edge dries quickly and wicks moisture away from the root zone.) Also break apart the base of the peat pot to free the roots at the bottom. Perennials also are sold in peat containers and other "plant-in-the-pot" options. Not all of those containers decompose in a timely manner. Either remove the plant from the container or make several slits down the sides so that the perennial's roots can break out. Burlap comes in many grades and not all of them decompose quickly. Untie any burlap wrapping and remove as much as you can before planting.

Seeds, unless noted otherwise, should be covered by soil at about the same depth as the seed's size. For example, tiny lettuce seeds need a scant covering of soil while a larger marigold seed needs about ¼ inch of soil covering. Space the seeds at the correct distance apart when planting directly into the soil outside—the seed package will provide the spacing recommendation.

Keep soil moist, but not wet, until seeds germinate and while they are growing. Do not let the soil dry out before they establish a good root system and show vigorous growth.

CARE

A low-maintenance landscape is not the same as a no-maintenance one! Some timely chores need

Container annuals require a bit more care but allow intensive planting in smaller spaces.

to be addressed throughout the growing season. Generally, trees are the least trouble once they are planted, settled, and growing. Problems arrive from poor drainage, weather stress, and insect damage, but overall, healthy trees are easy to maintain. Shrubs, too, are generally easy to look after. Pruning in winter or spring keeps shrubs tidy but is not always needed on an annual basis.

The flower garden takes a little more care. Perennials get overly large sometimes and need to be divided, and aggressive perennials need to be contained as soon as they break out of their allotted area. Perennials that produce runners have to be restrained, as do those whose flowers set viable seed. Take care of these enthusiastic growers by dividing often, digging out runners that sprout away from the main plant, and weeding out volunteer seedlings.

Annuals are definitely higher maintenance. Because they require more water and fertilizer, they are best "managed" when grouped together. Annuals benefit from having the dead blooms removed regularly, and they need to be removed after the first killing frost of the year. But the beauty of annuals is that they can fill in gaps where perennials or shrubs have not yet filled in. They look great in masses as well as under trees, around the mailbox, or on a slope.

Containers are also high maintenance, but the right plants in the container look stunning in the landscape. Placed by the door or hanging on lampposts along the driveway, they greet our guests; around a pool or on the patio and deck, they add color to what could be just drab concrete. The main task with containers is keeping them watered in hot summers.

WATER

Lawns, trees, shrubs, and flowers all need different amounts of water. Newly planted plants obviously need more water than established plants until they are settled, and smaller annuals need more water than trees. Good watering practices aim for getting the right amount of water to the lawn or garden *without wasting any*. Aim to optimize your time by grouping things that need more water together in the landscape.

Annuals, containers, and the vegetable patch all require daily watering. Placing a container with annuals at the end of your 500-foot driveway makes no sense unless you have a water spigot close by. Placing them in small groups around the landscape also requires moving the hose around, while grouping them together in one or two areas requires less watering time.

Timers and irrigation make watering the garden a low-maintenance task. With a little thought to how you set these systems up, your landscape, and even your containers, can be watered before you get up each day or even while you are on vacation.

FERTILIZE

We expect a lot from our landscape and that means adding a little boost from fertilizers to help keep it at its peak. Correct fertilizing is essential for containers, lawns, and the vegetable garden, but even shrubs and perennials benefit from an annual dose of good-quality compost or fertilizer. Fertilizer comes in myriad types and packaging (liquid, granular, and so forth) and getting the right one is sometimes difficult. In this section we help you decide what and when to fertilize.

Plants require nitrogen (N), phosphorus (P), and potassium (K) for good growth. These three, also known as NPK, are the major components of most fertilizers. All fertilizer bags and bottles display the NPK numbers on the front of the package. The numbers are in a ratio form, so 20:10:5 indicates that 20 percent of the total volume of the container is nitrogen, 10 percent is phosphorus, and 5 percent is potassium. (For more about NPK, see Fertilize in March.) Plants also need a number of minor nutrients; those are found sometimes in general fertilizers and sometime in preparations specific to that plant type, such as azaleas, tomatoes, or roses. Compost is derived from various plant materials and provides many minor nutrients. Alfalfa and seaweed composts are popular components in organic and vegetarian fertilizer mixes that contain a host of minerals,

Ready to Use

FERTIFEED

All Purpose Plant Food

12-4-8

FertiFeed Ready To Use All-Purpose Plant Food

Net Weight 4lb. 12oz. (2.15kg)

GUARANTEED ANALYSIS

Total Nitrogen (N)	12%
12.0% Urea Nitrogen	
Available Phosphate (P_2O_5)	4%
Soluable Potash (K2O)	8%
Manganese (Mn)	0.05%
0.05% Chelated Manganese (Mn)	
Zinc (Zn)	0.05%
0.05% Chelated Zinc (Zn)	
Inert Ingredients	76%

Information regarding the contents and levels of metals in this product is available on the Internet at http://www.regulatory-info-sc.com.

KEEP OUT OF REACH OF CHILDREN

Look to the fertilizer label to reveal its intended use for different plants and its nitrogen, phosphorus, and potassium analysis.

both major and minor. (Vegetarian fertilizers are those made without animal-based products.)

There are also chemical, natural, and organic labels on fertilizers. Chemical fertilizers get their prime nutrient—nitrogen—from urea; they tend to show a much higher NPK number on the bag than organic fertilizers do. Natural and organic fertilizers are based more on compost from chickens or mushrooms, or are derived from a single source such as alfalfa, and have a much lower nitrogen content.

Always read the application rate for fertilizer before you apply it. Excess lawn fertilizer not only causes lots of upward growth, but it can also "burn" the lawn due to excessive nitrogen. Accidental overfertilizing can be remedied by watering immediately and thoroughly to rinse the chemical into the soil and below the grass roots. Of course, this means you are now sluicing the fertilizer into the road where it enters storm drains, or into the underlying aquifers layers, which in turn take the nitrogen-rich fertilizer into the waterways where it can damage wildlife. Bottom line is to read the label carefully and apply in accordance with those instructions.

PROBLEM-SOLVE

Gardens are alive with insect life, above and below the soil. The landscape also plays host to butterflies and insects, some of which are not as welcome. Butterflies are attractive, but their caterpillar stage can be destructive.

Some insects prefer a specific plant like your azaleas, while others are less fussy and feast on the nearest perennial or shrubs. Japanese beetles are one of the less-choosy pests that visit *everything* in the gardens in July.

Good pest control depends on knowing what the insect is and deciding on your level of tolerable damage. Controlling the pest should begin with the least toxic method, which can be as simple as rinsing off plants with a hose to dislodge aphids. Encouraging birds to feed in the garden also helps control caterpillars and other small insects. Getting to know the insects is important because some of them are the good guys that eat other insects, and some are the bad guys that eat our cabbages. There

Deer have become acclimated to suburban life and are no longer just a threat to rural gardens.

Make sure you leave some space in your garden where you can sit and enjoy the beauty of your work.

are some insects, like the curious praying mantis, that eat both good and bad insects.

Other landscape damage is caused by large animals. Rabbits and deer destroy landscape plants across our whole region, and they browse in urban areas as well as suburban and rural areas. There are many powders and liquids that deter these pests, and there are some shrubs and plants that are not on the "favorites list" of deer (see Problem Solve in April for a list). Although one of the beauties of living in rural areas is that you get to see animals and birds in the wild, that does come with a downside too. A turkey taking a dust bath among your petunias could be just one of many trials. Dogs and cats will help keep some rabbits from your garden, but unless they are out loose at night, they'll miss most of them.

You can sometimes control animals and insects with fences and netting, but there is very little you can do about environmental issues like a long, damp spring. Weather-related fungal issues and mold problems are common from spring to fall. As with insects, getting to know the disease is an important step in learning how to control it. Cedar apple rust, for instance, is *not* an issue if you control it either on the apple or the cedar tree, because the organism needs to infect both trees to complete its life cycle. Continual rain in midsummer can create the right environment for late tomato wilts. If you are in an area where this is a problem, growing a tomato that is resistant to the wilt eases the problem.

As with other areas of pest control, look for the least-toxic remedy. Horticultural oils and soaps smother little insects and scale, while pyrethrum, which comes from the chrysanthemum, is a low-toxicity pesticide. Fungus and molds also have organically based remedies that should be your first choice.

It is also a good idea to meet other gardeners and roam public gardens and your neighborhood to see what others are doing and be inspired by them. Get to know your local Extension office where you can get your questions answered, and check the university websites for advice on all aspects of landscape care for New York or New Jersey. Both Cornell and Rutgers have a wealth of information online to help you.

I encourage you to spend time in the garden, and balance the work with time spent sitting down to enjoy it. Too often we'll spend all summer finding (and fixing) problems only to forget to enjoy the view. In winter, feel free to dream a little about the upcoming season in the garden.

Even in cities, where there is less space to garden, window boxes, stairs, balconies, and rooftops can still hold small but beautiful gardens.

HOW TO GET THE MOST OUT OF THIS BOOK

New York & New Jersey Month-by-Month Gardening aims to take the "scary" out of caring for your landscape. You will find clear and pertinent information about caring for each part of the landscape each month. I'll give you step-by-step instructions to correctly plant or apply fertilizer, but I'll also give you some great projects to do during those long winter days. Keep this book handy and make notes on your calendar as well as in the book about things that you want to remember.

This book shows how to care for your *whole* landscape. Each month features different tasks that need to be done and then divides that into the individual plant groups (some of which you'll have in your own landscape, and some that you may not; just ignore what doesn't apply). For each month, you'll get details for planning the garden, what should be planted that month, general care of the landscape, when and how to water, what to fertilize and how much, and how to solve problems that arrive in every landscape.

The major plant groups you will learn about are:

Annuals: Annuals play a vital role in many parts of the landscape, from filling containers to lightening up a dark corner of the landscape. Most annuals are planted after the last frost date for the area.

Bulbs: Most people think of bulbs as being daffodils and other spring-blooming flowers. But there are also summer- and fall-blooming bulbs. Many are perennial, and I include bulbs, corms, tubers, and rhizomes in this group.

Edibles: Herbs and vegetables are a common part of the landscape, and they can include annuals, biennials, perennials, or shrubs. Growing just a few edibles in the gardens adds fresh vegetables to your dinner table or lunchbox. Most common vegetables are easy to grow as well.

Houseplants & Containers: Our gardens are covered in snow for a good portion of most winters, and houseplants keep our green fingers busy. Containers decorate our front doors and patios, and they allow us to grow citrus and other tropical plants (which can be overwintered indoors).

Lawns: Almost every home has at least some lawn, and knowing how to care for it is important for curb appeal and for its overall health.

Perennials: What is perennial for some gardeners is considered an annual for others. It may depend on where you live (hardiness zone). Picking the right perennial for your landscape and giving it the correct amount of sun and care is important for its survival from one year to the next.

Shrubs & Roses: Shrubs are an investment in the landscape. They bloom and give visual interest most of the year. Picking the right shrub and planting it in the right place is a good way to get many years of service from your shrubs, whether they are foundation plantings or in a border. Roses are generally smaller than a lot of other shrubs but once they are planted in the right place—full sun—they give many years of satisfaction in the garden as well as blooms for your indoor vases.

Trees: Knowing how to pick the right tree for your property is just as important as how to care for it. Trees can be big investments, so they need to be chosen, sited, and planted properly.

Vines & Groundcovers: Vines decorate our fences and groundcovers, and they grow where other things cannot, such as on slopes and under trees. Vines are used for vertical height in a garden and can also be used in topiary.

USDA HARDINESS ZONES

Our region has nine cold hardiness zones that dictate which plants are likely to survive our winters. They range from Zone 7b all the way to Zone 3, with the majority of the population dealing with Zone 5 or 6 conditions. This does, however, mean that those living in the warmer areas will sometimes do things a month earlier in spring than suggested in this book, and those in colder areas may do things a little later. Check this hardiness map to see what zone you are in and use the book, along with your local conditions, to adjust your timing.

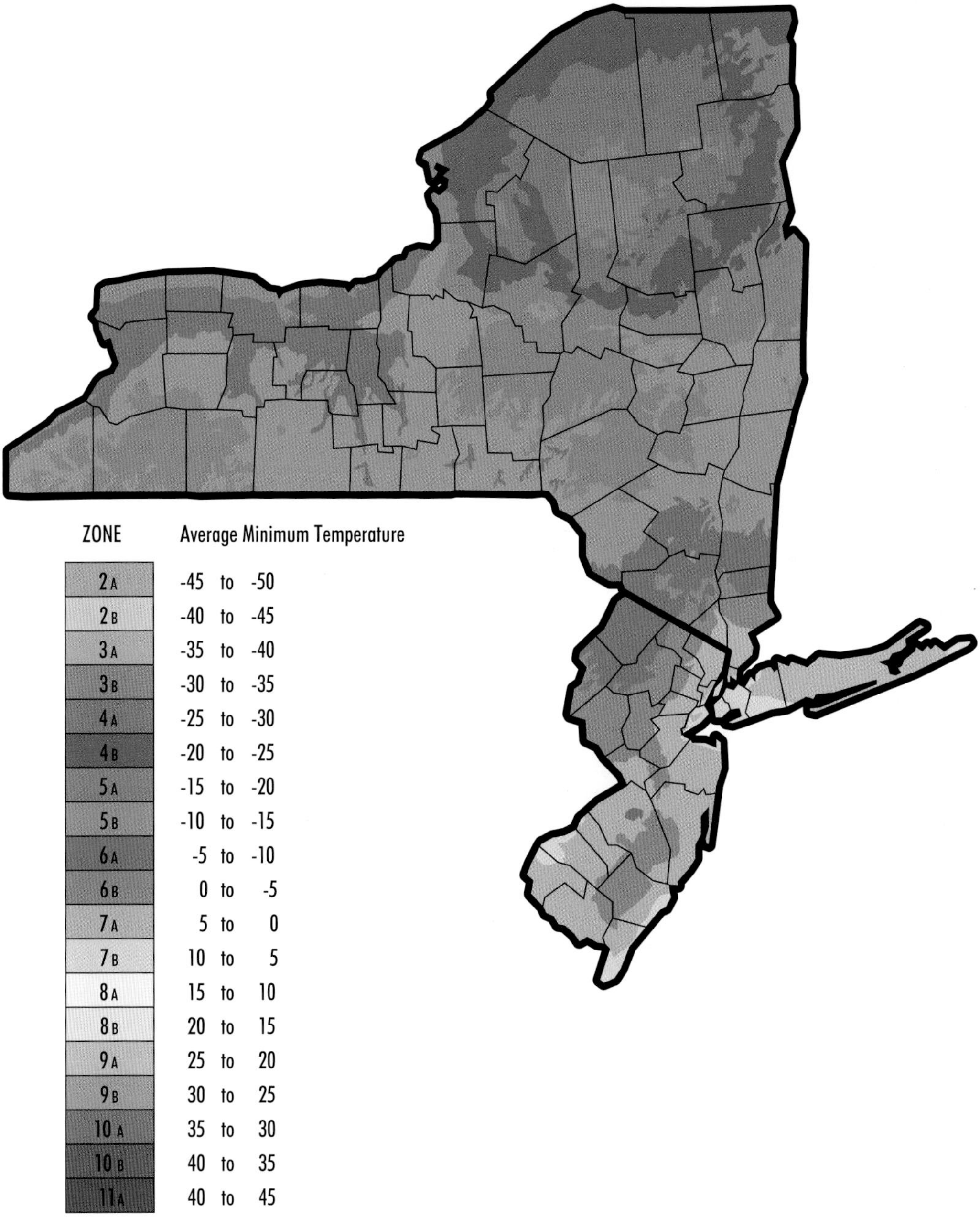

ZONE	Average Minimum Temperature
2A	-45 to -50
2B	-40 to -45
3A	-35 to -40
3B	-30 to -35
4A	-25 to -30
4B	-20 to -25
5A	-15 to -20
5B	-10 to -15
6A	-5 to -10
6B	0 to -5
7A	5 to 0
7B	10 to 5
8A	15 to 10
8B	20 to 15
9A	25 to 20
9B	30 to 25
10A	35 to 30
10B	40 to 35
11A	40 to 45

January

January gives us a fresh start—a time for plans and resolutions. It is also one of the coldest months of the year, with snowfall more common than rain, making it a perfect time to plan for the upcoming garden year.

You will need to check indoor plants for insect problems, but you'll have time to tackle a new indoor project like making a little terrarium, or even try your hand at winter-sowing hardy annuals.

Libraries and bookstores are full of great garden books and magazines meant to inspire you and help you visualize a new garden space. A great place to start the redesign is to stand at a window or sit in your favorite chair and look out at the barren, snow-covered landscape. What would you like to see? Stems left from last year's perennials make interesting features in the garden, as do conifer branches under a new snowfall. How about your den and dining area—do they need to have a more interesting vista to look at? While you are browsing books, check out some fascinating mysteries with gardeners as the sleuths, such as Mary Wingate, Anthony Eglin, and Susan Wittig Albert—these are great to curl up with on snowy nights.

When you are looking at your landscape, take note of sunshine patterns. Sunny winter areas tend to melt the snow first, making those spots the perfect space to plant early-blooming spring bulbs.

In January, you will also have new garden catalogs to browse and tempt you with the latest offerings. January is a great time to dream a little and visualize what a clump of giant alliums will look like at the back of your perennials or how that new zucchini will taste in summer. If you have gardening friends nearby, invite them to a seed party where everyone buys one or two packets of seeds. On delivery, you split the packets between everyone. Seed packets have anywhere from 25 to 2,000 seeds, so this is a great way to get a garden full of plants without having to buy packets of all the different seeds.

PLAN

January is a good month to plan what you are going to do in the garden this year. Look at pictures that you took last year and note if something is missing—a gap where a plant died or disappeared behind a more aggressive perennial. Sometimes our lives change and the challenge of caring for a large vegetable garden or annuals is too much. You might want to expand a particular garden—put in a cutting garden or expand the space for growing vegetables. January is the time to resolve to turn these thoughts into action. If you are living with deer roaming the neighborhood, eating everything you plant, research what deer don't like and plan to adjust your garden choices to those plants and shrubs that deer generally leave alone (see Problem-Solve in April for plants that deer don't like to eat).

Many seeds last more than one year—take a few minutes to sort them out and see what you have before you order more.

ANNUALS

Check the new varieties in your favorite catalog and order early before they sell out. Pick annuals for attractive containers and focal points. Cool-weather annuals including poppies and violas like to be planted very early in the year and flower before summer heat arrives, so order these in January.

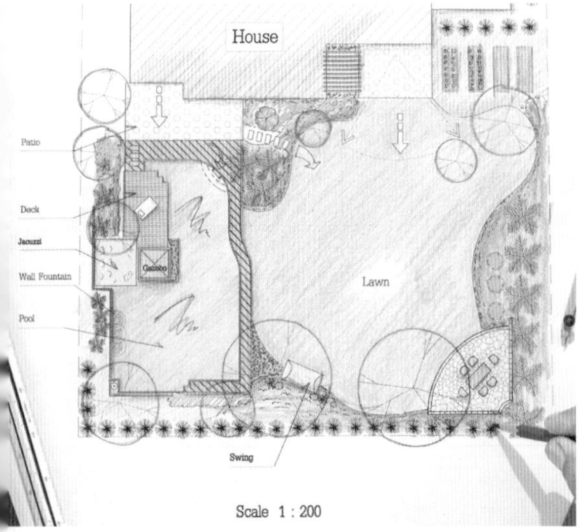

Draw a garden design on paper using one of the many landscape programs, or sketch the area using circles for trees and shrubs.

Spend a morning checking any seed you saved from last year. Make a list of the great varieties that you have on-hand before ordering more.

Annuals create a colorful contrast to evergreen shrubs and are perfect under trees where grass cannot grow. When looking through catalogs and planning where to use specific annuals, check how much sun they need, how tall they get, and opt for disease-resistant varieties if they're available.

BULBS

Summer bulbs are a boon to any garden—they are dependable and easy to take care of. Order some perennial summer bulbs to fit into your garden. Colorful alliums and old-fashioned lilies are hardy to Zone 3. Bulbs can be grown in containers; large, 24-inch containers can accommodate one or two full-sized dahlias; use some of the dwarf dahlias in containers that can sit on your deck railing.

EDIBLES

January is a perfect time to plan the vegetable garden. If this is your first vegetable garden, keep the plan simple and grow just a few things that you enjoy eating. Experienced vegetable gardeners should ask, "What worked last year and what didn't? Would expanding the garden correct those issues?" There are numerous new varieties to try each year, and even those with limited growing space can find varieties that grow well in containers.

Did you have seeds left over from last year? If so, many of them, like tomatoes and peppers, are still good for this year. Bring out all your seeds and discard any empty packets or any packets that look damp. Saving seeds from one year to the next is a great way to save money and reduce how many seeds you have to buy this year. Seeds of most common vegetables—like those in the cabbage group (*Brassica*), tomatoes, and peppers—are viable for four or five years.

If a short growing season is preventing your tomatoes from ripening, try some of the newer grafted plants. Grafted varieties have a strong root system that encourages fast, healthy growth as well as increased disease resistance. The root is grafted to a variety of tomato that you want to grow. Heirlooms and many favorite tomatoes are available on grafted roots. Tomatoes, peppers, and eggplants are all available as grafts.

One of the most frustrating parts of vegetable gardening is when "nature" harvests crops before you do. Deer, rabbits, groundhogs, birds, and squirrels cause chaos in the garden. Some of these are easier to exclude than others. January is a good time to plan your battle and arm your garden with fencing and repellants.

LAWNS

While most lawns are snow covered or dormant, plan for maintenance. A lawn service is great to help keep the lawn looking good, but other times, it is easy to do this yourself. Compare costs and

HERE'S HOW

TO DEAL WITH ANIMAL PROBLEMS

Birds: Most songbirds enjoy berries; a simple netting to cover raspberries and blueberries is an effective deterrent. Do not put netting over the crop until the flowers are set and the berries are growing. Remove after the crop is harvested. Larger birds such as turkeys are a little trickier to repel; their damage to young crops is more from picking at seed or having a dust bath in dry soil. Covering the bed with netting held above the bed can help.

Deer: Deer browse on green growth and shrubs or tree stems year-round; deer repellants, 10-foot fencing, and/or double fencing are needed for complete protection. Double fencing places a second, shorter fence about 2 feet inside a 4- or 5-foot fence. Deer like a solid landing, and their depth assessment is not good, so they tend to avoid jumping over both fences. Raised beds just inside a fence also work to confuse deer.

Groundhogs: From spring through fall, groundhogs are a problem. A persistent groundhog can climb 6-foot-high fences and dig underneath them too. Groundhogs dig under and uproot plants and spend a lot of time eating leaves and tasting vegetables. The best defense against climbing groundhogs is to install a standard 1-inch chicken wire fence that's 5 feet high and curved out at the top. To combat digging, bury a fence 2 feet in the ground. Lay chicken wire in a trench 3 feet (wide) × 2 feet (deep) so it reaches all the way to the buried fence.

Rabbits: Rabbits arrive in early spring, sometimes with their family, but rabbits don't jump very high: a 2-foot-tall perimeter chicken wire fence will keep them out.

Squirrels: Seen at bird feeders year-round, squirrels are not inhibited by high fences, but they do not burrow underneath fences. They nibble at seeds and crops alike and bury hoards of nuts in soft garden soil. Covering beds with netting or a cage of chicken wire is sufficient to repel them. Having some domestic animals that chase them is useful too (here, kitty kitty).

time and decide what works best for you. Signing up early for a whole season of lawn care sometimes saves money.

HOUSEPLANTS & CONTAINERS

Plan summer containers this month. Entrances are great places to put a container to greet guests. With careful planning you can design containers that are in bloom from early spring to late fall.

PERENNIALS

Perennials are the easy-care part of a garden. They need dividing every few years though, so plan where to put the divisions. At plant swaps in spring, common in April or May, you can give away a few divisions and come home with some new plants too.

Most perennials flower for two to four weeks but many continue from late spring to frost. Coneflowers, gaillardia, and threadleaf coreopsis (*Coreopsis verticillata*) are just a few long-blooming perennials. Swaths of similar colors look good in the garden, broken up with some accent plants or shrubs. Perennials range in height from spring-blooming groundcover phlox up to Joe pye weed, which ranges from 4 to 6 feet tall. Plan perennial gardens with taller plants at the back, lots of mid-sized plants in the middle, and a few low-growing plants along the edge. Vary heights within the bed and use clumps of plants rather than just singles.

To design a new perennial garden, first figure out the size and location, plus its overall shape. Curving lines look less formal than straight lines, and border beds are meant to be viewed from one side, whereas beds in the center of your lawn will be looked at from all sides. Transfer these measurements to a sketchpad and draw a scaled image of the intended garden—there are some landscape design programs that you could use for this as well.

Research plants to find those hardy for your area; learn how tall and wide they get, plus their bloom time. In a design plan, draw circles for the plants using larger circles to indicate a tree, fountainlike circles for small shrubs or grasses, and circles for groups of plants. Add color to the design to represent the flower colors and to see which plants work well together.

Allow plenty of room for larger perennials and less for smaller and more passive growers. Adjust the design to fit all the plants into the area and save it until you visit the nursery.

To get an idea of what your garden will look like in each season, make the basic plan and outline it in heavy pencil. Take three sheets of tracing paper and label them spring, summer, and fall, plus add an extra one for winter if you want winter interest. Lay each sheet over the basic design and trace the outline of the garden, then the perennials that will be in bloom that season. For spring, you'll probably add some bulbs, and for fall you could add an extra space for a perennial grass or chrysanthemum. Finalize the design to incorporate these extra seasonal ideas.

SHRUBS & ROSES

Shrubs in general are called the "furniture" in a garden, and carefully planned gardens include shrubs that bloom at various times, giving something to admire the whole season. Dark-leaved shrubs or shrubs with large leaves contrast well with annuals. Like everything else in the garden, make sure that your roses have full sun and that all your shrubs have the right conditions to thrive too. Check out which shrubs do well in sun and those that prefer shade in Plan in April.

Add some shrubs that provide winter interest to the landscape. Oak leaf hydrangeas have an attractive peeling bark as well as large white blooms in summer. Witch hazels start to bloom in late January, which adds much-needed color to winter gardens as well as lovely burnt orange foliage in fall. Some shrubs have multiseason appeal, which is perfect when you have limited space. Blueberries, for instance, put out a pretty white flower in spring, followed by edible berries in summer, and stunning red fall color.

New roses on the market include many that can be grown in small areas and some with great scent.

Roses make good blooms for indoor arrangements and come in a range of colors from white through yellows to deep red. There are climbing roses that can cover a fence or an arbor.

When picking a rose, you have the choice of single-blooming, multiple-blooming, climbing, and carpet roses, as well as the traditional shrub roses. Climbing roses grow 8 to 15 feet in one year which makes them perfect for arbors and other sturdy structures. At the other end of the spectrum are the carpet roses that spread out rather then up. These short, mounding roses are used on slopes as well as borders for perennial beds. Some names that you might come across when researching roses are:

Damask: Old rose, single bloom period

Tea: Repeat flowering, scented

Bourbon: Scented, tall, good on obelisk structures

Noisette: Climbing roses

Hybrid Tea: Single bloom, good for vases, high maintenance

Polyantha: Repeat bloom, low maintenance

David Austin: Modern hybrid roses, generally little or no scent

TREES

Trees provide color in spring and fall as well as shade in summer. Large, mature trees need professional care if they are near or high enough to fall onto a house, have limbs hanging over a roof, or are deteriorating with age. While there are no leaves on the branches, it is easy to see if there are any dangerous branches. Plan on getting these very large trees inspected by an arborist if there is any danger of falling limbs.

Not all trees get tall enough to be a hazard to the home. Small redbuds, star magnolias, and crape myrtles all fit well into urban and suburban plots. For a list of other small trees, see May.

By January, the Christmas tree is moving out of the house. Instead of throwing it away, recycle it. Some big stores accept trees (without any ornaments or decorations) and in return they deliver a truckload of mulch. Others give you a small tree to plant. A tree can also be recycled to use as mulch. Saw the limbs off the tree and lay them onto perennial beds to give a little extra winter protection.

VINES & GROUNDCOVERS

Each spring, gardeners are surprised by how much a particular groundcover has spread. Sometimes this is great; others times you might need to plan on removing some or limiting where it wanders.

Vines can be annual or perennials, and there are many woody varieties too. Annual vines are good for fast cover and look good on decks and gazebos where you sit in summer. Some fun annual vines include cup and saucer vine (*Cobaea scandens*), black-eyed Susan vine (*Thunbergia alata*), and cardinal vine (*Ipomoea*). Perennial vines such as climbing hydrangea (*Hydrangea anomala* subsp. *petiolaris*) and sweet pea vine (*Lathyrus latifolius*) are good for covering fences and climbing up a trellis. More woody vines like climbing roses, trumpet vine, and wisteria need a sturdy support but work well for pagodas and arbors.

PLANT

January is not the best time to plant, but there are some things that you can plant. Winter-sown seeds are put outside (see below), and perennials as well as some very early vegetables can be started indoors. The key to success with starting seedlings in January is to provide good light, which usually means supplementing with a grow light. Plant in February has more details on successfully growing seedlings.

ANNUALS

Winter-sown annuals are a great way to start seeds without having to use window space for seedlings. The idea is that nature self-seeds many annuals (including edibles, which are mostly annuals). Consider the stray tomato plant found growing in

Cosmos is just one of the many hardy annuals that sows its own seed each fall.

the compost pile. These seeds manage to survive winter and grow when the weather turns mild. Gardeners across the country have capitalized on this and sow some seeds in milk cartons, which sit outside in the snow until nature tells the seeds it's time to germinate. Cut a milk carton (plastic or cardboard) almost in two so that you have a hinged top. Punch a few holes in the base for drainage and leave the cap/lid off so that the carton gets moisture but is also vented. Fill the base with a damp potting mix and then seeds. Secure the hinged top to the base with duct tape, label, and put outside in the snow. Come spring, the container warms up and seeds germinate in their own little greenhouse.

Good seeds to winter sow are lupines, delphiniums, bachelor buttons, larkspur, and cosmos.

BULBS

Amaryllis bulbs are a popular holiday gift. Plant a bulb in a container not much larger than the bulb itself (usually the box includes a container). Fill the container's bottom with potting mix and settle the bulb so that its tip and shoulders are above the soil (about half the bulb).

Any spring-flowering bulbs that you didn't get around to planting last fall can be planted in a container indoors and forced into bloom early. Spring bulbs do need several weeks of cold temperatures below 50°F, so if your bulbs were stored in a cold garage they will be fine. If they were stored in a cool basement, put them in a refrigerator for about two months before planting in a container. Containers can be planted and left outside in the cold until mid-February or March when they are brought indoors to bloom. If you want to force blooms with less fuss, plan to order some warm-climate bulbs next fall. These southern bulbs only need minimal cold storage—two to three weeks or even less.

Bulbs that need chilling are tulips, some daffodils, hyacinths, and crocus. Do not chill amaryllis, freesia, or tender daffodils (paperwhites).

EDIBLES

Some of the earliest vegetables can be started in January in warmer areas. Kale, spinach, and Swiss

Amaryllis are great winter bulbs—plant them now for late winter color.

HERE'S HOW

TO GROW HYDROPONICALLY

Hydroponics has been around a long time, but only recently has it been available through mainstream retailers. The idea is that you use a liquid to nourish plants rather than a soil medium. Plant roots need air and nutrients, which is accomplished by running a small pump in the system, which then circulates the water with air through the system.

Small plants or seeds are placed in a soilless medium (fibers or sponges are common). The sponge is placed into the system and the pump started. The air-enriched water bubbles over the seeds and as a seedling grows, its roots extend down into the water. Specially formulated liquids are added to the water so that the roots can grow and support the plant. After a few weeks, the lettuce or herbs are ready to harvest. For some systems you need to provide a light source; others include a light.

Other leafy vegetables can be grown in these systems and even patio tomatoes can be grown.

These systems are small and convenient for most kitchens and are a great way to garden in January as well as to get some fresh vegetables.

chard are planted outside in very early spring, so starting seed in late January is a good way to get a jump on the early vegetable garden. Cold-tolerant kales, onions, and lettuce can also be winter sown (see Annuals for more detail). Lettuce and salad greens can be sown in containers for an indoor garden.

HOUSEPLANTS & CONTAINERS

Terrariums were popular in Victorian parlors, and they have made a comeback in modern homes. They are small, contained, low maintenance, and create a talking point as well. For more indoor container gardens, see December.

HERE'S HOW

TO PLANT A TERRARIUM

Occasional watering, monitoring, and venting are needed to keep a terrarium healthy, but with biweekly attention, they are a low-maintenance part of the houseplant routine.

1. Start with a clean glass container. A terrarium is (usually) a covered system like a small greenhouse or bell jar on a base.
2. Select the plants that you want in the container: one focal-point plant or a group of small plants works.
3. Pick a soil base that suits the plants (such as cactus mix for cacti or succulents) or a general-purpose potting mix.
4. Line the terrarium's bottom with a thin layer of activated charcoal over the layer of pebbles to filter the water.
5. Add a layer of sphagnum moss.
6. Add the potting mix, deep enough to cover the roots of the plants.
7. Plant your terrarium with the chosen plants.
8. Sprinkle the plants with water to settle them into the soil.
9. Close the terrarium's lid.
10. Locate the terrarium in a bright, but not direct, light and enjoy.

PERENNIALS

Some perennials take a long time to germinate and grow very slowly the first year, so starting them 10 to 12 weeks before they can be transplanted is a good idea. Research perennial seeds carefully. Some, such as coneflowers, need to be kept refrigerated for a few weeks to imitate winter before you put them into a garden.

CARE

Outside, most of our area is covered with snow and plants are dormant. If the cold weather breaks in late January, you will have a chance to go outside and see how things are doing. While snow looks great on conifers and other evergreen shrubs, it also protects the roots and crowns of herbaceous perennials and keeps them dormant regardless of the cold arctic masses that come down each winter. The arrival of polar air is more problematic for warmer areas where there is less than 2 inches of snow to protect plants. In these areas, make sure that your plants are still covered with a 2- to 3-inch layer of mulch. Always shovel snow onto the flower beds and shrubs to increase the protection, but keep deicing salts applied to driveways and walks away from the beds where it can contaminate the soil and damage the plants.

■ *Cannas are not winter hardy for most of us and are stored inside in a cool, dry place for winter.*

BULBS

Did you store cannas or dahlias in the basement last fall? Check those to make sure they're still healthy and dormant. Remove any that are soft and decaying.

EDIBLES

If you've started seeds, make sure that they are kept watered and under a strong light. If you are growing herbs or edibles hydroponically, check the nutrient level. As seedlings grow they need more nutrients in the water to stay healthy.

HOUSEPLANTS & CONTAINERS

Now that the holiday season is over, it is a good idea to wipe the leaves of indoor plants, particularly those with large leaves. Dust lands on the leaf surfaces and can block the tiny holes that allow them to photosynthesize and absorb sunlight, and it generally causes leaves to lose their shine. A damp teabag, a room-temperature spray in the sink, or even a trip to the shower are ways to freshen up houseplants.

If you want to keep a holiday poinsettia for another year, trim the plant down to within 4 inches of the soil surface and water sparingly. It will put out new leaves, and by spring it'll be ready to plant into the garden. Next fall you'll bring it inside to condition it and force it into bloom for the holidays. (See Plant in September.)

PERENNIALS

In areas where the snow melts regularly and you can see the garden bed, check perennials to make sure their roots are not being heaved out of the ground where they'd be vulnerable to cold temperatures. Resettle the plant in the ground or, if the ground is frozen, find some mulch or pile of leaves to cover the roots until spring.

SHRUBS & ROSES

Late January, particularly in eastern areas, can have some mild sunny days that give gardeners a chance to do light winter pruning. Shrubs that bloom in summer can be pruned while they're dormant. Leave unpruned any shrub that blooms early in the year like lilac and forsythia, because

HERE'S HOW

TO FORCE BLOOMS

Branches from early-blooming shrubs like forsythia, pussy willows, and lilacs can be forced into early bloom indoors (apple tree branches work too).

Take a few branches from each shrub—no more than one-quarter of the shrub. For tall vases, stems should be about 3 or 4 feet long. For table vases, just 2 feet is usually tall enough. Place the stems in a bucket in an out-of-the-way room and change the water every three days. As the blooms swell and start to open, place the stems in their decorative vase and move to the vase to the final position in the home.

Bright yellow branches of forsythia inside your home, viewed against a backdrop of snow outside, make a welcome sight.

you'll be pruning off their buds. Do not prune if temperatures are close to, or below, freezing. It is okay to trim a few forsythia branches to bring indoors to force.

TREES

Remove any branches on small trees that have broken under the weight of snow. Large, heavy, or out-of-reach branches on mature trees should be taken care of by professionals.

VINES & GROUNDCOVERS

Large summer-flowering vines like clematis can be trimmed if necessary while the vine is dormant.

WATER

Plants need *much less* water in winter, and too much water around roots kills a plant rather than revives it. Moisture levels should be slightly on the dry side for most indoor plants, but keep germinating seed damp.

BULBS

Keep amaryllis bulbs moist while the flower stem is growing. Enjoy the bloom, then reduce the water. They just need a little water to sustain growth until you plant them outside in spring; keep potting soil damp to slightly dry.

EDIBLES

Consistently water seedlings that have germinated. Rosemary should be kept slightly dry but will need water if it is on a sunny kitchen windowsill. If you are overwintering an outdoor rosemary in a cool room, water it only once or twice a month.

HOUSEPLANTS & CONTAINERS

All houseplants need to be watered when their soil dries out. As salts can accumulate in the soil medium, set the houseplants under a faucet and water slowly until water runs out the bottom of the container. Let the container sit until all the water drains out before placing it back on the shelf. Do this every two to three months.

TREES

Trees do not need watering unless they are newly planted and you haven't had much winter moisture. A gentle trickle of water from a hose for about an hour keeps the roots of these trees healthy. Place the hose nozzle about 6 to 8 inches from the trunk of the new tree. This does not need to be done more than once or twice over winter and only if the overall moisture levels are low and the ground is not frozen.

A shallow dish filled with water and gravel under a small container helps to keep the area humid.

HERE'S HOW

TO MAKE COMPOST

Compost can be started anytime and can be located in an informal corner of the garden or in a variety of containers. There are three components for great compost: raw materials, decomposing materials, and finished compost.

RAW MATERIALS

Green and brown garden material is the bulk of the raw material needed to make compost. You'll need about one-third brown and two-thirds green material.

Green material includes clippings from kitchen vegetable prep and overripe fruit or vegetables found at the back of the refrigerator drawer. Untreated lawn clippings can be added but refrain from putting in anything that has weed killer or other chemicals—they can remain active in the compost and kill container plants next year. You can also add weeds that are not in flower.

Brown material includes leaves in fall and garden waste, such as spent flowers and dead stems from fall cleanup.

DO NOT ADD

- Kitchen waste of meat/fish, which can attract rodents.
- Any plant material that has disease, such as tomato wilt.

TO MAKE COMPOST

1. Start with a soil layer to incorporate lots of soil microbes.
2. Add a green layer, then a brown layer.
3. Water the pile (just enough to dampen).
4. Continue to add green layers through winter.
5. Add dried leaves and other brown material in spring.
6. Turn the pile every month to get the whole pile hot (do not be surprised in winter if the compost pile steams—that means it's working).
7. In spring, or when the compost looks like dark soil, take a bucketful to the garden.
8. Sift the compost to remove any woody stems that have not decomposed. You can pick larger twigs out by hand.
9. Spread on the garden bed.

Note: If you have room, a three-bay compost system works great. The first bay is for raw materials that you are actively adding over time; the second bay starts the composting (and no further material is added to this pile); the final bay holds finished compost ready to screen and use. Commercial composting bins allow access to the finished compost through a door at the bottom. Remember to open and water these systems.

FERTILIZE

Fertilizer stimulates growth, so nothing outdoors needs to be fertilized at this time. Most indoor plants are still only growing slowly; they really do not need any fertilizer either.

Compost makes a great fertilizer for containers as well as garden beds. Making your own compost is very easy and a great way to recycle leaves, untreated grass clippings, and kitchen scraps from fruit and vegetables. Compost tea is a great way to use a diluted form of compost on plants. Newer compost tea bags allow you to make simple compost tea year-round. Just put the compost tea bag into a watering can, fill with water, and steep overnight. Use compost tea on seedlings and indoor plants as well as for soaking pea and bean seeds before planting.

EDIBLES

Indoor herb gardens can be lightly fertilized to keep them healthy and productive.

PROBLEM-SOLVE

The middle of winter is when indoor plants (and those overwintering indoors) start to show signs of stress due to low light conditions. Aphids, whiteflies, and scale are just some of the opportunistic insects that can cause problems. Check plants regularly, particularly under their leaves, and treat any signs of infestation promptly. Seedlings can struggle with low light too—add a lamp to increase the light level.

BULBS

Amaryllis bulbs sitting in too much water or too-wet soil can rot. If the leaves start to droop, take the bulb out of the pot and check to make sure it is not soft and black. Discard the bulb if it shows signs of decay.

EDIBLES

Rosemary leaves go brown, then fall off if the soil moisture levels are too high. Resist watering rosemary too often.

In addition to aphids on indoor herb gardens, mold can be an issue—try running a small fan to keep the air circulating to avoid mold issues and check them carefully each week. See Houseplants & Containers for ways to treat aphids and scale.

HOUSEPLANTS & CONTAINERS

Check for and treat any whiteflies or scale that you find. Remember to check stems and *under* the leaves for eggs and insects. Avoid using toxic treatments and opt for nontoxic remedies. Aphids and flies can be dislodged with a spray in the sink—wrap the container in a plastic bag so that you can turn the plant upside down in the sink to rinse underneath the leaves without losing all the potting mix. Eggs and scale are best treated with horticultural soaps or oils. Horticultural soaps and oils are found at most nurseries and larger hardware and home-improvement stores. They are safe for most plants, as well as for pets and children. Check labels for recommendations or cautions when using on specific plants such as edibles.

SHRUBS & ROSES

Watch shrubs for signs of deer or other animal damage. A ragged stem close to the ground is an indicator of small animals such as rabbit, while sharper stem ends and leaves disappearing higher up is typical of deer browsing. Spraying animal repellant can help to minimize this damage.

Winter deer damage on trees is a common problem.

February

For many of us, particularly those in the western and northern areas, February is just a repeat of January. Those on the eastern end of New York and in southern New Jersey fare slightly better, and by the end of February the weather usually shows some signs that winter is slowly receding everywhere. So there is light at the end of the tunnel, but it is not too late to work on those plans that you started in January or even start a new plan to redesign a garden space.

Clear blue February skies may not be warm, but it is great to walk outside in the garden and look at what is happening. Many shrubs are still dormant, but early-blooming shrubs are already starting to show swelling buds. Winter pruning of summer-blooming shrubs and grasses is just one of the jobs that can be done outside when the sun comes out. The first deliveries of dormant shrubs arrive this month from Internet orders made last fall; they are always a surprise when they arrive.

By the end of February, day length has increased; indoor plants come out of dormancy and need some attention.

February is a popular month for seed swaps, so take a look in your local paper to see if anyone has organized one nearby. Entry costs vary, with some charging a few dollars or the equivalent in seeds donated to the swap; others do not charge anything and you can leave with some great seeds for both the vegetable and flower gardens. It is also the right time to start seeds for those cold-tolerant vegetables that grow well in cool spring weather, such as kale and spinach. Getting the seed trays clean and ready for the major seed-starting in March all gets done in February. Do you have a place to put the seedlings where they can get lots of light?

Overall, February is the end of the quiet winter months and the last time to relax before garden chores are on your agenda.

PLAN

February is another month when you can fine-tune gardens for the new year. Last year, did you plan on putting some culinary herbs in a convenient spot, only to find there's not enough sun to do so? These changes in plans are easier to handle in February when you can get outside and see how much sun the garden gets. Walk around with your plans in mind and double-check that they'll work. Note where the sun is at midmorning, midday, and around 4 p.m. Plants requiring full sun need six or more hours of sun after 10 a.m. Part-sun conditions are between four to six hours of direct sun, and shade conditions are less than four hours of sun. Shade is usually found on the north side of a house. Remember that a sun pattern under a deciduous tree will change when the tree leafs out, but also that summer sun is higher in the sky than in February, which may increase direct sun in some areas.

ANNUALS

February is the right time to decide which annuals you'll grow this year. Annuals brighten most areas of the landscape, so plan to use them in a variety of locations. Decide which colors you need, and order seeds so that you can have plenty to fill both the shady and sunny areas of your garden.

Getting young children into the garden and interested in nature starts when they are toddlers or at least preschoolers. Plan a garden they can enjoy by adding plants with different textures for them to feel, colorful flowers that attract insects for them to watch, and tall sunflowers that tower above them. Vines (or even sunflowers planted close together) make teepees that are great places to hide or indulge in imaginative play. Herbs and vegetables can be attractive to young children as they can feel and smell the leaves of sage or basil and taste fresh, ripe berries from the blueberry bush.

BULBS

Bulbs that you are forcing into early bloom, like daffodils and crocus, should be growing by now. Find a bright spot somewhere out of the way for these containers while their little flowers grow. Move them to their final locations to display when the flower buds are just showing.

Order summer-blooming bulbs this month so they arrive in plenty of time. Alliums, dahlias, and lilies are planted in April or May so that they'll have time to grow and bloom in summer.

EDIBLES

What are your plans for the early vegetable garden? Succession planting gives a long crop of early-spring lettuces as well as kale (see Plant for more on succession planting).

LAWNS

Check lawns carefully as the snow melts. Some early fungus issues affect lawns that have been covered too long, and you will need to know how to identify and treat snow mold and other problems. See Problem-Solve in June for more on identification of grass fungus and mold.

HOUSEPLANTS & CONTAINERS

Plan the outdoors spring container display. Pansies go on sale at the end of the month or early March in some locations, and they make great spring container plants alongside miniature daffodils or little early-blooming iris.

Pansies and early daffodils look great together in spring containers.

PERENNIALS

Most perennials are still dormant, but if you left the stalks standing from last year, trim those back. Grasses are trimmed back before new growth starts, though they add some interest to the garden in winter, particularly when the low angle of winter sun catches them.

When planning perennial gardens, if you plan to add more, use the color wheel to help select colors.

SHRUBS AND SMALL TREES FOR A YEAR OF COLOR

SHRUB / SMALL TREE	*FEATURE*	*TIME*	*HARDINESS ZONE*
Red twig dogwood (*Cornus sericea*)	Bright red or yellow stems	December/March	2–7
Witch hazel (*Hamamelis vernalis*)	Orange/yellow blooms	February/March	4–8
Oregon holly (*Mahonia aquifolium*)	Yellow flowers	March/April	4–7
Star magnolia (*Magnolia stellata*)	White flowers	March/April	4–8
Bridal wreath spirea (*Spiraea* × *vanhouttei*)	White flowers	April	3–8
Kerria (*Kerria japonica*)	Yellow blooms and bright green winter stems	March/May	4–9
Lilac (*Syringa vulgaris*)	Lilac/purple or white flowers	April/May	3–7
Chokeberry (*Aronia arbutifolia*)	White flowers	April/May	3–9
Azaleas/rhododendrons (*Rhododendron* spp.)	White/purple flowers	May/June	Variable with variety
Ninebark (*Physocarpus*)	Dark red leaves, white flowers	May/June	2–7
Hydrangea (*Hydrangea arborescens*)	White, pink, or blue blooms	June/July	3–9
Summersweet (*Clethra alnifolia*)	White flowers	August	4–9
Viburnum (*Viburnum carlesii*)	Blue/black berries, red to orange fall leaf color	September/October	4–8
Blueberry (*Vaccinium corymbosum*)	Red/orange leaf color	October	3–8
Oak leaf hydrangea (*Hydrangea quercifolia*)	Orange fall leaf and exfoliating bark	October	5–9
Fothergilla (*Fothergilla major*)	Orange fall color	October	4–8
Beautyberry (*Callicarpa japonica*)	Purple berries	October/November	5–8
Fall witch hazel (*Hamamelis virginiana*)	Yellow flowers	November/December	3–8
Holly/winterberry (*Ilex verticillata*)	Red/orange berries	November/December	3–9

On the color wheel, complementary colors are adjacent while contrasting colors are opposite each other.

Yellow and blue are contrasting colors on the color wheel and look great together, while pink blends well with reds and dark blues or purples.

SHRUBS & ROSES

Shrubs are considered the permanent part of the garden; once growing, they prefer not to be moved. Choose shrubs that will give a full year of color somewhere in the garden.

Some shrubs do get a little too big, and these need to be pruned well. Check under Care in this chapter for how and when to prune multi-stemmed shrubs. Shrub bloom times vary for colder areas of New York State and warmer coastal areas of New Jersey.

TREES

Keep an eye on the weather and watch for branches falling under the weight of late snow or brutal winds. Deal with broken branches as quickly as possible after the event. Do you have a trusted arborist or landscape company that can help clear branches from the road or pathways? Now is a good time to find one. The American Society of Consulting Arborists has a list by state or zip code on its website (www.asca-consultants.org).

If your plans include adding a few fruit trees this year, decide how much and what size you can accommodate. Fruit trees come in full standard size (about 15 to 20 feet tall), semi-dwarf (12 to 15 feet), and fully dwarf (8 to 10 feet). You can also find container and colonnade fruit trees. All fruit trees benefit from planting two trees, and with many varieties it is essential that you have a second, compatible fruit tree for pollination. Apples, pears, plums, and cherries need two different varieties that bloom at the same time in order for pollination to occur. Peach and apricot trees are self-fertile, but they still produce better yield with another tree close by. When ordering bare-root trees from a reputable source, a tree's best pollination partner will be mentioned in the catalog. Note this is not the same as when most home-improvement stores have fruit trees on sale in spring. Those lovely young trees, often complete with flowers or young fruit, mislead you into thinking that the tree will fruit the same for you next year. Without a pollinating partner, they won't. Before you buy one of these trees, check to see if the pollinator is on sale as well and buy both trees.

Here, a groundcover is used between irregular stepping stones in this informal pathway.

VINES & GROUNDCOVERS

Groundcovers can be used in a variety of places in the landscape. There are groundcovers that are good under trees where it is shady in summer: small bulbs such as bluebells and lily-of-the-valley both do well in these areas and are delightful when in bloom, and sweet woodruff works well under shrubs as a living mulch. Winter aconite is a groundcover that tolerates some shade but works well on tough-to-mow sunny slopes; it's also deer resistant but can become overzealous in some gardens. Woolly thyme, creeping phlox, and basket of gold (*Aurinia saxatilis*) look good casually draped over retaining walls to soften the edges. Many groundcovers can cover large open areas that you cannot tend to easily, either because of location or time constraints. For variety in these large areas, pick groundcovers that have different textures, leaf color, and height as well as flowers.

Give your seedlings lots of light as soon as they germinate.

The first leaves a seedling puts out are the simple leaves, or seed leaves. True leaves grow in after that.

PLANT

Everything out of doors is still cold and covered in snow, so very little planting is done outside in February. Everyone can still do some winter sowing (see Plan in January under annuals). Warmer areas can start cool-weather vegetables inside from seed this month, as well as some perennials, which take a long time to grow.

ANNUALS

Some spring-blooming, cold-hardy annuals, such as Canterbury Bells and Bachelor Button, like to be planted on top of snow. If you didn't winter-sow your poppies and other cottage garden annuals, sprinkle a few seeds where you want them to grow (on top of snow or cold ground) and let nature take over to germinate them at the right time. To prevent animals from nibbling on the seeds or eating the tender young shoots, cover the seeded area with an old towel, horticultural cloth, or even an old screen door.

BULBS

It is too early to plant summer bulbs, but in mild areas where the ground didn't freeze, there is still time to plant a few late-flowering spring bulbs. Those that are labeled as being suitable for Southern states do not need a long cold spell and include both daffodils (most jonquil and tazetta classes of daffodil) as well as single late-blooming tulips. Success will largely depend on what the weather in February and March brings, but there's a good chance they'll grow and bloom. In general, Southern bulbs need six weeks or so below 50°F, which even the mildest of our winters can usually give them.

HERE'S HOW

TO START SEEDS INDOORS

The outdoor growing season for annuals begins after the last frost of spring and ends with the first frost of fall. To get a few weeks ahead of the outdoor calendar, gardeners start seeds inside and transplant seedlings into the garden when they're ready. Tender flowers and vegetables are transplanted outside in May or June (usually), when all danger of frost has passed, whereas some hardier plants can be transplanted a little earlier. Fall vegetable seedlings are transplanted as soon as they have two or more sets of true leaves.

Starting plants from seed is popular because the cost per plants when purchased as seeds is much lower than the cost of a transplant. There is also more variety when growing from seed. Online sites and catalogs have *pages* of heirloom tomatoes or beans, not to mention every possible shade of petunias. Successful seed starting relies on two basic needs of the seed—light and moisture.

TO START

Assemble clean containers, trays, potting mix or pellets, and seeds.

1. For a batch of seedlings, moisten the potting mix in a bucket rather than the seed tray. Most commercial mixes include peat moss, which takes a while to absorb all the liquid. If you're using peat pellets, place the pellets in the tray and add enough water to expand the pellets fully. Drain the excess water from the tray underneath the pellets before you plant them.
2. Fill the trays with potting mix and level the surface.
3. With a skewer or a pencil, make a small hole in the surface where the seed is going to be planted. **Note:** Most peat pellets already have a pre-made hole.

4. Read the seed packet for specific instructions regarding how deep to plant the seed and if the seed likes to be covered. A few seeds, such as parsley, zinnia, and cosmos, require darkness to germinate (I put them in a black garbage bag under the bed) and some, like petunias, salvias, and nicotiana, require light to germinate. The rest like some soil on the seed but are not overly bothered by bright light or total darkness, so either your floor or the top of the refrigerator is fine. Most summer annual seedlings like a warm room to germinate—about 70°F—and they germinate in 10 to 15 days.
5. Cover the seedling tray with plastic wrap or the plastic cover that came with the tray.
6. Let the seedlings germinate. Seedlings germinate at different rates. Most common annual flowers and vegetables germinate

in 5 to 10 days but celery takes closer to 20 days. Perennials take a week or two, so check the seed package to get an idea of how quickly you should see their seedlings pop up. Old seed that you saved from a year or two ago will likely have a much lower germination rate than fresh seed, so if nothing happens within the expected time, replant with fresh seed.

If you are in doubt about the viability of the seed, place a dozen or so seeds onto a damp paper towel. Fold the towel over and put in a warm place for a week or two (check the packet or Internet for typical germination times). Most seeds start to swell and show signs of germination (a little white root breaking out of the seed capsule) within this time. If none of the seeds germinate, discard the whole packet and purchase new seed.

7. As soon as the seedlings break the surface of the soil, they need light—and lots of it. Ideally you'll have a south-facing windowsill or table. Growing systems with shop lights are available. With these the light source can be lowered to just above the seedlings for maximum light (about 2 inches above is the best distance). Put a timer on the light so the seedlings get 12 to 14 hours of light per day.

8. Fertilize the seedlings after about a month. Use half-strength if you are using a general fertilizer or, if you're using a fertilizer labeled as suitable for seedlings, and follow the package directions.

9. Seedlings in a tray or in small cells of less than ½-inch diameter can be transplanted to larger containers when they have two sets of true leaves. The first set of leaves that the plant puts out are known as simple (*cotyledon*) leaves, and they rarely show the true leaf structure of the plant. The first true leaves appear about a week after these simple leaves. True leaves look like the leaves of the mature tomato or marigold or whatever plant it is that you are growing.

10. To transplant, lift the seedlings *gently* out of the tray complete with roots and growing medium. The waiting planting container should be ready with damp potting mix. Make a hole in the mix that is sufficiently large enough to accommodate the seedling roots. Fill the hole to secure the seedling and water well. Some seedlings, such as tomatoes, need to be transplanted two or even three times (into successively larger peat pots) before you can put them into the garden. Annual flowers are ready to plant in 8 to 10 weeks; common summer vegetables are ready in 6 to 8 weeks.

■ *Winter-sown seedlings germinate in milk cartons outside.*

EDIBLES

Early-season vegetables can be started in seed trays. The onion group (onions, leeks, scallions) takes a long time to mature when they are started from seed. Start them in a deep container, *now*, so they're large enough to plant outdoors in April or May. Kale, chard, mustard, and spinach are also started from seed this month. Onion seeds can also be sown in fall and winter (see Plant in January).

Plant garlic bulbs outside as soon as you can work the ground. Garlic is planted in fall for an early crop, but planting now will give a second crop in mid- to late summer.

HOUSEPLANTS & CONTAINERS

Plant seeds for fun theme gardens in your containers this month. Try a red, white, and blue garden with bright red geraniums, white petunias, and blue salvia; or plant a moon garden with white zinnias, dusty miller, and alyssum draping over the side. For color in a shady spot, try contrasting pale caladiums with vibrant red begonias. Support your favorite football or school team with colors—for a black-and-gold theme, try *Scabiosa* 'Black Knight' paired with golden marigolds.

PERENNIALS

Perennials that you didn't sow last month can be started from seed this month. Check the information on the seed packet and online guides to determine how long the perennial takes to germinate and grow, as well as the best conditions for growing seedlings. Some perennials need to be cold-treated for a few weeks; others like to be uncovered and exposed to light to germinate. Perennials often take three to six weeks or even longer to germinate, so be patient.

Mistletoe is a favorite for Christmas decoration, and you can have your own crop if you saved the seed from the previous year. (Really! But you'll need some patience.)

SHRUBS, ROSES & TREES

If you live in the milder Zone 7 or 8 areas, you could find that dormant fruit trees, roses, and shrubs are delivered in February. This is fine if your garden is tillable. Other years, snow and cold lingers well into this month. If the snow has cleared and you can see the ground, dig holes for woody plants as soon as they arrive. If the ground does not permit this, keep trees dormant and outdoors if possible. Most will have damp, torn newspaper around their bare roots. Put trees into a bucket with the damp paper, mulch, or peat moss and keep them moist but not wet until you can plant. Anything that has already broken dormancy and is putting out leaves should be kept cool but protected from frost.

HERE'S HOW

TO SOW MISTLETOE SEEDS

1. Seeds should be fresh. The ones that you saved from fall and kept in a bright location should still be viable.
2. Pick a host tree: apple, oak, and willow trees are all possible hosts.
3. Lay the sticky seeds evenly along the bark.
4. Label the area.

Mistletoe seeds have a low viability, so use lots of seeds. The first phase is a little green leaf shows growth has started. It takes four or five years before the plants create the familiar berries, so be patient.

HERE'S HOW

TO PLANT BARE-ROOT TREES AND SHRUBS (INCLUDING ROSES)

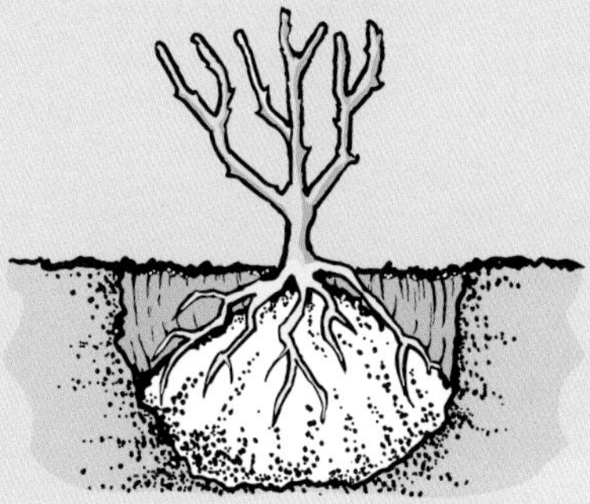

Buying bare-root trees and shrubs or roses from a nursery means you can get woody plants delivered to your home with much less packing and lower shipping costs. The plants are shipped dormant, making damage less likely. Along the stems or trunk of the shrub you will notice small swellings where new buds will break through in a few weeks. The lower part consists of the root mass. Sometimes the roots are almost at a 90-degree angle from the main stem (the trunk, on trees), but more often they spread out and down from the stem.

Many fruit trees and roses are grafted. When a plant is grafted, the upper part of the tree (or rose) is the variety that you want to grow, while the roots are of a different variety; this is done mainly to enhance cold hardiness. The roots of the tree that is taken to be the root stock of a graft has characteristics such as dwarf sizing, disease resistance, or extra cold hardiness. When grafted to a rose or ornamental tree, those characteristics are seen in the upper part of the shrub, making the shrub palette much larger for homeowners.

You'll need to identify the graft by looking at the junction of the roots to the stem. Frequently this is a painted line, but it will look like a swelling on the trunk. The rootball should be positioned so the graft junction is placed *just above* the soil level when you plant the shrub.

Caution: Before you start to dig holes for trees, check the utility markings. Cable, Internet, and electrical wires are not something that you want to sever.

TO PLANT

1. Spread the plant's roots and dig a hole that is wide and deep enough to comfortably accommodate all the roots. Set the excavated soil from the hole to the side.
2. Add some compost to the pile of excavated soil—about one-third compost to two-thirds soil.
3. Loosen or scuff up the soil at the base of the hole to make a "soft" base to the hole.
4. **For raspberries and other plants with lateral roots (those that travel at a 90-degree angle):** Lay the roots on the loosened soil with the root/stem junction at the soil level.

   For roses and other shrubs and trees: Scoop the loosened soil into a pile in the center of the hole into a cone shape. Roses need a much higher "cone" than most shrubs or trees. Assess how high you need to make this by looking at the plant's root system. A tree's central trunk should settle on the top of the pile with roots fanning out around it.

   Seat the bare-root shrub so the root/stem junction or graft is just above the soil line.

   Spread the roots around the pile of soil in the hole; add some of the soil/compost mix underneath if needed to get the height correct—that is, so the graft or stem is just above the soil line.
5. Refill the hole with the waiting soil and compost mix.
6. Water well to settle.

VINES & GROUNDCOVERS

Start perennial groundcovers indoors this month. Sweet woodruff (*Galium odoratum*), candytuft (*Iberis sempervirens*), and dead nettle (*Lamium maculatum*) are hardy to Zone 3 and are deer resistant too.

CARE

Most garden activity is indoors, but the change in seasons can be felt. Get tools and equipment ready before you need them. There is still time to finish late-winter pruning.

ANNUALS

Clean seed-starting equipment. Discard any broken seedling trays. After you have cleaned all soil residue off the trays, rinse them with 1:10 bleach-to-water solution. Replenish your supply of seed-starting mix or pellets.

BULBS

Trim spent flowers off amaryllis, along with any other spent flowers on forced bulbs. Move bulbs that are actively growing to a bright location until their flowers are almost out. Then move the container to a living area to be enjoyed.

EDIBLES

Toward the end of the month, longer days and sun prompt rhubarb to break dormancy. Put a clay pot, glass cloche, or plastic "walls of water" over the emerging crown to force the rhubarb a little early.

PERENNIALS

The edges between the perennial/shrub garden and the lawn tend to get disturbed from snow, ice, rain, and weather in general. Take a few minutes to tidy the edges. A sharp straight-edged spade or edger slices through the grass roots that are heading toward the garden and makes a neat edge to the lawn. A sharp edge is easier to keep tidy when mowing and trimming the lawn.

HOUSEPLANTS & CONTAINERS

As the sun gets a little higher and stronger in the sky, some indoor plants start breaking dormancy

Edge pathways and perennial beds with a sharp, straight-edged spade.

(just like outdoor ones, particularly rosemary). Rotate their containers a half-turn weekly if they are located close to a window. One-sided light creates stems that lean toward the window, and this soon creates an unaesthetic look to the plant.

Check tender perennials like *Pelargonium* (scented geraniums) that you are overwintering indoors. Weaker winter sun from December and January creates leggy growth, which can be trimmed back to about 6 to 8 inches, depending on how big the plant is.

LAWNS

Toward the end of February, before the lawn starts to grow, get your mowing equipment ready for use. If you did not clean your mower last fall, now is the time to do that. Refill the tank with fresh fuel and oil when mowing season starts—March or April for some in our area—so getting the mower in good shape this month is one less thing to do when you need to use it. See Care in October for further details on cleaning a mower.

SHRUBS & ROSES

Prune summer-blooming shrubs this month, if needed. Pick a day that is above freezing and use clean, sharp tools. Clean tools by wiping with rubbing alcohol. Daily cleaning during the season can be accomplished by plunging the spade/fork

Prune roses while they are still dormant.

and other large tools into a bucket of sand before hanging in the shed. This removes dirt and keeps the implements sharp.

All ornamental grasses can be cut back and divided if needed.

TREES

Trim small trees to remove any branches that are crossing or are going to cross another branch.

Brush snow off trees, particularly conifers, after heavy snow falls. Heavy snow weight can break the boughs.

HERE'S HOW

TO PRUNE SUMMER-BLOOMING SHRUBS

Shrubs come in two basic forms: those that have main stems that branch farther out as they grow (roses) and those that have multiple stems coming out from the base of the shrub. Not all shrubs need to be pruned every year and only occasionally will you find a very overgrown shrub that needs major reduction in height. Always remove dead or broken branches first.

TO PRUNE SINGLE-STEM SHRUBS, LIKE ROSES

1. Look at the overall shape of the shrub and visualize the shape you want to finish with.
2. Reduce (prune) evenly around the shrub to a junction between a side stem and the next larger stem *or* to an outwardly facing growth tip. The place where the new growth will start can be identified as a swelling on the side of the stem. Some of the swellings indicate that the new stem will grow toward the inside of the bush while others are on the opposite side of the stem and indicate the new growth will grow out from the bush.

TO PRUNE MULTI-STEM SHRUBS, LIKE HARDY HIBISCUS AND LACECAP HYDRANGEAS

Multi-stem shrubs not only grow upward from the ground but they also increase their girth by sending up new shoots around a plant. Pruning can reduce one or both, depending on your needs.

1. Remove as many side shoots as you wish from the perimeter of the shrub to reduce its overall spread. They can be trimmed down to the ground or even dug out if needed.
2. Prune back the remaining stems to a growth point or a side stem at an appropriate height. Note that you are trimming last year's wood and growth. This year's growth will add to the level that you leave. For instance, if you want to reduce the final *summer* height to be lower than your neighbor's fence, take that into account now. Trimming back individual stems is also called "heading back."

HERE'S HOW

TO PRUNE FOR A MAJOR REDUCTION IN SHRUB SIZE

Some shrubs, when left alone, grow out-of-bounds quickly and may need major pruning to restore them to a reasonable shape and size. This can be done in one single step or over several years. With boxwood, there are two schools of thought; one camp prefers cutting to the ground, which looks ugly for a while because the shrub puts out new growth evenly. This group says that multi-year pruning creates thick branch angles inside the shrub that catch and retain water, causing rot. But I have seen both ways be successful.

For a single-step reduction: Take all the stems down to the first junction. For multi-stemmed shrubs such as forsythia or lilac, you can also dig and remove the lateral stems. Note that the shrub may look woody and unattractive for a year or two and may not bloom this year, but it will recover. The advantage with this way is that it's a single step, which saves time, and in the case of a vastly overgrown and crowded landscape, it's the best way to clearly see what is there. Roses recover to a decent shrub size in a year or two, but boxwood and holly take four or five years to look like a good foundation shrub again.

For a multi-step reduction and continuing care: Climbing roses and many shrubs put out new growth and continue to add to the existing growth each year. Because they flower on new growth, the flowers can be many feet in the air, while the rose's stem that you see at eye level is brown and old—that does not make an attractive looking rose. For this and many other overgrown shrubs:

Year 1: Remove one-third of the oldest stems (older than the previous year's growth). Reduce the overall height of the remaining stems.

Year 2: Remove another one-third of the oldest stems and reduce overall height of remaining stems if needed.

Year 3: Remove the oldest one-third of the shrub. By this time your overall shrub is younger, smaller, and more floriferous. In successive years, continue the maintenance pruning by annually removing the oldest one-third of the stems and trimming overly long stems back.

Reduce each stem to regain a neat overall shape to the shrub.

Severly overgrown shrubs can be taken down to just above the first junction.

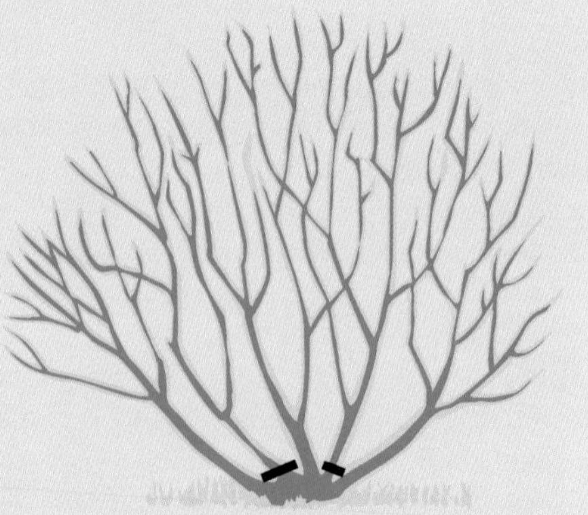

Really old shrubs can be rejuvenated by taking select stems (no more than a third) right down to the ground.

SUMMER SHRUBS THAT BLOOM ON NEW WOOD

These common summer shrubs bloom on new wood created the previous spring. They can be pruned this month.

SHRUB	BLOOM COLOR/SEASON	HARDINESS
Abelia (*Abelia × grandiflora*)	White flowers all summer	5–7
Caryoperis (Blue mist shrub) (*Caryopteris × clandonensis*)	Blue flowers, summer	6–9
Hydrangea-lacecap (*Hydrangea macrophylla*)	White/pink flowers, summer	5–9
Mock orange (*Philadelphus coronarius*)	Fragrant white flowers, early summer	4–8
Potentilla (*Potentilla fruticosa*)	Yellow flowers, summer	2–7
Smoke bush (*Cotinus coggygria*)	Fuzzy pink flowers, early summer	4–7
Spirea (*Spiraea japonica*)	Various pinks and whites, late spring and summer	4–8
Summersweet (*Clethra alnifolia*)	White, fragrant flowers, early summer	4–9
Rose-of-Sharon (*Hibiscus syriacus*)	Pink/white/mauve flowers, all summer	5–8
Viburnums, summer flowering (*Viburnum cassinoides* and *V. dentatum*)	White flowers, early to midsummer	3–8

VINES & GROUNDCOVERS

Perennial vines become very woody with age, not to mention a tangled mess of stems. Annual maintenance goes a long way toward keeping them looking good year-round.

WATER

There is no need to water outdoors. Most landscape trees and shrubs are still dormant, and melting snow provides more than enough water. What's more of an issue is the top layer of snow or ice melting at the surface and having nowhere to drain to because of a still-frozen subsoil. This causes root rot problems for many woody perennials and shrubs: heaping snow on the perennial beds and good soil drainage in the area helps.

Lawns, perennials, vines, and groundcovers are also mainly dormant and don't need watering.

ANNUALS

Any seedlings that have germinated will need gentle watering. Self-watering seedling trays that water from the bottom help keep their small roots moist while not damaging the tender seedling stems.

BULBS

If you forced bulbs and planted them last month, they will be sprouting by now and should be treated like any other container plant. Keep the soil damp; do not let the container sit in water or dry out. As the roots grow, the plant will need a little more water than before.

EDIBLES

Cold-weather seedlings will need watering as they grow. Keep the soil damp but not wet, and check daily.

Over time, the plants in hydroponic systems take up nutrients from the liquid as well as transpire,

HERE'S HOW

TO PRUNE COMMON FRUIT TREES AND VINES

The purpose of pruning fruit trees is twofold. You'll create a well-balanced tree that allows airflow and sunlight into the middle of the tree. In addition, a pruned tree is easier to harvest. Always remove branches that are crossed or close to crossing, dead branches, and those with a narrow angle to the main trunk. An angle of less than 60 degrees means inherently weaker joints that are subject to winter damage.

A young tree has a main trunk that heads up. This is called the "leader," and on most fruit trees, this controls the overall height of the tree; it's cut to reduce upward growth in favor of side branch growth. "Head off" is used in reference to cutting off a whole limb close to the next limb. It also refers to cutting the leader to control height. "Spurs" are small "bumps" on the sides of the branches where the flowers and fruit are produced.

Pruning is a big topic, so for more on pruning fruit trees, consult your local Cooperative Extension office.

Apples: Prune apple trees to create a central leader and well-spaced side branches.

Apricots: Apricot trees bloom on spurs. Trees are very early blooming, which means they're frequently damaged by late frosts; delay pruning until after flowering.

Peaches: Peaches bear fruit on new wood. The leader is cut on three-year-old trees to stop any further height to the tree. Prune side branches to allow good spacing and airflow.

Pears: Young pear trees don't need to be pruned. After three years, prune to a central leader to encourage more side branches to form.

Plums and cherries: Generally, plums and cherries need very little pruning. Flowers and fruit are produced on spurs, and any pruning should be done after flowering.

Kiwis: Kiwis are very fast growers. Yields are best on younger wood, so take off anything older than three years. Prune in winter to open the vine up and allow airflow to the interior. (**Note:** You'll need one male plant for every four female plants to get fruit.)

Grape vines: Prune grape side canes close to the main stem. Allow two or four side branches to develop to the side of the main stem.

Apple trees are pruned to have just one stem growing upright; the rest of the branches come off to the side.

Peach trees are pruned to have limited upward growth and all branches growing outward.

HERE'S HOW

TO PRUNE WOODY VINES

Most woody vines start at ground level with a main root and stem. Over the years, more roots grow from the base, adding width to the vine. Some vines, like some clematis, die back to the ground each year and return the following year.

For those that die back to the ground each year, remove all top growth and mulch the crown just as you would other perennials.

For vines that bloom on this year's wood, including some clematis, roses, and grapes:

1. Trim these vines down to the ground each year and allow to return in spring from the base.
2. If you want a larger vine, leave a few branches and trim a few to the ground. This gives a fuller vine overall and is a good way to maintain the vine long-term.

For woody vines that bloom on last year's wood, including American bittersweet, some clematis, and wisteria: these vines get very large and tangled if they're not attended to regularly. Trim these vines after they flower.

1. Look at the vine and support structure and see how far along the structure the vine is. This gives an overall status of the vine. Young vines that are less than two years old may not need to be trimmed at all.
2. See how many stems are sprouting up from the base; remove some of these.
3. After flowering, trim back all the stems to about one-third of their length.
4. Selectively trim about one-third of the stems back to the ground.

Very woody, old vines, whether the vines bloom on new or old wood, can be pruned down almost to the ground. Those that bloom on old wood will not bloom this year, but an overall healthier vine will be back in flower next year.

1. Remove top growth to about 8 inches from the ground.
2. Remove about one-third of the oldest, woodiest stems.
3. Remove a few side stems to reduce the overall girth of the vine at ground level.

both of which use water. Check the level of water in hydroponic systems weekly and change every two weeks.

Keep rosemary barely damp and in good light.

HOUSEPLANTS & CONTAINERS

With a little more sun and longer days, houseplants are starting to come out of dormancy and need a little more water. Check the potting mix daily and maintain an even but not wet moisture level.

African violets have slightly higher water requirements as the plants don't really go through a dormant period. A wick arrangement is recommended for these delightful plants.

FERTILIZE

Give all indoor plants a little fertilizer in February, but there's no need to fertilize outdoors for a few more weeks.

ANNUALS

Once the seedlings are up and growing, add a light fertilizer to the water and feed every two to three weeks. Compost tea is great for seedlings as it is not very strong. If you are using a regular liquid fertilizer, read the label carefully for use on seedlings. Generally, one-quarter strength is suitable once the first true leaves form.

BULBS

Indoor bulbs such as amaryllis, orchids, or forced daffodils don't need any more fertilizer until their flowering is over. At this stage, remove the flower stem, place the bulb container in a bright room, and give a *light* dose of fertilizer.

EDIBLES

As with the annual seedlings, a little fertilizer when the first true leaves develop is a good idea but not necessary. Err on the side of under- rather than overfertilizing hardy kale and other cool-weather vegetables. The taste of such plants is concentrated in the leaves, and rapid growth due to nitrogen fertilizers tends to dilute their flavor.

Blueberries like a slightly lower pH than other plants, so adding a little elemental sulfur to the blueberry patch this month allows it to seep into the ground and change the pH just in that little area. Using a product formulated for azaleas also lowers the pH of the soil (locally).

HOUSEPLANTS & CONTAINERS

Houseplants coming out of dormancy benefit from a light fertilizer. Start with a half-strength fertilizer for most plants when you see the first signs of new growth. African violets use a particular fertilizer formulated for them; follow the product's guidelines.

PERENNIALS

Lavender prefers "sweeter" soil (meaning a higher pH) than many landscape plants. If you burn wood in your fireplace, spread a shovel of wood ashes around lavender to raise the pH just a little in that one specific area.

PROBLEM-SOLVE

Problems in February are mainly indoors with just a few outdoor issues stemming from winter storms that continue through the month.

ANNUALS

Most problems for annuals this month come from poor light. Poor light produces weak stems and unhealthy seedlings prone to diseases and insects. If you're growing annual seedlings and you have a very bright window, turn the seedlings each day. Without a window, they will need extra light (such as from a grow light) that should be placed about 2 inches above the seedlings.

Once seedlings have at least one set of true leaves, they can be fertilized.

When seedlings do not get enough light, they lean toward the window. This creates a thin, weak stem without true leaves.

BULBS

Check tender bulbs that are being stored inside for damp areas and rot. Remove any spoiled bulbs and thoroughly air the others so that they continue to be dry. In a matter of weeks, they will start to sprout, but for now they need to stay dormant.

EDIBLES

Edibles seedlings are subject to the same light issues as annuals.

If you kept rosemary alive over winter by bringing it indoors, check it for insects such as aphids and scale as well as molds. Use a pesticide registered for indoor and edible plants to treat aphids and oils for scale (horticultural soaps and oils work on most insects). A fan placed near a plant to increase air circulation often helps avoid fungal and mold issues, which cause many rosemary plants to fail.

HOUSEPLANTS & CONTAINERS

After several weeks indoors, houseplants are apt to develop a few issues with whiteflies, aphids, and scale. Be watchful for insects that look like little scabs on branches or take off in a cloud when you brush against a plant. Deal with these promptly so that they don't get too severe. Severe infestations can kill a plant. Good airflow and healthy plants go a long way in preventing these problems. Check Problem-Solve in July for dealing with common insect problems.

LAWNS

Lawns are still dormant, so there aren't any problems—yet.

PERENNIALS

In some areas, a break in winter weather is sufficient to cause some new growth on perennials. Even though this is early in the year, there's not much you can do, and although this growth will be injured if a severe frost arrives, the plant will generally be fine. Push a little extra mulch over the perennials to keep them dormant as long as possible, but don't panic about some early growth.

SHRUBS & ROSES

A few early-blooming shrubs like witch hazel and star magnolias (although this may be more of a small tree) will show some swelling of the buds. Check the buds to make sure that there are no little bugs waiting to take advantage of the new tender growth. Look for little black dots close to the emerging buds.

In milder areas, check outdoor shrubs for winter damage. Eggs can lay dormant on the plant and hatch as soon as the spring growth arrives. Viburnum leaf beetle is not unknown in February, and is just one pest that can be avoided by checking the shrubs now and removing its black eggs. For eggs and scale on other shrubs, use a dormant oil treatment to forestall damage. Colder areas will check for insects and treat next month.

TREES

Occasionally, an unseasonable warm spell in late February stimulates new growth, particularly in warmer zones. Late frost kills this growth, but as with shrubs, the trees will be fine. Secondary leaves will replace the killed leaves, and the tree will look normal by the end of spring.

Spider mites find winter homes in conifers of all sizes. Hold a piece of white paper under the branches and shake them. A smattering of dark dots indicates spider mites. Treat these with a *miticide* (not a pesticide) and keep the trees well watered to reduce the persistence of mites. A strong spray or water can also dislodge this pest.

March

March is the first of the transition months that bridge winter into spring, with weather changing from mild and back to snow again on what seems like a weekly basis. The march of crocus, primroses, and daffodils starts at the Atlantic coastline before heading west and up into the mountains in April. For the gardener, this is a great month—perennials start to show signs that they made it through winter, the trees put out new leaves and blossom, and the nurseries ramp up selling seed-starting supplies, seeds, and yes, plants too.

The flowerbeds and lawn areas are seen again for the first time since maybe November, and winter damage can be clearly seen. This is when the benefits of snow cover become truly evident. Brutally cold polar air masses that dropped across our states are sometimes cold enough to kill all the branches of shrubs and hedges above the snow line. This leaves a bizarre line as the snow clears. Damaged branches and dead limbs are still easy to see and are easier to remove in March. The lawn, when cleared of snow, quickly turns from dirty brown to a welcome green as the temperature moderates.

Damage from deer and rodents is seen when you get closer to your shrubs. Deer, particularly toward the end of a long, snowy winter, often browse on ornamentals. Usually this is not sufficiently damaging to distort the shrub and stops as soon as other foraging is available. Make a note about where you see the nibbled stems and keep a watch on it—you might need to treat it with repellent if the animals start nibbling the tender new growth.

March is also when major home and garden shows are held that include great ideas and educational programs. New York and New Jersey each have several shows to get you in the mood for gardening and maybe encourage you to start something new in the garden. Take a good pair of walking shoes, a camera to remind you of specific designs, and a notepad to jot down names of plants that you want to research.

PLAN

March is a colorful month with the appearance of the first spring bulbs, but snowstorms and frosts are still with us for a while yet. This is the big seed-starting month. Find out your last frost date, and schedule when to start seeds, when to fertilize the lawn, and when to buy tender plants. Find your last spring frost and your first fall frost at www.plantmaps.com.

March is a good time to take a soil test. Lawns, vegetables, shrubs, and many perennials rely on the correct nutrients, but for nutrients to be available the soil must have the correct acidity or pH. A soil test helps you decide if you need to adjust pH with chemicals, as well as what nutrients you need to add.

ANNUALS

Have you ordered annual seeds? If not, do that this month. Annuals are great to fill spots where young perennials are growing or to lighten shady places. Brightly colored marigolds come in a variety of sizes, and colorful zinnias grow quickly from seed and fill in sunny spots, while the rich foliage of coleus does well in shady locations. All are easy to grow from seed.

BULBS

Spring bulbs are up and showing in March, making great displays in the garden. Late-spring irises are peeping up and tender bulbs like dahlias and cannas, which you kept stored in the basement or back room, will be ready to break dormancy this month. As you look at the bulbs in bloom, make a note of where you would like to add more.

When early daffodils finish flowering, allow the leaves to go brown. Many gardeners are tempted to snip the unattrative leaves off too soon—don't. A better way is to plant a perennial such as a peony

HERE'S HOW

TO TAKE A SOIL TEST

1. Dig a hole by removing the top 4 to 6 inches of soil from a perennial bed, vegetable garden, or lawn. From the sides of this hole, scrape about ½ cup of soil to get a representative sample from the whole depth where the plant roots will grow.
2. Put the sample into a bucket or jug. Repeat this step for several other areas so that you have a representative sample from an entire perennial bed. Lawns particularly benefit from several areas being sampled, such as areas that are close to buildings or streams.
3. Mix the samples from one bed, or the lawn, together in the bucket. Put about one cup of mixed soil into a baggie or box. University Cooperative Extension offices provide testing services, and they often have boxes to submit samples. Place your sample soil in the appropriate box with paperwork; the office will mail or submit the sample for you. A modest fee is usually charged (less than $20).

   Private laboratories also perform soil tests. Generally, upon being contacted, they will send a container with labels and the proper paperwork to submit.

   Results are usually sent by email. For help interpreting the results, contact your local Cooperative Extension office or the private testing lab.

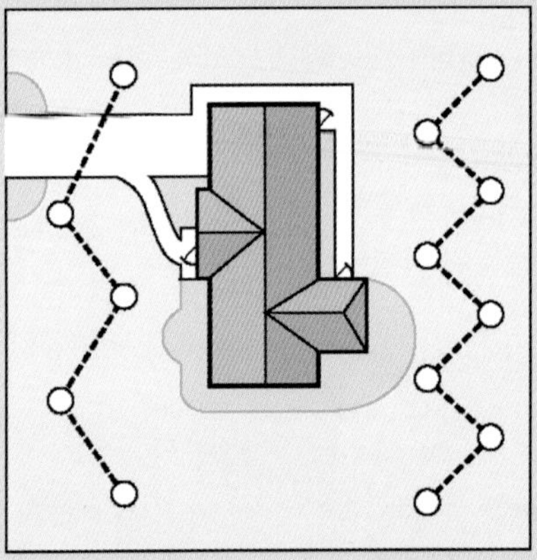

Take samples from different areas of the lawn or garden and mix them together to make an average pH of the whole area.

or ornamental grass—something that emerges from dormancy early—in front of the daffodils and block the sight of the decaying leaves until you can remove them.

Primroses are one of the early perennial plants in the garden.

EDIBLES

Some cold-hardy kale and vegetables can be hardened off and moved into the garden. This frees up space so tender vegetable seedlings like tomatoes can move to the space on the windowsill.

HOUSEPLANTS & CONTAINERS

Along with daffodils outdoors, indoor bulbs will be blooming. When their blooms are over, what is your plan? The bulbs can be planted outdoors in a week or two, or composted. Forced bulbs are rarely successful a second year; paperwhite daffodils, in particular, should be composted after you have enjoyed their blooms. For regular, hardy daffodils, wait until after the bloom has finished, then keep the bulbs in a cool, sunny area until the leaves start to turn brown. To plant outside, wait until outdoor daffodils and crocus are going dormant, then plant the forced ones to the landscape. They may not bloom the next year, but should be fine their second year. Amaryllis bulbs are the exception to the one-year limit of successfully growing forced bulbs. When the amaryllis bloom is over, cut the bloom stalk down but leave its green leaves. Put the plant into a bright room so that the leaves can replenish the bulb. In summer, after danger of frost has passed, plant the bulb in maximum sunlight. In September, bring the bulb inside, induce dormancy, and bring it into bloom again in time for the holidays. (See September for the how-to.)

SCHEDULE FOR PLANTING COMMON VEGETABLES

PLANT	*4–6 WEEKS BEFORE LAST FROST*	*2–4 WEEKS BEFORE LAST FROST*	*AT OR AFTER FROST*
Chard	Start indoors	Transplant outside	
Kale	Start indoors	Transplant outside	
Lettuce	Start indoors	Start indoors	Transplant outside and plant seeds directly outside
Spinach	Start indoors	Transplant outside	
Peas	Plant seeds outside	Plant seeds outside	
Beans		Plant seeds outside	
Tomatoes		Start seeds indoors	Transplant outside
Peppers		Start seeds indoors	Transplant outside
Summer squash		Start seeds indoors	Plant seeds outside/ transplant seedlings outside

LAWNS

Spring sunshine melts the last of the winter snow, and the lawn is visible again. Check drainage patterns in the lawn and note which areas have snow the longest. If you have a dog, you'll probably see evidence of their favorite part of the garden, which will need attention soon. (See this month's Problem-Solve.)

If you plan on reseeding the lawn or replacing areas with sod, plan now so that the ground will be weed-free and ready for the new grass. You need to know the square footage. Use a tape measure to calculate the width and length of the lawn and multiply that to get the square footage (area). Add the square footage of all areas of the lawn—side, front, and back—so that you know the total square feet in order to buy the right amounts of fertilizers and other treatments.

Plan the year of lawn care this month. Both New York and New Jersey have laws regarding how and when you can fertilize lawns. Read about lawns under Fertilize and the tips for annual lawn care.

PERENNIALS

Did your perennials come back? Even "perennials" may not, depending on the severity of a winter. Early spring is a great time to walk around the garden to see where perennial leaves are showing through the mulch. Resist the temptation to pull all the mulch away from the plants, particularly in colder areas, because snow and ice are still very possible, and they'll need that mulch.

This patio uses groundcovers both in place of and between concrete stones.

SHRUBS & ROSES

Do you know which shrubs are spring-blooming and which are summer-blooming? This is important when you decide to prune. Roses bloom on new wood but lilacs bloom on "old" wood that grew last year. Check the list in February to see which shrubs you can safely prune this month.

TREES

The earliest trees to bloom are those that do so before they put out leaves. Star magnolia is a beautiful small tree that blooms very early and is hardy though Zone 4. Plant this tree where you can admire it from indoors on cold days.

VINES & GROUNDCOVERS

Hardy groundcovers such as pachysandra and ivy start to show green this month. Sometimes they've travelled too far and you need to pull them back. This is easier to do in early spring than in summer when new growth is already well established.

Large areas of the same groundcover tend to look monotonous. Consider planting a few different groundcovers in swaths or in different sections. Spring and summer bulbs, plus some small perennials coming up through the mass, help alleviate that overpowering feeling a block of a single groundcover can give.

Plant groundcovers with smaller leaves among patio stones, as well as among stepping stones, for interest.

PLANT

For Zone 7 and coastal regions, March is usually the start of planting. If the ground is damp and cool, likely in central New York or even the higher elevations of New Jersey, wait to plant. March and April are both iffy months for weather; some years it is fine, others it is dismal. Let nature be your guide.

You'll probably find that any bare-root roses and trees you ordered are delivered this month. Assuming the ground is not frozen, plant right away. Plant dormant crowns of perennial vegetables like asparagus, horseradish, and strawberries this month. For successful planting, it is critical that the soil is free of ice and frost.

Before you start digging holes for trees or a new perennial bed, call the utility marking company in your area. In New Jersey, use New Jersey One Call (www.nj1-call.com), and in New York City, use New York 811 (www.newyork-811.com). The rest of New York State can use Dig Safely New York (www.digsafelynewyork.com). These services try to arrive within a few days and will mark cable and electrical lines and water and sewer pipes. They do not mark private utilities such as well water lines, septic lines, or geothermic/solar power lines or irrigation system pipes. These have to be marked by the company that installed them or a private company that can trace these lines. Once you have the lines marked, you can easily avoid them.

Plant early crowns now, such as asparagus and strawberry plants.

ANNUALS

Plant hardy annual seeds outdoors this month if you did not plant them last fall. Poppies and snapdragons are just two cold-tolerant annuals that like to be planted as soon as the ground is free of ice and snowpack.

BULBS

Summer bulbs suitable for smaller containers can be planted indoors this month. Small varieties of dahlias look great in deck containers as well as in the ground. Keep the containers indoors until spring weather settles and the chance of frost has passed in May.

Lettuce grows well in early spring sunshine. Keep a few plants in a container for early harvest.

EDIBLES

Cold-tolerant kale, spinach, chard, and mustard can be planted outdoors sometime this month. In warmer areas, March 1 is the traditional date to plant potatoes, but for most of us that is much too early. The soil should be well drained and free from ice. Plant asparagus, strawberry, and rhubarb crowns, as well as bare-root, dormant fruit bushes such as raspberries and blueberries. (See February for instructions on how to plant bare-root shrubs and dormant perennial plants.)

Lettuce and cabbages can also be started indoors in March. These plants *do not* thrive in hot summer weather, so they yield better in early gardens. Lettuce seedlings will be transplanted into the garden in April; you can start them now. Plant some lettuce in containers and start hardening them off on bright March days. If a cold snap arrives, bring the container indoors for a day or two. In milder winter areas, the seedlings can be hardened off in late March.

HOUSEPLANTS & CONTAINERS

If you started pansies from seed in early February, they can be hardened off and placed in a container outdoors at the end of March or in April (they usually take about 10 weeks, though, so count the weeks). When the daffodils and early-spring flowers pass their peak, add a few little spring perennials like creeping phlox or sweet William to give color until you transition to summer annuals. In shady containers, bleeding hearts and columbines work well. Later in May, when summer annuals are ready, remove the perennials and replant them in the garden.

LAWNS

Early March can be mild enough to encourage some green growth on the lawn, which reveals areas of dead grass. When the lawn is fully drained and free from snow, these areas to be repaired can be prepared and seeded. This can occur as early as mid-March or as late as April; let the ground and weather be your guide. (Check out the notes on reseeding in April.)

PERENNIALS

Perennials arrive in local stores this month, but delay buying them until the ground is easy to dig. Damp, cold soil often causes the roots of perennials to rot before they have time to grow and produce a healthy plant.

Plant peonies when they are delivered. They will grow this year, but won't bloom. Peonies like to be established before they bloom, but once they start they continue for years.

SHRUBS & ROSES

Dormant roses are safe to plant this month, along with any other dormant shrubs. Forsythia and lilac are the most common shrubs on sale this month in much of our area, and they're safe to plant if you can dig a hole without getting into frosty subsoil. (See February for tips on planting bare-root trees and shrubs.)

TREES

As with shrubs, dormant trees can be planted if you are able to dig the hole easily. If you cannot, keep the tree dormant: cover tree roots with damp newspaper and burlap to keep them moist but not frozen and store the tree in a sheltered location outside. As soon as conditions improve, plant.

VINES AND GROUNDCOVERS

Start these annual vines indoors this month about six to eight weeks before the last frost. Plant them in peat containers so that you do not have to disturb the roots when transplanting.

CARE

The garden starts to come out of dormancy in March, and sometimes it's apparent that not everything made it. But don't be too quick to dig out remnant crowns because some plants like daylilies take longer to break dormancy. It all depends on how harsh your winter was and how much snow protected them.

ANNUALS

Sweet peas are planted early, and they need a support to climb. Put their support in place before the seedlings get higher than an inch or two.

When seedlings have at least one set of true leaves, thin them to just one or two per cell. Remove the excess carefully or use nail scissors to cut them.

FAST-GROWING ANNUAL VINES		
Cypress vine (*Ipomoea quamoclit*)	White/red flowers	Full sun
Corkscrew vine (*Vigna caracalla*)	Blue and white	Full sun
Black-eyed Susan vine (*Thunbergia*)	Yellow and black	Full sun
Morning glory (*Ipomoea*)	Varies	Full sun
Hyacinth bean (*Lablab purpureus*)	Purple/pink	Full sun
Nasturtium (*Tropaeolum majus*)	Yellow/oranges	Full sun
Cup and saucer vine (*Cobaea scandens*)	Purple/white	Full sun
Spanish flag (*Mina lobata*)	Red and yellow	Full sun
Canary vine (*Tropaeolum peregrinum*)	Yellow	Full sun
Cardinal climber (*Ipomoea* × *multifida*)	Scarlet	Full sun

Remove the weakest seedlings so that only one per cell or container remains.

BULBS

Early bulbs are past their best in late March but their leaves are still green. Let the leaves stay until they turn brown. The leaves nourish the bulbs, which is necessary to create healthy bulbs that survive the following summer and winter.

Sometimes daffodils put out lots of green leaves but never produce any flowers. This is due to overcrowding. It is too late to remedy that this year, but make yourself a note to dig the bulbs after the leaves have turned brown and divide them; see June to learn how to do this.

EDIBLES

Watch early seedlings that you've planted outside or that are in a cold frame, and protect them when frosty nights are forecast. Using old towels and sheets can prevent seedlings from getting too cold. Most frosty nights are dry, so the weight of a towel or sheet is fine for one night. Remove these promptly the next morning, after the frost melts. Although kale can tolerate a frost, it is not a good idea to subject seedlings to frost too often; it will slow their growth.

Before putting any crops back into the vegetable garden this year, turn under cover crops that you sowed last fall and refill raised beds with compost.

HOUSEPLANTS & CONTAINERS

As spring progresses, houseplants come out of dormancy. March is a good time to assess their light. Dormant plants that you placed in a back bedroom for winter can now be put into a brighter location. Other plants need to be moved farther away from the window so that they don't get burned by the warmer sun or drafts from open windows.

LAWNS

Most New York and New Jersey lawns contain cool-weather grasses, which include rye grass, fescues, and Kentucky bluegrass. These stay green from the time the snow melts through the first snows of next winter. They are great for areas with cool summers and adequate moisture. They have a tendency to go dormant (brown) in very warm weather (mid- to upper 80s for more than a week or two).

Warm-season grasses do not do well in freezing temperatures, so they're only found in the southern coastal areas of New Jersey. These grass are brown in winter but perform very well in hot, humid summers. Bermuda, centipede, and Zoysia grasses are considered warm-season grasses.

Fertilizer: For the cool-season grasses, the best time to fertilize is in fall after the stress of summer has passed. The grass grows in spring as well, but an excess of nitrogen at this point encourages upward green growth at the expense of roots, which are needed to survive summer. So a light fertilizer in mid-spring (usually late March or early April) is applied, followed by a second fertilizer in September.

Warm-season grasses perform best with early season fertilizer. A second summer application is preferred to a fall application when the grasses are going dormant (they go dormant at about 50^{0}F).

Weed/insect control: Weeds can wreck the appearance of a lawn. There are two ways to treat them: before they germinate or after they germinate. For annual weeds such as crabgrass, the best treatment is a pre-emergent applied just before the seeds germinate—usually April. A rough guide to application timing is to treat when forsythias just finish blooming. **Note:** Do not apply pre-emergents if you plan to reseed any portion of a lawn this summer.

For perennial weeds such as dandelion or violets, a post-emergent is applied. Most broadleaf (non-grassy) weeds are treated by a generic weed-and-feed product. Violets and biennial thistles are best treated with an herbicide sprayed directly onto the weed.

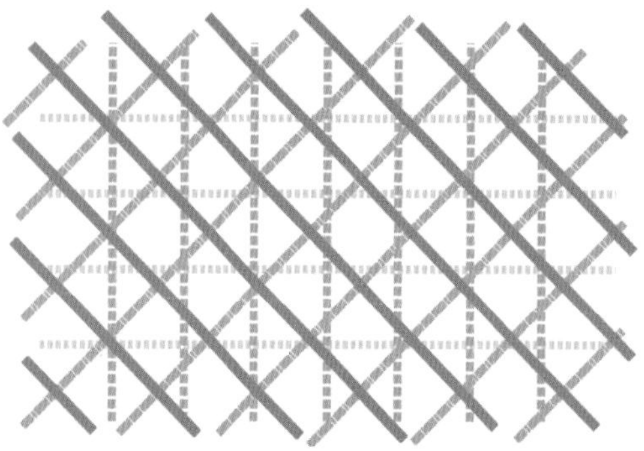

Alter mowing patterns between straight lines and diagonal lines on the lawn.

Mowing: Cool-season grasses are best mowed to about 3 inches. A thick cover of 3-inch-tall grass prevents many weed seeds from reaching the soil surface and thus reduces weed incidence as well. Taller grasses also help retain moisture and keep the soil a little cooler.

Organic lawn care: For those who prefer not to use lawn chemicals, there are organic options. These include lots of commercial fertilizer products as well as some lawn care companies with organic offerings. Organic pre-emergent treatments are based on corn gluten, which in itself is not organic, but it's not toxic to waterways and wildlife. In terms of weed killers, there are some organic herbicides, but these kill lawn grasses as well as weeds and that is *not* what most homeowners are after. You can spot-kill weeds that are already in the lawn as a post-emergent treatment. (See May for details of spot-treating weeds.) Once a lawn is well established, it is much easier to transition to organic treatments, but all lawns can be treated organically; it just takes a little longer to regain control over the weeds than with conventional methods.

Thatch: Excess thatch causes lawn problems. Thatch is a mass of surface or near-surface grass roots, under-decomposed clippings, and debris that accumulates at the base of the grass stems. Too much thatch keeps water and nutrients from getting into the soil and thus compromises a lawn's growth. Thatch is created by excess nitrogen, lack of moisture, and poor mowing habits. Thatch should be removed in fall (see September for instructions).

If your lawn suffers from thatch, plan this summer to address the cultural issues like watering, correct mowing, and reducing nitrogen applications.

PERENNIALS

In warmer areas, perennials are up and running, so it is safe to pull mulch away from their crowns. In cooler zones, continue to protect perennials from heavy frosts.

Carefully remove any dead growth from hellebores, which start to put out new growth this month. Use clippers rather than pulling the old leaves off.

If you didn't edge all the perennial beds last month, March is a good time to finish that. Grass invades flower beds every year, and edging with a sharp straight-edged spade will sever any roots that are heading that way.

Any new garden beds that you made last year are almost ready to plant. Add a new layer of compost to the bed if you didn't last fall, and top off with 2 to 3 inches of mulch. You can make new beds this month, too. A no-till method is great for planting between trees as you don't want to disturb tree roots with tilling. (For turning grass into a flowerbed, as well as the no-till method, see September.)

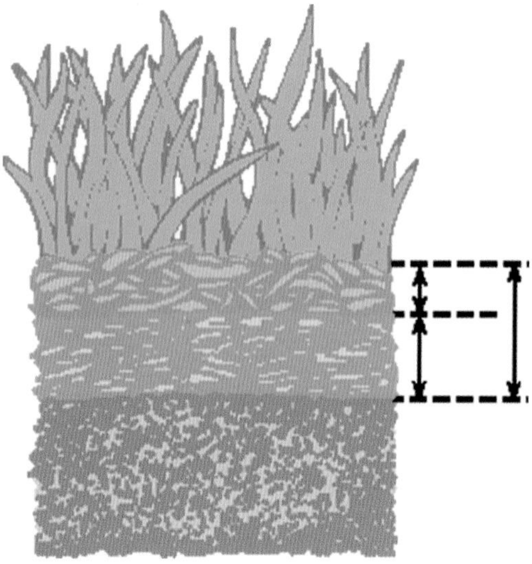

Thatch is a layer of dead leaves and grass that impedes water and nutrients from getting to the roots.

SHRUBS & ROSES

Complete any pruning of roses and summer-blooming shrubs this month. Summer-blooming shrubs form their flowers on stems that start to grow in spring. Cutting off new growth when it is already growing delays development of the flowers. See February for a list of summer-blooming shrubs that *can* be pruned this month.

VINES & GROUNDCOVERS

In areas where the groundcovers are greening up and growing, you can see how far they have travelled.

Use a sharp-edged spade to dig into the vines where they encroach upon steps or sidewalks so that they are not a hazard to walk on. Remove bits of vines plus their roots. Edge areas where the lawn meets groundcovers in the same way. Gently rake or manually remove any leftover winter debris, leaves, and weeds.

Prepare garden beds for groundcovers around trees with a no-till method (see September).

WATER

Generally, March brings plenty of rain, sometimes way too much rain. Excess rain causes flooding, and drainage is affected wherever that occurs. Lawns and established gardens can survive a day or two of flooding, but any more will cause some waterlogged plants to die. Soil erosion is another concern of flooding, so inspect the garden as soon as you can to correct site problems promptly.

River or lake flooding tends to leave a layer of silt over the ground, which disappears into the soil and in most cases is good for the soil. Saltwater flooding from ocean storms is slightly more problematic. Sometimes sand is dragged up with the waves; this can be raked off if it is too deep, but salt contaminates the ground. After the water recedes, rinse flooded areas thoroughly to wash salts through the ground (most areas are sandy so this isn't too difficult). Invest in salt-tolerant shrubs and landscape plants that can cope with salt exposure.

Try to water seedlings from below and let the planting medium absorb the water.

ANNUALS

Although March rains usually keep the ground moist, there are years where the temperatures rise and rain is sparse. Keep any area with annual seedlings moist by watering from a hose if necessary.

BULBS

If you planted tender bulbs such as dahlias in an indoor container, keep them moist until they come out of dormancy. Those bulbs that are going straight into the garden in April or May should still be dormant and don't need watering yet.

EDIBLES

Edible seedlings transplanted outside need to be kept evenly moist. This is particularly important if you planted them in a cold frame because cold frames stop rain from reaching the soil (as well as protecting against cool winds and frosts).

HOUSEPLANTS & CONTAINERS

Slowly increase watering of growing houseplants, particularly if they are close to bright sunny windows. Water flowering bulb arrangements, even after they have stopped blooming.

If you have a warm spring day and the plants are in small containers that are easy to carry, take them outside for a long shower soaking and spray. The spray removes winter dust from the leaves and a good soaking with water removes salts that build up in the soil over time. Let the plant's foliage dry and let the container drain thoroughly before bringing back inside.

HERE'S HOW

TO PRUNE A TREE

Trees purchased as 5-foot saplings often grow to 25 or even 40 feet tall. The stage during the growth of a tree at which you decide to opt for professional tree help depends on what you're comfortable doing and how tall a ladder you have. Basic tree care, though, is two-fold: removing certain limbs for safety or the health of the tree and trimming to maintain a good-looking tree.

When cutting into tree limbs, look for the collar, which is close to the main stem or next branch. This is a small, slightly swollen area that circles around the younger branch. Trim the branch to this collar area—not flush with the next branch or 8 inches away. What should you cut?

1. Start by removing any dead branches.
2. Remove any crossing branches or branches that are going to cross another one. Branches that sit on other branches rub against one another, making abrasions, which in turn invites disease. One or the other of the branches is also more likely to break in a storm.
3. Trim any water sprout growth. These are fast-growing branches that usually head straight up vertically from a branch or around the base of the tree. They are weak branches that fail quickly as well as mar the overall look of a tree.
4. Stand back from the tree and look at its overall shape. Note any branches that are sticking out of the overall shape and remove them.
5. Remove any dual-header branches. These too grow upward and compete with the leader stem in a tree. Remove one of the header branches.

HOW TO REMOVE A TREE LIMB

1

2

3

4

LAWNS

Generally, spring is wet enough that a lawn doesn't need added water, but if you reseeded an area, then those seeds need to be kept moist until they germinate. Just occasionally, in warm, sunny weather, you may need to water more than just once a day.

PERENNIALS

When you plant new perennials, water them immediately. If there's no rain for 48 hours, check the plants to see if they're wilting; if they are, water by hand to keep the area moist. After about a week, check every few days. Most perennials will happily settle into the ground, put down new roots, and start growing in just two or three weeks.

SHRUBS & ROSES

Water newly planted dormant shrubs only if there is no rain for a few days. Check on them but resist watering every day. Shrubs and bare-root roses are just coming out of dormancy and do not need much in the way of extra water.

TREES

Water bare-root trees or balled-and-burlapped trees when you plant them. A tree needs water at its root zone rather than at its top, so watering is best done with a dripping hose rather than overhead watering. See tips on watering in Water in May.

FERTILIZE

Everything is coming out of winter dormancy—established lawns, perennials, shrubs, and trees all start growing in March or April, and a little all-purpose fertilizer is a great way to give the garden a boost. Always check the rate of application on the package before you fertilize anything.

ANNUALS

Seedlings being grown for summer bedding plants or containers benefit from a half-strength liquid fertilizer in March. They still have a while to go before they can go into the ground, so giving them a boost is fine.

BULBS

Spring bulbs growing outside don't need fertilizing this month. The summer bulbs that you took out of winter storage and planted in a potting mix that includes a fertilizer don't need any further fertilization. If they are in a mix with no fertilizer, give them a boost with a general bulb fertilizer.

EDIBLES

Fertilize seedlings with more than two true leaves. Some seedling mixes container a fertilizer, others do not, but most seedlings grow rapidly and have small roots, so a boost is a good idea. Water at half-strength about once a month.

Windowsill herbs are harvested continually and benefit from a dose of fertilizer to keep them going until the outdoor perennial herbs can take over.

HOUSEPLANTS & CONTAINERS

Just like outdoor plants, the indoor plants are coming out of dormancy and benefit from a boost. If you plan on repotting them next month, you can skip fertilizing this month.

LAWNS

Fertilizing the lawn is a major part of lawn care, but doing it too early wastes money and chemicals. First, assess what stage of spring you are in. If the weather has been mild all month and the grass is nicely greened up from winter, then a first application of fertilizer is fine. If you still have a soggy lawn with areas of snow or water that is more brown than green, then hold off until April.

Herbs work hard for us all winter, so a dose of fertilizer is welcome in March.

ABOUT NPK

All fertilizer containers display three numbers on the front of the bag, even if one of the numbers is zero. These are known as NPK. The letters represent nitrogen, phosphorus, and potassium, the three main nutrients necessary for good growth, and the numbers represent the percentage of each nutrient.

N: Nitrogen stimulates greening of lawns and general leafy growth of plants. Too much nitrogen on an annual can promote lots of green leaves at the expense of flowers.

P: Phosphorus is rarely a problem in soils, except in very sandy areas that leach out all nutrients very quickly. In general, phosphorus is needed for good root growth and overall health of the plant. Excess phosphorus, which drains into waterways, contaminates lakes and rivers and has a detrimental effect on wildlife that depends on those waters. Both New York and New Jersey restrict the use of phosphorus in lawn chemicals and household cleaning products.

Ready to Use

FERTIFEED

All Purpose Plant Food

12-4-8

FertiFeed Ready To Use All-Purpose Plant Food
Net Weight 4lb. 12oz. (2.15kg)

GUARANTEED ANALYSIS

Total Nitrogen (N)	12%
12.0% Urea Nitrogen	
Available Phosphate (P_2O_5)	4%
Soluable Potash (K2O)	8%
Manganese (Mn)	0.05%
0.05% Chelated Manganese (Mn)	
Zinc (Zn)	0.05%
0.05% Chelated Zinc (Zn)	
Inert Ingredients	76%

Information regarding the contents and levels of metals in this product is available on the Internet at http://www.regulatory-info-sc.com.

KEEP OUT OF REACH OF CHILDREN

K: Potassium is important for overall cell production and health of the plant. Too much potassium slows growth and affects the taste of vegetables.

Good mowing that allows the clippings to return to the lawn can yield an estimated ½ pound of nitrogen per 1,000-square-feet of lawn.

PERENNIALS

Applying a general fertilizer is fine for perennials. A better way to fertilize the garden is to spread a 2- to 4-inch layer of compost or shredded mulch over the whole bed in early March as perennials are just peeping though the ground.

SHRUBS & ROSES

A layer of compost is far more beneficial than granular fertilizer, but if you don't have access to compost, then a sprinkling of a general fertilizer is fine as a spring boost.

TREES

Established trees more than 10 years old really do not need fertilizer unless they are under stress and look weak (sparse canopy, deformed leaves, dead areas). Check with an arborist or your local Cooperative Extension office for advice on trees over 15 feet high to correct these problems, which could be due to mineral deficiency or poor soil conditions. Young fruit trees benefit from a light fertilizer when the leaves are coming out.

VINES & GROUNDCOVERS

If vines and groundcovers are putting out new leaves, then fertilize lightly with a general fertilizer. If they are only just starting to recover from winter, wait until April. Try to get the fertilizer on the soil surface rather than on the leaves.

PROBLEM-SOLVE

March is a tough month for gardeners—nice sunny days are mixed with cold frosty nights.

HERE'S HOW

TO CALCULATE HOW MUCH FERTILIZER IS NEEDED

Without a soil test, a typical recommended lawn fertilization rate is about 1 pound of nitrogen per 1,000 square feet. A 20-pound bag of 26-0-10 indicates that you have 26 *percent* nitrogen in the bag, which means you would have 5.2 *pounds* of nitrogen (20 × .26), which would cover 5,200 square feet of lawn at 1 pound per every 1,000 square-foot application.

Note: To get pounds of nitrogen per bag, multiply the number of pounds of the complete bag (20 pounds, in this example) by the percent of nitrogen (26 percent or .26 in this example). Nitrogen is always the first of the NPK numbers on the bag, and the number represents a percentage of the total contents. (This calculation works for other fertilizer needs too. Just combine the square feet of annual and perennial beds to get a total, assuming they all need the same rate of fertilizer.)

If your soil test recommends more than 1 pound of fertilizer per 1,000 square feet of lawn, do not put down more than 1 pound at one time. For a recommendation of 2 pounds per 1,000 square feet, apply the first pound to the lawn then four to six weeks later, apply the second dose.

For an even distribution of chemicals, divide the chemicals into two equal parts. Fill the hopper of a spreader with one-half of the product, and walk up and down the lawn, checking that you overlap with each run. Always shut the spreader off at the end of a strip when you turn around. The first half of the application should cover the whole lawn area.

Return to your starting point and refill the hopper with the second half of the product. This time walk up and down the lawn at right angles to the first application. This ensures fertilizer is evenly applied to a lawn.

Sweep up all chemicals that end up on the path or driveways to keep the product out of the street or storm sewers.

The garden takes its own time in getting back to spring growing, and some plants emerge later than others. Don't assume a perennial or shrub is dead because it is still brown. Problems this month include slow drainage of ice-cold snowmelt particularly when the subsoil is still frozen. Areas that are well drained in spring and summer act like poorly draining clay in early spring.

BULBS

Deer avoid daffodils but *love* tulips. The only remedy is to plant tulips in containers on the deck (where determined deer might still find them) or plant them inside a fenced area. Other bulbs disappear due to rodent damage (voles, squirrels), which is helped by replanting in a "cage" of chicken wire.

Early daffodils up this month are often felled by late snow. Cut the fallen blooms and put them into a vase to enjoy. The foliage will recover as soon as the sun returns.

EDIBLES

Fresh new seedlings in the garden attract hungry rabbits and other animals. If your seedlings are disappearing down to the ground or have large chunks taken out of the leaf, cover them with netting or surround the area with a fence that is tall enough to stop rabbits getting in—about 2 feet high should be sufficient.

LAWS AFFECTING FERTILIZER USE

NEW YORK

- No lawn fertilizer can be applied between December 1 and March 1.
- No fertilizer with more than 67 percent phosphorus can be used unless you are establishing a new lawn *or* your soil test shows a phosphorus deficiency.
- A 20-foot buffer zone has to be left between the lawn being fertilized and any waterway.

NEW JERSEY

- No lawn fertilizers can be applied between November 15 and March 1 (commercial companies have until December to complete customer applications).
- Twenty percent of the nitrogen must be slow-release in all fertilizers.
- No phosphorus is allowed in lawn fertilizer unless your soil test (done within the last three years) shows a deficiency, *or* you are establishing a new lawn, *or* you are overseeding an existing lawn, *or* it is a subsurface application.
- A 25-foot buffer zone has to be left between the lawn being fertilized and any waterway (10 feet if a drop spreader is used, or you are using a rotary spreader with a deflector).

HOUSEPLANTS & CONTAINERS

Tender new growth on houseplants is attractive to whiteflies and other insects. Check for eggs under leaves and for little flies to dance off plants when you ruffle their leaves. A pyrethrum spray helps control insects, and horticultural oils are good for dealing with immobile insects and eggs.

Be aware of drafts this month. Nice sunny days are great for opening windows to air out the house, but while 62°F and a light breeze may seem pleasant to you, it is a bit of a shock to plants used to much warmer, quieter conditions. Move them to the floor for a few hours while you open the windows. Look for drying, browning leaves on just one side of a plant to indicate this may be a problem with cold drafts.

LAWNS

Lawns tend to look scrappy in March: detritus from snow and fallen branches make them look rather brown and messy. This is normal and very temporary.

Snow mold results from lawns being covered for a long time; it's commonly seen this month. Snow mold looks like a gray or pink cobweb on the lawn. The issue disappears as soon as the weather clears and the lawn fully dries out from winter.

Dead areas where your dog relieved himself will be visible and should be treated this month. After a dog has used the same place all winter, nitrogen and salts from the urine produce a locally bright green or brown patch. Irrigate affected areas well and soon after the dog has used the area. Training your dog to use a spot other than the lawn helps. As spring moves along, the grass will green up to disguise these "enriched" areas. If the brown areas do not green up, remove the top 4 inches of the lawn and reseed.

Spot-treat dandelions and violets that arrive very early in the season. These are both perennial weeds and are best treated as soon as they arrive and before they produce seeds. Spot treatment is either by digging by hand or using an herbicide aimed directly at the weed.

PERENNIALS

Perennials are coming back to life but rarely have problems this month. Areas of poor drainage cause some perennials to die and some just plain disappear over winter. This can also be caused by rodents eating the roots or winter temperatures getting too cold before sufficient snow cover was established.

SHRUBS & ROSES

Watch for insects or even larger creatures attacking new growth. Whole leaves and young stems disappearing is most likely deer damage,

Hand-dig single weeds.

whereas holes and small areas of leaf damage are more symptomatic of insects. Groundhogs and rabbits eat bits of leaves close to the ground (under 2 feet); the most effective remedy is a fence they cannot breach. Treat insects by removing them or using a horticultural soap/oil. Larger animals can be repelled with a number of natural commercial products.

TREES

Trees generally don't have problems this month, assuming they are showing signs of coming out of dormancy. For those that are late in this process, it's too early to be concerned. A few trees, such as redbuds, actually put out the flower before the leaves. Seasonably mild March temperatures start the process in most trees, whereas a snowy, cold March delays it. Occasionally, very warm March temperatures encourage early blooming trees to put out new leaves and blossom, only to have them frozen off when cold April temperatures arrive. This is particularly problematic when early blooming apricots and peaches put out blooms. Be assured that although new leaves and blossoms, along with any developing fruit, are killed, the tree itself is fine. New leaves soon emerge again and by summer the tree will look normal.

Genetically, some trees such as crape myrtles need much warmer temperatures to bring them out of dormancy, and it may be the end of April or even May before this happens. So do not give up on your trees and shrubs just because they are not showing signs of spring yet.

VINES & GROUNDCOVERS

As vines come out of dormancy, look for brown stems turning green. Clematis is late to green up, so don't give up on vines that do not show signs of new growth this month, particularly in colder areas.

SALT-TOLERANT SHRUBS AND OTHER PLANTS

Each year, some areas of New York or New Jersey get high tides with storm surges that bring the ocean closer to our homes than we'd like. Creating a garden that can deal with these deluges is tough, but some plants are reasonably tolerant of ocean salt. These plants also do well at curbside in the Snow Belt where salt trucks throw a snow/salt mix off the road.

PERENNIALS	SHRUBS
Agapanthus	Beautyberry
Crinum lily	Holly (some varieties)
Daylilies	Junipers
Gaillardia	Mock orange
Goldenrod	Red osier dogwood
Santolina	Rose-of-Sharon

For a more complete list of trees, shrubs, perennials, and annuals, check: www.ces.ncsu.edu/files/library/71/Salt%20Tolerant%20Plants.pdf.

Santolina.

April

April is the second transition month that edges us closer to summer. Almost all areas are free from snow and ice. Mild temperatures last for several days, and cool nights replace cold winter temperatures. Snow does happen in April, though, and northern areas in particular should be watchful of the weather. Garden centers capitalize on spring fever and fill their shelves with summer flowers and already-flowering summer tomatoes. This can be dangerous for the gardener who is lulled into thinking that frosts are a thing of the past and summer has truly arrived—not so! The average last frost (for virtually all of us) is not until next month for even the warmest areas in the region, so hold onto your wallet, enjoy browsing, but let the stores keep the plants safe for another week or two.

The warm days of April are perfect for hardening off seedlings and taking care of the weeds that arrive. There is time to finish the last of the pruning of summer-blooming shrubs such as roses and some hydrangeas as well as tidying up the garden in general.

You will find lots of plant sales this month. Everyone from garden clubs to historic houses and public gardens have plant sales where you can find a variety of quality plants and some less-common items, such as unusual shrubs. Most of these plants are grown and tended by the people who are selling them and who can attest to the delight of the plant as well as the best growing conditions. Talk to the people selling the plants about the conditions that suit the plants (sun or shade) and ask if it can be planted immediately. This last point is important because sometimes you find peppers and other tender annuals that should not be put into the ground until at least May.

Cool or damp days are great to start seeds for annuals that will fill out the landscape, containers, or vegetable garden. In the garden, admire the early spring blooms of little *Iris reticulata*, daffodils, hellebores, and early tulips.

PLAN

If you did make garden plans this past winter, they should be dusted off and adjusted or updated with this year's conditions. You can also work out the step-by-step process to put the grand plan into action. The last frost date is still a ways off, but garden plans and seed schedules can be drawn up, and you can get started with the first steps.

One of the first jobs outside is to refresh mulch on all garden beds and around trees. Adding 2 to 3 inches of mulch to garden beds is much easier to do when the perennials are just peeping through than it is in May when they are growing well.

ANNUALS

April is also a good time to get a seed schedule together for starting annual seeds. Mark the average last frost date on your calendar and count back four to six weeks from that date. Check www.plantmaps.com for the last frost date.

BULBS

Now that your stored bulbs are sprouting, you can assess how many remain viable for planting this year. Canna's white rhizomes are similar to potatoes in that they produce "eyes" where new stems grow, and cannas have a tendency to create large rhizomes with many growth points. They can be divided easily; just remember all those little cannas grow to full-sized plants, so decide where in the landscape you're going to plant them. Each canna reaches 3 or even 4 feet tall, making them great for the back of a sunny border. They average about 18 to 24 inches across, so a planting of just six canna rhizomes in a group is sufficient for a great tropical look.

Comfortable April temperatures are perfect for mulching and other heavy garden chores.

EDIBLES

Seed starting is a fun time for vegetable gardeners, but we tend to overplant. With tomatoes, for instance, there are many varieties with some producing early cherry-sized tomatoes and others yielding fruit that is great for tomato sauces for pizza and lasagna. Growing one of every sort takes a lot of room, so unless you have a lot of time, space, and energy, decide which traits and varieties you really want and grow just enough for your needs.

LAWNS

Lawns revive this month, and evidence of problems will be apparent. Dead areas, lawn weeds, and other issues need to be addressed early. If your lawn wasn't as lush as you would have liked last year, get a soil test done (your local Cooperative Extension office can help), and check for any nutrients that are lacking. (See March to learn how to do a soil test.)

HOUSEPLANTS & CONTAINERS

Final design ideas for outside containers can be made, and if you need annuals for those containers, check your seed packages and start them this month. A basic container design includes a tall feature, a layer of mid-sized plants to contrast, and something that drapes over the sides. Shade options include coleus, begonias, and impatiens. You can include perennials such as hostas or coreopsis that are often on sale this month and are small enough at the start of the season to work well in containers. At the end of summer, transplant them into the perennial garden.

Containers can hold just one plant or you can group several containers of varying sizes and contents together. Smaller containers can be placed on porch steps or sit on top of pedestal features in the flowerbed for give extra height.

Containers can mix shrubs and perennials, as well as annuals.

PERENNIALS

Take advantage of spring sales to add a few new plants to your perennial garden. (See Plant, Perennials in this chapter for directions on dividing perennials.)

SHRUBS & ROSES

Shrubs make a great backdrop for perennials as well as serving as an attractive border. There are great shrubs for sun and shade.

Roses are putting out new growth, and their overall health can be assessed. Dead branches are not uncommon on rose bushes; these will become apparent as new growth starts. Selectively trim some of the old, straggly stems of climbing roses to keep the shrub healthy. (See February for more on pruning roses.)

TIPS FOR A PLANT SWAP

Plant sales or swaps are great events to meet other gardeners and get interesting plants for your garden. Usually the people who organize the event are knowledgeable gardeners, but attendees may not be. When it comes to labeling plants, most sales leave a lot to be desired, and pertinent information is often missing, so be careful about what you pick up. Be aware that some common plants in a plant swap are there because they frequently run out of bounds and will be aggressive in your garden too. Ask questions, use the browser on your phone to research, and have fun finding jewels in selections.

When donating cuttings:

- Pot up divisions of perennials three to four weeks before the sale.
- Label each pot with the plant name, sun or shade needs, mature height, and bloom color. A piece of a slat from an old plastic window blind works well for labels.
- Water divisions well.

When picking up plants:

- Take a couple of bags or a leftover plant tray to put the new plants in.
- Check to see that all the information is on the label—if not, ask.
- Check plants for bugs or problems. Holes in leaves, discolored leaves, and rotting crowns are just a few signs of problems.
- Once the plants are home, plant as soon as possible.

GREAT SHRUBS FOR SUNNY AREAS		
PLANT	*HARDINESS*	*CAN TAKE PART SHADE?*
Abelia (*Abelia × grandiflora*)	5–8	yes
Buttonbush (*Cephalanthus occidentalis*)	3–11	no
Carolina allspice (*Calycanthus floridus*)	4–9	no
Blue mist shrub (*Caryopteris × clandonensis*)	5–9	yes
Daphne (*Daphne cneorum*)	4–7	no
Deutzia (*Deutzia gracilis*)	4–8	yes
Flowering almond (*Prunus triloba*)	3–7	no
Fothergilla (*Fothergilla major*)	4–9	yes
Virginia sweetspire (*Itea virginica*)	5–9	no
Mountain laurel (*Kalmia latifolia*)	5–8	yes
Spirea (*Spiraea*)	3–8	no
Wiegela (*Weigela*)	4–9	yes

GREAT SHRUBS FOR SHADY AREAS		
PLANT	*HARDINESS*	*CAN TAKE SOME SUN?*
Dogwood (*Cornus* spp.)	3–7	yes
Ninebark (*Physocarpus opulifolius*)	2–7	yes
Fragrant honeysuckle (*Lonicera fragrantissima*)	4–8	yes
Snowberry (*Symphoricarpos albus*)	3–7	yes
Spicebush (*Lindera benzoin*)	4–9	yes
Koreanspice viburnum (*Viburnum carlesii*)	4–7	yes

TREES

Trees are putting out blossoms and leaves, so you can easily see which branches were killed during winter. Sometimes whole areas of a tree will decline, indicating a problem. Look for a sparse leaf canopy and deformed leaves. As the season moves on, look for early changes in leaf color or premature leaf dropping. Any tree pruning should be completed this month, including removing any dead or crossing branches.

VINES & GROUNDCOVERS

Any young vines planted last year may not have grown past their first nursery-sized trellis yet. This year they probably will, and a more permanent support should be installed. Purchase string or ties so that you are ready to secure the vine to a support (if necessary) and encourage the vines to reach the support or nearby fence when they need it. Like many hardy shrubs and trees, vines sometime take a year or two before they really start to travel. Training young vines is always a lot easier than persuading an overgrown vine to sit on a trellis.

PLANT

April is a good month to plant everything that tolerates a little frost. That includes perennials, shrubs, and trees. If you can schedule a day before a gentle rain to plant, that works well for the plants and helps them get settled in.

ANNUALS

Start annual seeds for bedding plants this month. Most take four to six weeks to be large enough to transplant to the garden or outdoor containers.

Hold off buying tender annuals on sale at the store. When frosty nights arrive in mid- to late April, they'll perish and you'll be back to a store for replacements. If you do buy petunias or zinnias, do not plant them until next month. Keep them well watered, in a sunny position close to the house, and bring them quickly inside on cold nights.

BULBS

The bulbs that you wintered over indoors can be put outside this month. The bulbs can take a light frost but the tender young sprouts should be covered if frost is forecast. Plant cannas just under the surface; plant larger bulbs like dahlias or ornamental alliums 2 to 3 inches below the surface. Wait until next month to plant more tender bulbs such as elephant ears.

EDIBLES

Peas and potatoes are the main crops to plant now. Plant potatoes in a 6- to 8-inch-deep trench and cover with soil. As the potato plants grow, mound new soil up around the stems and leaves, with some leaves exposed. Perennial asparagus, rhubarb, and strawberries can still be planted this month, along with fruit bushes and trees. Cool-weather lettuce can be hardened off and carefully transplanted into the garden toward the end of this month. Be prepared to cover them if a late frost arrives.

Peas benefit from being treated with an inoculant. This is a black powder containing microbacteria, which helps peas (and beans) take nitrogen from the air/soil and convert it into a form that the roots can use. Soak pea seeds for an hour in water or light fertilizer such as a compost tea, drain, and dust with inoculant before planting. Peas can be planted directly into the ground where they're to grow and sprinkled with inoculant if you prefer. The key factor is to get the inoculant in contact with the pea seed. Inoculant is available from all main online suppliers of seeds as well as some local nurseries.

LAWNS

Renovation and reseeding of the whole lawn can also be done this month but, if possible, delay until fall. (See Lawns in September.)

Potatoes are planted in trenches.

PERENNIALS

Take advantage of spring garden shows and plant specials to get more perennials. Assuming the ground is free from frost and snow, perennials can be planted this month.

Get perennial seedlings ready for planting outdoors in mid- to late April depending on weather. Aim to plant on a cloudy, calm, mild day after the seedlings have been hardened off. (See Care for directions on hardening off seedlings.)

SHRUBS & ROSES

Dormant roses, potted roses, and shrubs can be planted this month. Check February for how to plant bare-root and dormant roses.

TREES

Trees are sold bare root and dormant, balled and burlapped, or in a container (usually in leaf and bloom). Plant bare-root trees as soon as you can and before they start to put out new leaves. Container as well as balled-and-burlapped trees can

HERE'S HOW

TO RESEED SMALL AREAS OF LAWN

1. Prepare the area by scraping away any dead grass, weeds, stones, and roots from the area.
2. Add about a 1-inch-deep layer of compost.
3. Rake the area smooth and flat.
4. Evenly spread seed over the prepared area.
5. Cover with a little compost or topsoil—no more than ¼ inch.
6. Cover with straw to help retain moisture (optional).
7. Water to moisten the area, and continue to keep the area moist (but not wet).
8. Continue to keep the soil moist until the grass has filled in and is growing well.
9. When the grass is about 3 inches tall, you can give it the first mow.

Note: Keep children and pets off the young grass if possible until after the first mowing.

be held a day or two but should be planted as soon as you buy them, if possible.

VINES & GROUNDCOVERS

Start planting perennial groundcovers this month. Sweet woodruff (*Galium odoratum*) is a great option for filling in under shrubs, and creeping thymes make great groundcovers for sunny areas. For fast cover, decrease the plant spacing from about 8 inches to 6 inches, depending on the size of the original plants.

CARE

April is a busy month for gardeners. New growth on shrubs and young trees is attractive to insects and the bark of larger trees is a target for deer to rub their antlers against. With an abundance of warm days, it is a rude awakening to see frost or even light snow in the forecast. This scenario can abort fruit production on early-blooming fruit trees such as apricots and peaches. There's really not much you can do, apart from protecting smaller trees and shrubs by throwing a sheet over them. The cold will not kill the tree, but it can make it look like a mess for a few weeks until more new leaves arrive.

April is a good time to renew landscape mulch. Aim for between 2 to 3 inches of mulch over all the flowerbeds as well as around trees and shrubs. There are several categories mulches on the market—organic and inorganic.

Organic mulches are made from trees or pine needles that have fallen. Lawn clippings and chopped fall leaves are also organic mulches.

ANNUALS

The second part of April is a good time to start clearing out annuals from the windowsill and hardening them off. (See page 78 for how to harden off plants and seedlings so that they're not shocked by the direct sun or wind.)

BULBS

As spring bulbs die back, their leaves turn brown. This is a good sign that most nutrients have been returned to the bulb, and it's safe to trim off the dying growth. If your daffodils didn't bloom, dig up the bulbs and divide them.

EDIBLES

Don't rush seedlings out until the weather is settled and the soil is warm and well drained.

Young plants growing in a cold frame can dehydrate quickly in spring unless you open the frame's lid when the sun is out. They also aren't able to take advantage of rain, so watering is important for these plants. If the weather is mild, leave the lid of the cold frame open all day and night.

The raspberry patch needs attention this month. Raspberries and blackberries send out shoots that erupt and grow anywhere in a 2-foot radius from the mother stems. The fruit is borne on last year's wood, and in some cases, this year's wood. Older brown stems are not usually as productive. The problem comes with all these stems tangle around one another, making harvest impossible. To sort them out, visualize a line where you want the stems to grow. Remove stems growing away from that line, and secure last year's stems to a post or wire. Remove any older, brown stems and old remnant flowerheads from last year. Weed and compost the area when you can access it. For an old berry patch, you should consider trimming everything down and clearing out pathways in the patch. As new stems grow this year, restrict them to the line(s) you established.

Leftover milk cartons and jugs make easy protection from excess winds as well as cutworms.

HERE'S HOW

TO DIVIDE PERENNIALS

Perennials are easy to divide in spring when their growth is just showing. Later in the season and in fall, they can still be divided, but the foliage is more likely to get damaged. Perennials usually spread by increasing their root mass or crown. Hostas have a solid crown, whereas coreopsis has more of a mass of intertwined roots. Both are divided in the same way.

1. Dig up the whole plant.
2. Sometimes a plant will fall apart into several pieces without your help and can easily be split by massaging the roots apart. If it doesn't, use a flat-edged spade and slice down into the roots to divide the mass into two (or more) parts.
3. Replant each section in a new location.

1

2

Early in the year when there is very little growth on perennials, you can often just slice down into the ground to remove a section. This method works well with perennial groundcovers.

Note: Most perennials benefit from division every three to five years. The center of the plant becomes crowded, woody, or the plant will spread too far.

Perennial grasses can be more of a challenge. Their thick, matted root zones increase in girth quickly making it almost impossible to break the mass into smaller pieces. Divide these at least every other year unless you have a chainsaw handy to split the mature grass apart.

HERE'S HOW

TO PLANT POTTED SHRUBS, ROSES, AND SMALL TREES

Shrubs (roses, small trees) are much larger than perennials, but they're similar in the way they're planted.

Before you start, it's important to know where your utilities are before digging; if you don't know, find out. Check the mature size of the shrub (height *and* width) so that you can site it where it's not going to grow into your neighbor's yard. Also check the plant tag to see if the shrub needs full sun, part sun, or shade. You might find additional information by scanning a QR code that's commonly found on plant tags.

HERE'S HOW TO PLANT:

1. Place the containerized plants where you want them to grow.
2. Dig a hole that is approximately the same size as the container and place the excavated soil on a tarp. (The current advice from academic sources says no soil amendments are needed; the differences in soil/amendment textures cause uneven water absorption rates.)
3. Lay the plant on the ground and remove its container. This is not always easy but try not to yank the plant out of the container by pulling on its stems (and do not pull a tree out by its trunk—you'll damage the whole tree if it breaks). If it's stuck, use a knife or sturdy scissors to cut the container away. Or try rolling the container on its side.
4. Check the hole against the container and adjust if needed by making it deeper or wider to accommodate the rootball.
5. Check the roots of the plant; look for dense, matted roots. Pry the roots apart to free the root mass. If the root mass is tightly coiled, take a knife and make one or two slits in the sides of the root mass (about 2 to 3 inches deep). Then roots should be able to be spread.
6. Place the plant in the hole and check the depth. The soil level in the container should be the same as in the hole. To check the level, lay a straight edge such a piece of wood or broom handle across the hole, which now contains the plant. The plant should not be below the handle, nor should it raise the bar above the edge. If it does raise the bar, remove the plant and make a deeper hole; if below the bar, add a little extra soil to build up the base of the hole.
7. Place the rootball in the hole and slowly refill with the excavated soil, making sure that the soil gets to the bottom and sides of the hole. Continue until the hole is filled.
8. Check the plant to see that it is upright and not leaning.
9. Water the plant well, checking that soil around the stem is still level with the surrounding soil line after watering. Add more soil around the shrub if necessary.
10. Add a 2- to 3-inch layer of mulch, but do not let the mulch touch the stem.
11. Periodically check that the plant is securely planted. Small shrubs and trees that start to lean within a few days of planting can usually be straightened. Add a stake to keep small trees upright.
12. If the tree shows wilting, know that some wilting is normal just after planting. A good watering should help, but do not overwater. A good, 15-minute weekly watering should be sufficient.

April is a good time to spread a 2- to 3-inch layer of mulch over the top of the vegetable bed before adding seeds, or you can lightly incorporate it into the soil before planting.

LAWNS

You'll probably need to mow the lawn this month. Keep the mowing height about 3 inches for fescues and Kentucky bluegrass. Don't cut more than one-third of the height at one time. If vacations or wet conditions prevent you from mowing, adjust the mower height to accommodate the taller grass, and mow twice, a week apart, to regain the proper height.

HOUSEPLANTS & CONTAINERS

Trim houseplants that are going outside for summer, such as *Pelargonium*, back this month to accommodate fresh new growth.

PERENNIALS

Uncover perennials by removing mulch over the perennial crowns and divide if needed (see this month's Plant, Perennials section). Shasta daisies are one perennial that increase in girth quite rapidly after their first year.

Harden off any perennial seedlings that you've been growing. They can be put into the ground at the end of the month.

SHRUBS & ROSES

After spring-blooming lilacs and other shrubs finish blooming, prune them if necessary. (See February for how to prune shrubs.) Small or new plants don't necessarily need pruning, but keeping a regular maintenance schedule before these shrubs get too large is a good idea. Evergreen shrubs, holly, boxwood, and so forth are putting on new growth. Pruning these is best done after the first flush of new growth has slowed—May or even June. Otherwise, you'll be pruning a second or even third time to keep the bushes closely clipped.

Borderline shrubs like rosemary and crape myrtles in central and southern New Jersey or Long Island, New York, may take longer to break dormancy than other plants in the garden. Watch them and do not rip them out thinking they're dead until at least June. Likewise, any gardener who is growing

HERE'S HOW

TO PLANT BALLED-AND-BURLAPPED TREES

Balled-and-burlapped trees are dug from a field, and the rootball is wrapped in burlap, then secured with twine or a metal basket. The burlap is *usually* biodegradable, but that takes a long while, and some trees are wrapped in non-biodegradable material, so remove as much of the covering as you can before planting.

1. Dig the hole as described on page 72, making sure the depth and width will accommodate the tree's rootball. For burlapped trees, it is very helpful to measure the deep and width of the rootball (while it's still in the burlap) with a tape measure and check that the hole is large enough to accommodate the tree.
2. Lay the tree down and remove the metal or twine—some soil or mud will probably fall out too.
3. Pull as much of the burlap off the rootball as possible.
4. Place the tree in the waiting hole.

1

3

plants that are borderline for an area will notice some delay in those breaking dormancy.

TREES

Check stakes on small trees. During winter winds and storms, ropes and ties can cut into bark, and gnawing rodents can fray ropes. Adjust or remove stakes if needed (see May).

VINES & GROUNDCOVERS

All perennial vining plants, like clematis and trumpet vines, should be attached to a sturdy trellis or fence. On walls, use masonry nails and string a wire between them to support the vines. For easy cleaning behind the vine, a trellis that is fixed at the base and has a hinge will allow access to the back side of the trellis.

WATER

Outdoor plants should be getting enough water this month, but indoor seedlings and plants need to be watched. However, young plants outside and in containers can still dry out in brisk spring breezes and warm sun, so keep a close watch on them.

5. Straighten the tree.
6. Refill the hole and water well.
7. Add a layer of mulch (2 to 3 inches), around but not touching the stem.
8. Stake, if needed. See more about staking trees in May.

A third way to plant large trees is with a (commercial) tree spade. Very large spades dig the hole and fetch a mature tree, which is then plugged into the waiting hole. There are many advantages to using a tree spade service, the main one being that you'll install a full-sized tree instantly. The large rootball included when the tree spade digs up the tree minimizes transplant stress, and survival rates are high. The downside is the cost of the service and the source of trees.

4

6

ANNUALS
Water annual seedlings carefully so that you don't knock them over. Newer seed trays allow bottom watering from a reservoir under the seed-growing medium. When watering from above, mist with a hand spray or use a fine "rose" spray on the watering can.

BULBS
Water newly planted rhizomes, such as irises, when you put them into the ground and water every day or two if needed.

EDIBLES
Maintain watering schedules for seedlings indoors and outdoors as necessary. Remember to water seedlings that are in the cold frame.

LAWNS
It is rare that lawns need watering in spring except for newly seeded areas, which should be kept moist until the grass is well established. Check the directions for lawn treatments to see if they need to be watered within 24 hours. Keep pets and children off the area until the chemicals have been dissolved by rain or watering.

HERE'S HOW

TO PLANT AN AREA WITH GROUNDCOVERS

Groundcovers are used to cover large areas under trees or on slopes that are difficult to maintain. They are also used under shrubs. Typically, but not always, they're low-growing plants that act as a living mulch, suppressing weeds and keeping soil cooler.

Prep the area you want to plant a groundcover by first amending and loosely turning the soil.

For groundcovers under shrubs:

1. Measure the whole area to be covered.
2. On a diagram, draw the area to scale (approximately).
3. Add circles for the shrubs.
4. Estimate the area of the shrub bed (length × width for a rectangular garden bed).
5. Estimate the area of a shrub base—leave about 2 to 3 inches around a shrub so that the groundcover does not start to climb through the shrub.
6. Add all the shrub areas together and subtract from the overall garden area.
7. Pick the groundcover—either for shade or sun—and note how far apart they are planted and how far they typically spread. You'll find spacing advice on the plant tags.
8. Divide the total area to be covered (from step 6) by how far apart the plants need to spaced. This figure tells you how many plants you need.
9. Space the plants around the shrubs and garden area, then plant (see May for how to plant perennials).
10. Mulch between the groundcovers and water well.

As the seasons progress, the amount of needed mulch decreases and the area of groundcover increases. Eventually you'll need to dig out some groundcovers each spring so that remaining plants have room to grow.

For a large empty area:

1. Start by getting the overall area of the planting bed (width × length).
2. Pick the groundcover and divide the total area to be covered with the distance between each groundcover plant. This gives the total number of plants required.
3. Plant and mulch—steps 9 and 10 above.

For more interest in a large area, add a few different groundcovers or a few small shrubs.

TWO TYPES OF MULCH

ORGANIC MULCHES

Pine or hardwood nuggets: This is the coarsest wood mulch and can draw nitrogen from the soil as they decompose. They do a decent job of insulating soil and suppressing weeds.

Shredded hardwood: This is much finer than nuggets and usually decomposes within a season. It's great for weed retention.

Pine needles: These are more common in the South, but pine needles spread easily if you can get them.

Cocoa hulls: Cocoa hulls are newer to the market than the hardwood mulches, and they should be avoided if you have dogs—chocolate is poisonous to dogs. The hulls are light and tend to blow around until a few rain showers have arrived.

Straw: Straw is popular to use on strawberry beds and newly seeded grass. Straw breaks down quickly, but it's good for moisture retention.

INORGANIC MULCHES

The downside with inorganic mulches is that they don't decompose, so if you change your mind you have to manually remove the mulch. It is also difficult to plant through these mulches.

Pebbles, river rock, and gravel: These look good when they're newly spread. They're good for weed retention for the first year, but as annual seeds disperse, they'll root in the rocks, so weed protection is limited.

Rubber mulch: This is mainly made from recycled tires and works well for moisture retention and weed suppression. But, it does have an odor when it gets warm in summer. Rubber mulch is *not* environmentally friendly, and you'll have a real issue when you want to replace it.

Landscape fabrics and plastic: These are often called "mulch," but they are really more of a weed suppressant. The fabrics do allow water through and seeds do settle on top. Plastic is best used just to warm the vegetable bed in spring. Plastic does not allow water to penetrate and does not break down to help the soil. On a slope, plastic acts as a slide for any mulches that are put on top.

A word about dye-colored mulches: The chemicals in the dye are supposed to be fine for plants and animals, but I don't recommend colored mulch around edible crops. Because dyes disguise the origin of the wood chips, it is harder to ensure they did not come from chemically treated wood.

HERE'S HOW

TO CALCULATE THE AMOUNT OF MULCH YOU'LL NEED

A basic calculation includes the length × width of a garden bed, multiplied by 0.25 if you're working in feet (3 inches of mulch is one-quarter, or .25, of a foot). Bags of mulch vary from 1 to 4 cubic feet per bag. For most landscaping projects, bags of mulch are fine. More complicated calculations come in when you need *a lot* of mulch. For instance, for a garden bed that is 15 feet × 3 feet:

15 feet × 3 feet = 45 square feet × 0.25 cubic feet = 11.25 cubic feet of mulch

Bulk mulch is sold in cubic yards and is delivered by truck right to your driveway. There's usually a delivery cost, but when you need more than a cubic yard (27 cubic feet), it's less expensive overall.

HOUSEPLANTS & CONTAINERS

Warm spring sunshine can dry out containers quickly. They need to be watered at least every other day if the sun is out. Self-watering containers can help maintain moisture levels and ensure that the container does not dry out. After heavy rain and storms, remember to check the saucers under the outdoor containers as they retain water and impede drainage of the containers.

PERENNIALS

Except for just-installed plants, perennials usually get plenty of moisture.

SHRUBS & ROSES

Any new container-grown shrubs or roses should be watered as needed. If you have no rain for three days, check to see if the shrubs need a little extra. Put your finger into the soil around the shrub to see if it's dry or look for wilting leaves on the shrub. This is particularly important in areas where the subsoil is sandy and drains moisture very quickly.

HERE'S HOW

TO HARDEN OFF SEEDLINGS

Young plants have spent the early part of their lives in a warm, still atmosphere. Acclimating seedlings to wind and direct sun is something that takes a few days. This adjustment is call "hardening off."

1. Pick a calm day to take the seedling tray outdoors for the first time.
2. Place the tray in the shade and bring it back in after about four hours.
3. Repeat this on Day 2.
4. On Day 3, leave the seedlings out all day and return them in the evening.
5. By Day 4, you can introduce seedlings to direct sun for three to four hours and then return them to shade.
6. On days 5 and 6, leave seedlings in full sun for a longer time (four to six hours).
7. By Day 7, seedlings should be able to stay outside in the sun all day and night (check the temperatures). While outdoors, seedlings dry out faster, so continue to monitor the water level and protect them from storms and high winds.

TREES

Most trees will be fine this month. However, take particular care that newly planted trees don't dry out too much.

VINES & GROUNDCOVERS

These should get enough water this month from natural sources.

FERTILIZE

If the landscape was not ready for spring fertilization last month, make a note to do that this month—see March for general landscape fertilization.

ANNUALS

Annuals are still waiting to go into the ground, and a half-strength general fertilizer will give them a boost until you pass the last frost date in May, when it's safe to transplant them into the garden.

BULBS

If container-planted bulbs and rhizomes of cannas, dahlias, and other tender plants have sprouted, then a light fertilizer is fine. If the bulbs are still dormant, save fertilization until they go into the ground at the end of this month or next month.

EDIBLES

Spring peas are up and growing, so a sidedressing of compost is a good idea. Other spring salad items don't need any more fertilizer, as they don't stay in the ground very long. Indoors, frost-tender vegetables such as tomatoes and peppers should be given a half-strength dose of organic fertilizer every month, or water with compost tea every week. Continue this until the seedlings are planted outside.

LAWNS

If you fertilized the lawn last month, then leave it be for this month. For those who live in colder climates, the grass wasn't dry enough for you to apply fertilizer last month, so an application of general nitrogen fertilizer now is fine.

HOUSEPLANTS & CONTAINERS

Maintain a regular schedule with houseplants that is suitable for that plant; African violets have different needs than orchids. As a general rule, a half-strength general fertilizer twice a month is sufficient for most houseplants. If a white crust forms on the top of the soil, it's an indication that you're overfertilizing. If this happens, repot the whole plant in fresh mix and stop fertilizing for a month (most potting mixes include a fertilizer), then resume biweekly applications.

Side-dress by applying fertilizer around *the plants.*

PERENNIALS, SHRUBS, ROSES, TREES, VINES & GROUNDCOVERS

Like lawns, perennial beds, shrubs, trees, and vines only need one spring application of fertilizer, so skip this if you did that last month.

PROBLEM-SOLVE

In addition to your landscape coming out of winter dormancy, animals, rodents, and insects do too. Integrated Pest Management (IPM) is a way to deal with any pests; it involves scouting for problems and treating them early. Critical to successful IPM is identifying not just the problem but the best time to treat it. For instance, Japanese beetles lay their eggs near the soil surface in late summer. The eggs hatch and small grubs start eating—and growing. As the temperatures drop, they burrow down into the ground. In spring, the now much-larger grub returns to the surface where it feasts on grass roots before pupating, and finally turning into the beetle that we see in summer. Spring is when we notice the damaged lawn and see the nasty grubs, but the best time to treat a lawn for grubs is in late summer when they are small, close to the surface, and require less eradication formulas. (See July for more about using IPM to help solve landscape problems.)

ANNUALS

Check indoor seedlings to make sure that they are not leaning toward the light source or getting leggy from poor light. Turn their tray daily and add another light source if the seedlings are spindly.

BULBS

If your spring bulbs didn't come up this year, they may have been attacked by rodents. Various remedies include enclosing bulbs within a buried wire basket; see October for more on protecting bulbs. Aboveground, tulip leaves are a favorite of deer. Plant these delightful spring flowers inside a protected, fenced area.

Check iris leaves as they come up and look for little notches on the side that indicate borers are present. Dig the iris and inspect the rhizomes for holes where borers enter. Discard afflicted rhizomes.

EDIBLES

Rabbits and groundhogs may become an issue in the vegetable garden this month and for the rest of the summer. Granular treatments are available that deter most animals, but groundhogs are tough to control. If you see large holes coming up through the raised bed, or a 6-inch-wide hole going down through the bed—it's likely a groundhog. Fencing the bed is about the only thing that stops these pesky critters. Check January for information on animal problems including how to construct a fence to deter groundhogs.

Seedlings that are outside can be attacked by anything from cutworms, damping off issues, and rabbits. A 4-inch "pipe" made from the inside of paper towel roll can be used as a collar around seedlings to help protect against worms and rodents. Sink the collar about ½ inch into the ground around the seedlings. Damping off disease is a soil-borne fungal disease and can be an issue in cool, damp springs and/or poor soil drainage.

LAWNS

Scout for insect and vole problems under the surface. To assess if your lawn has grubs, carefully remove a 1-foot square section of lawn plus the underlying grass roots. Damage to the root zone or grubs, if present, should be evident. Repeat this for several areas of the lawn. A general threshold for treatment is six to eight grubs per sample; if this number is exceeded in most areas, you have a problem. If there are grubs in just one area, treat just that area. Counting the number of grubs is effective this month, but leave the actual treatment until fall. Lawn pesticides, when used, should always be used judiciously as pesticides also kill earthworms and other helpful insects in the subsoil as well as being dangerous to pets and children.

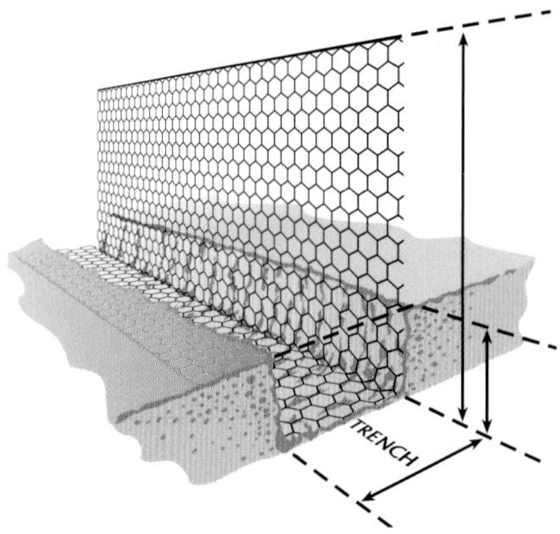

This fence is for groundhogs, which both burrow and climb. Rabbits are fine with a smaller fence as they neither climb nor burrow.

If your newly seeded grass did not come up or had poor germination, did you use a pre-emergent or crabgrass treatment within the past eight weeks? These affect seed germination. Weed killers and other general herbicide residue can also kill the seeds before they grow very tall. Check the herbicide label to see how soon after treatment you can sow new seed.

HOUSEPLANTS & CONTAINERS

Watch for insect problems on indoor plants. Whiteflies (seen when you brush against the plants) and mealybugs (white fuzz on the stem or under the leaves) are just two pests that can be treated early, before they become problems. Look for products labeled for houseplants and that are suitable for indoor use, such as some Neem preparations. Follow the instructions for the treatment and always keep them away from food, children, and animals. Horticultural pyrethrum-based sprays are safe for indoor use.

PERENNIALS

Deer damage to perennials is sometimes an issue. Look for truncated stems, stems missing leaves, and hoof prints around plants. Sprinkle or spray deer repellant around the garden to help deter browsing.

SHRUBS & ROSES

Deer damage on shrubs is similar to that on perennials.

Check for beetles on viburnums as they leaf out. The beetle egg can be seen on the stem just as the leaf buds swell. Handpick beetle eggs if possible. A pesticide may be needed if the beetles are severe. Females lay about five hundred eggs on or in the bark each summer that then eat and destroy the leaves and branch. Eventually this kills the shrub.

TREES

After the fruit has set on fruit trees, selectively remove some, particularly on young trees. Too many heavy peaches or apples on small limbs can cause them to bend and even snap under the weight. Ideally, fruit trees under four years old should only have one or two fruits per branch. Groups of multiple fruits growing close together should be reduced to allow just one to mature.

Cedar and apple trees are alternate hosts for cedar-apple rust. The disease is a fungal issue that starts in damp springs on cedar trees. As the fungus grows, it swells to show a bright orange gall on the cedar branch. The gall releases spores, which become airborne and travel to an apple tree where it appears as orange to brown spots on the apple leaves. In mid-summer, spores from the apple tree returns to the cedar to start another cycle. Buying rust-resistant trees helps. If this was a major issue last year, treat apple trees with preventive fungicide. Small cedars can also be treated. For the most part, damage is not serious on either tree and is limited to some disfigurement only.

Cedar apple rust on cedar trees.

Scout trees for insect problems. Spring tent worms form at the junction of branches on a tree (compared to fall webworms, which form at the tip). In mature landscape trees, you'll probably not be able to reach the tent, but they rarely are severe enough to cause problems. Birds help by feeding on the worms.

VINES AND GROUNDCOVERS

Some vines, such as ivy and pachysandra, are more aggressive than others and need to be restrained before they damage steps, walls, or other buildings. Trim vining tendrils of pachysandra before they bend down and root. For aggressive, invasive, or nasty vines, such as honeysuckle or poison ivy, dig them out where you can and use an herbicide to catch a vine before it destroys trees or invades the garden.

DEER-RESISTANT SHRUBS

Almost all shrubs are susceptible to deer browsing in late winter, but this rarely damages shrubs. More serious damage is done when deer continue to browse as the tender new growth arrives and they destroy the new growth and stems. There is nothing that is completely deer-proof, but this list names a few shrubs, perennials, and annuals that are not on a deer's favorite menu:

Bridal wreath spirea	Baptisia	Annual vinca
Boxwood	Basket of gold	Cleome
Forsythia	Bleeding heart	Larkspur
Most holly	Catmint	Nicotiana
Lilac	Hellebore	Snapdragon
Redbud	Spotted deadnettle	Strawflowers
Viburnum	Sweet woodruff	Sweet alyssum
Witch hazel	Pulmonaria	Poppy

A full list of shrubs, annuals, and perennials can be found at www.njaes.rutgers.edu/deerresistance.

May

The end of May officially kicks off summer, and frost is something that we all see the last of this month. The official last frost of the season is mid- to late April on coastal areas and late May many western areas. Planting tender annuals after Memorial Day is recommended for Zone 4 areas of upstate New York, as well as western areas toward Buffalo. The last frost date for your specific county can be found by contacting your local Cooperative Extension service.

The end of frost is only part of the story regarding when to plant seedlings outside. Other considerations include soil temperature and daytime temperatures, which play a big role in whether the tender plants thrive or not. Tomatoes, peppers, and basil like day temperatures to be consistently warm, which is why they are not planted until a few weeks after that last frost date. Beans, however, fair reasonably well even if the early summer temperatures are not as warm as we would like.

May is warm enough, though, to bring out spring perennials as well as blossoms and leaves on trees and shrubs including azaleas and other late spring-blooming shrubs. These shrubs form their flowers the previous year, which allows them to bloom early in the year. After these have bloomed, trim the blossoms off, and tidy the shrubs if needed. Forsythia in particular can get very large, so a good prune will keep it in bounds. Other plants of the garden are putting out new stems, which will produce flowers later in the summer. Rose-of-Sharon and roses are two shrubs that form their blooms on new wood.

Warm May days are great for finishing up the general cleanup of the garden, starting a good lawn care program, and moving plants out of the house and into the garden. Rain is also a big part of the weather scene most Mays, so while the garden does not usually need water, it is a good time to assess your irrigation set-up for containers and the garden in general.

PLAN

May is a great month for doing rather than planning, but there is a lot to do: scheduling dates for direct seeding, hardening off seedlings, and planting are important. Prioritize outside chores, particularly if your garden work is limited to weekends. Check on the weather forecast to see if you can schedule your work accordingly. Planting is good on cloudy days, particularly if rain is forecast, but some lawn treatments require a lawn to be dry for 24 hours for them to work.

ANNUALS

By the end of May, most gardeners can put tender annuals into the ground. Those in western New York around Buffalo and Zone 4 areas should wait until June to plant petunias, marigolds, tomatoes, and pepper plants. Annuals can be planted into containers this month. Not everything that you grew yourself will be in bloom, so note bloom colors as well as the variety of the seedlings on their tags. When considering where you would like annuals to go, think about their maintenance, particularly for watering. Small groups of annuals scattered around your property take time to water and deadhead, but if they're in larger groups they not only look more attractive, but are also easier to care for.

■ *The plant tag should indicate how much sun your plant needs as well as how big it is going to get.*

■ *Cold frames help to harden off tender plants before they go into the garden.*

BULBS

The last of the daffodils and tulips should be ready to trim back this month. Remember to wait until the leaves start to go brown before you trim. If you need to move or divide bulbs, mark where those particular bulbs are so that you know which ones need to be divided and so you'll be able to find them if they're dormant.

EDIBLES

The last frost may be a thing of the past for most of us, but the soil needs to be warm for basil and squash to be planted. Usually two weeks after the last frost date is a good date for planting these warm-season vegetables. Some years have mild weather in April and May, and if that's the case, it's fine to put beans into the ground at the beginning of May and tomatoes by mid-May. Other years the ground is so damp and cold that tomatoes cannot go in until almost June.

LAWNS

If you don't have a professional lawn service, get a plan together for fertilization and weed control. Most fescues and cool-weather grasses do better with a fall fertilization and a small boost in spring. Preventative weed control for crabgrass can be scheduled for this month.

Decide now if you want to keep the lawn green or let it go dormant when summer heat and droughts arrive. Cool-weather lawns can be kept green with frequent irrigation, but without that they'll return to green when summer temperatures moderate.

HOUSEPLANTS & CONTAINERS

It is still early to put tender plants outside, but toward the end of the month you can carefully transition them. It takes a week or two to get houseplants and other tender plants that overwintered indoors used to direct sunshine and breezes. This is similar to hardening off seedlings and needs to be accomplished before you move them to their permanent summer location.

PERENNIALS

There is plenty of time to add a few perennials to fill in gaps in the garden. When you're at the store or nursery, pay particular attention to perennials and make sure that they are well watered and adjusted to outdoor weather. Check the tags on perennials and look for key words such as "drought tolerant" or "deer resistant" if these traits are important to you, as well as whether they need sun or shade.

Arrange perennials in groups for easy watering if needed. Placing perennials with like needs together cuts down on watering chores this summer.

SHRUBS & ROSES

Any spring-flowering shrubs can be scheduled for pruning back this month. Pruning as soon as possible after the shrub has bloomed allows it to put out lots of new stems with blooms for next year. Container-grown or balled-and-burlapped shrubs as well as roses can be planted this month. Perhaps add a scented rose that you can clip for indoor vases. If you're buying roses for a specific color or scent, wait until it's actually in bloom before you buy it—sometimes labels are lost or put into the wrong pot.

TREES

Picking the wrong tree or planting it in the wrong place can lead to a whole bunch of headaches down the road. Key to deciding what tree to choose is researching varieties before you head to the nursery. Check the tag on every tree before you buy it. Things to look for on tags:

Mature height and width: Oak trees can reach 40 plus feet in height, whereas a redbud is closer to 12 feet in height.

Growth rate: Some trees are fast growers, and you have probably read that they are great for an almost-instant hedge. But the fast growth is often associated with weak limbs, so these aren't great choices for windbreaks. Other trees are much slower growing and take years to reach maturity, so they are not good choices for instant screens.

Where to plant: A small tree that you can easily lift and plant looks great until it starts to grows out of bounds. In a few years, it can shade out certain areas of the garden. So think before you plant.

- Trees should not be planted under or near power lines—we have all seen utility workers struggling to clear lines from overly tall trees planted just a few feet way. A 10-foot clearance is best.
- Likewise, don't plant over buried cable or electric lines or septic fields. Tree roots can penetrate septic fields and surround underground cables, making maintenance of these areas problematic.
- Be respectful of your neighbor's property when you locate a tree. Trees should be planted so that they don't grow across property lines and (eventually) don't provide dense shade over a neighbor's perennial garden.

VINES & GROUNDCOVERS

Groundcovers quickly fill empty areas of the garden such as areas where grass doesn't grow because of shade or tree roots. Research groundcovers like mosses that can be planted in these areas to keep the design interesting.

Tiny green-leaved creeping thyme (*Thymus praecox* 'Minus') or red creeping thyme (*T. praecox coccineus*) is slow growing and low to the ground, making each perfect for growing in cracks and between flagstones. Woolly thyme (*T. pseudolanuginosus*) spreads faster than these but makes a wonderful groundcover, falling over a wall and between sun-loving shrubs.

GOOD TREES FOR SMALL PROPERTIES			
TREE	*HARDINESS*	*SUN*	*AVERAGE HEIGHT*
Shadbush (*Amelanchier arborea*)	4–9	Part sun	15–20 feet
Eastern redbud (*Cercis canadensis*)	4–9	Full/part sun	15–20 feet
Smokebush (*Cotinus coggygria*)	4–8	Full sun	10–15 feet
Crabapple (*Malus*)	4–7	Full sun	15–25 feet
Hawthorne (*Crataegus crus-galli*)	4–7	Full sun	20–25 feet
Saucer magnolia (*Magnolia × soulangeana*)	4–9	Full sun	20–25 feet

PLANT

May is a good time to plant most of the garden. Temperatures may be variable: Some days have high temperatures followed by a week of cloudy, wet weather. It's worth keeping a close eye on rain and temperatures during this time. As a general guide, plant on cloudy days when there is a good chance of gentle rain.

ANNUALS

Even though the area has passed its last frost, the ground may still be cold, and daytime temperatures can be too low for many tropical annuals like begonias. Wait until about two weeks after the last frost date and, if the weather has settled to warm days and mild nights, go ahead and plant. Planting annuals in soil that is too cool affects the early plant growth; although they don't die, they certainly don't thrive, and a weak plant is more susceptible to insects and fungus.

BULBS

Continue planting summer-flowering bulbs such as alliums and gladioli. Amaryllis can be planted outside too.

EDIBLES

It may be too early in some areas to plant tender summer squash and peppers, but you can plant beans and beets. In eastern areas, assuming the forecasted temperature is mild, plant tomatoes and peppers beginning about the middle of May. Western and mountain areas should wait until the end of the month, even after Memorial Day.

Perennial herbs can be put into the ground this month, as well as cilantro seeds.

Plant a group of bulbs in one hole for a clustered, natural effect once they bloom.

LAWNS

Small areas can still be repaired. Larger areas that need to be addressed immediately can be seeded or laid with a few pieces of sod. Repairing a small area with seed is covered in April. (Large areas and reseeding the whole lawn is covered in September.) To repair an area with sod, start with well-hydrated, fresh-looking sod with no sign of decaying roots at its base.

HOUSEPLANTS & CONTAINERS

Even areas with late May frosts still get some warm spring days for gardeners to play outside. Plant containers with your chosen annuals and perennials.

HERE'S HOW

TO PLANT ANNUALS AND PERENNIALS

The containers in which annuals and perennials are sold vary in size from just over an inch for 6-pack annuals to 4 to 8 inches for perennials. The amount of roots inside a container also varies depending on when it was planted. Most plants come clean out of the container: you will see a mass of roots and some potting mix that holds the shape of the container.

1. Check the label for a plant's sun or shade preference and how big the plant will grow or spread.
2. Make a hole in the ground about the same size as the rootball.
3. With your fingers, tease the roots apart so they're free from circling and most of the ends are free too. Place the plant gently into the waiting hole so that the soil level is similar to the soil level in the container. Refill around the rootball with waiting soil, or, in the case of little annuals, just push the surrounding soil around the plant.
4. Press down firmly to settle the soil around the plant.
5. Pinch off any flowers on annuals. Perennials only flower for a few weeks, so it's fine to leave those on if you choose.
6. Water the plant well and resettle the surrounding soil.
7. Spread a little mulch over the area to keep the moisture in, about an inch or so.

Over the next few days and weeks, make sure that the new plants get plenty of water so that they do not dry out, but don't keep the area wet. After about a week or two, the plants start to show new growth and are off and running for summer.

HERE'S HOW

TO PLANT SMALL AREAS OF SOD

1. Clear the area of vegetation (grass, weeds, and so forth) with an herbicide or dig them out.
2. Square off the area so that the sod fits easily.
3. Lightly till.
4. Add a 1-inch layer of compost.
5. Rake the area smooth.
6. Place the first piece of sod snug against the existing lawn area.
7. Lay the second piece of sod so that it butts up closely to the first piece.
8. Cut pieces to fit the area needed and continue to fill the area with pieces of sod.
9. Tamp all down firmly.
10. Water the area and avoid walking on it until new growth is well established and the edges of the lawn/sod interface are no longer noticeable.

1

2

6

9

Plant an herb container with perennial oregano, French tarragon, thyme, and chives plus annual basil and marjoram. Add parsley (a biennial) and you'll have enough fresh herbs for the season. Many containers are suitable for herbs, including traditional strawberry pots and containers that hang over the edges of railings.

If you kept your poinsettia alive, trim back any leggy growth and plant outside in a sunny location. Remember to harden it off before you plant it.

PERENNIALS

Continue to plant perennials this month, particularly those that bloom all summer like daylilies and *Gaillardia* (both hardy to Zone 3 or 4, depending on variety).

If you kept a chrysanthemum from last fall for planting this year, now is the time to plant. Pinch back any straggly early growth at the same time you plant.

TREES, SHRUBS & ROSES

May provides the last shot for planting trees, shrubs, and roses. By June, the weather turns summery with frequent high temperatures and drought. Avoid balled-and-burlapped trees unless they look fresh and well tended.

VINES & GROUNDCOVERS

Annual and perennial vines can be planted. Plant the seeds of fast-growing black-eyed Susan vine (*Thunbergia alata*) and nasturtiums now, and by midsummer the trellis will be filled with colorful blossoms. Plant fast-growing annual vines to grow among spring-blooming shrubs or other vines. Sturdy perennial vines like wisteria take on a second season of interest when the scarlet blossom of the cardinal climber or the bright white flowers of a morning glory vine show through the vine's green foliage.

Continue to plant groundcovers particularly in shady areas such as under trees and shrubs. Just a few shade-loving plants help retain moisture at the root zone for the shrubs, just as a mulch would do. Pretty pink-flowering periwinkles (*Vinca minor*) and sweet woodruff (*Gallium odorata*) work well under shrubs. Many annual vines can be used as groundcovers too.

CARE

May marks the end of spring and the arrival of summer, and in the midst of our treasured perennials and shrubs, opportunistic weeds and bugs arrive, too. Prompt removal goes a long way toward controlling them. A new 2- to 3-inch layer of mulch should be applied to all perennial and shrub areas as well as around trees.

ANNUALS

Harden off the seedlings that you kept indoors before planting them outside (see Care in April). Self-seeded cosmos, cleome, and other outside annuals emerge this month, and often there are way too many of them. Remove seedlings that are growing under perennials or where you plan on planting something else.

BULBS

The last spring bulbs should be done by now and are ready to have their leaves trimmed. Some late-blooming daffodils are still around. Most smaller

ANNUAL GROUNDCOVERS	
Moss rose (*Portulaca*)	Various colors
Nasturtium (*Tropaeolum majus*)	Yellows and orange
Poached egg plant (*Limnanthes douglasii*)	Yellow and white flowers
Pumpkin and melon vines (*Cucumis*)	Green leaves and yellow flowers
Sweet alyssum (*Lobularia maritima*)	White or pink flowers
Periwinkle (*Vinca minor*)	Pink and white flowers
Wave® petunia (*Petunia* 'Wave')	Various colors

FLOWERING PERENNIAL GROUNDCOVERS

PLANT	COLOR	BLOOM TIME	HARDINESS	SUN
Creeping St. John's wort (*Hypericum calycinum*)	Green with yellow flowers	Summer	5–9	Full sun
Thyme varieties (*Thymus*)	Green with white, pink, or red flowers	Late spring	2–10	Full sun
Lily turf (*Liriope spicata*)	Green with purple flowers	Early summer	4–10	Full sun
Sweet woodruff (*Galium odoratum*)	Green with white flowers	Spring	4–8	Shade
Bugleweed (*Ajuga reptans*)	Purple leaves, blue flowers; some green ones too	Late spring	3–10	Shade
Spotted deadnettle (*Lamium maculatum*)	Light green leaves, blue or pink flowers	Late spring	3–8	Part shade/shade
Stonecrop (*Sedum*)	Green, gray, purple, or burgundy leaves	Summer/fall	3–10	Full sun

LAST FROST DATES

The average last frost date is relied on by gardeners as a safe date for planting tender seedlings outside. However, the average is calculated over the past 25 years or so, and the two weeks on either side of that date can, and sometimes do, get light frosts. Hence, your local weather forecast is critical in deciding what to plant into the garden.

The other factor affecting planting is the soil and air temperatures. Some springs are long and cool with snow arriving well into April. During these cool springs, the soil temperature remains cool and won't really be ready for tender sun- and heat-loving petunias and begonias, which prefer warm soil. Additionally, a cool May that is frost-free can have temperatures that hover in the mid-50s with nights in the 40s. Basil and peppers really need warmer temperatures where the daytime heat reaches into the 80s and night temperatures don't drop much below 60°F.

Empty a bag of mulch where you want to use it.

Use a rake to spread a layer of mulch evenly around the plants.

spring bulbs (snowdrops and crocus) don't need to be trimmed at all because their narrow leaves break down quickly after flowering.

EDIBLES

All those seedlings should be ready to harden off this month to get them ready to go into the garden. Tomatoes, peppers, and lettuce have spent their time indoors with constant moisture and still air. When preparing to put them outside into the real world, they need to be hardened off. Sunlight, even from a sunny window, is far weaker than the effect of direct sun, which can shrivel a seedling in hours. Start with any remaining lettuces that enjoy cool to warm weather and wait until you are well past frost before you plant tender summer vegetables. See page 78 for more on how to harden off seedlings.

HOUSEPLANTS & CONTAINERS

Just as annuals were slowly transitioned to life outside, houseplants should be too. Patio hibiscus and citrus plants that adorn patios can be taken outside this month. Many are too big to bring inside every day (in the event of frost) so wait until the weather has settled before starting this transition. Keep the plants close to the house and keep a towel or two handy in case of windy, cool nights. After a week in a protected area, transition to a shady area close to where you'd like them to be permanently. Keep the containers well watered and move to the permanent sunny area after a week or two.

LAWNS

Around the time that forsythia blooms end, it's time to apply a pre-emergent to the lawn to prevent crabgrass and other annual weeds. Don't apply pre-emergent if you plan on reseeding a lawn because the treatment stops germination of *any* seed, including grass seed, for as long as three months.

PERENNIALS

Deadhead and tidy early blooming perennials such as phlox and hellebores. If you see ants on your peonies, don't worry—they are attracted to the peony but don't do any damage.

SHRUBS & ROSES

Schedule any spring-flowering shrubs for pruning this month. Pruning as soon as possible after a shrub blooms will allow it to put out lots of new

Remove (deadhead) old blooms from perennials.

stems with blooms for next year. Deadhead roses after blooming and remove spent blooms on shrubs. Follow the guidelines for general shrub pruning in Care in February.

TREES

Tidy and remove fallen blossoms. Add a layer of mulch to the area around the tree, but don't mound it up to the trunk or let it touch the trunk. A 2- to 3-inch layer, kept 2 to 4 inches away from the bark, works well.

When you plant a new tree, it takes a while to settle in and may not show much growth for the first year or two. When trees are planted incorrectly, it is in the third year that they fail.

It takes fully grown trees a while to respond to severe climate conditions like long-term drought or flooding. It may be two or even three years before you notice a decline that is linked to one of these catastrophic weather events.

VINES & GROUNDCOVERS

Vines and groundcovers should be growing well this month and need very little extra care. Handpick any weeds that arrive.

If you are using liriope as a groundcover, mow it this month to encourage general tidiness. If liriope is in a perennial bed, trim it as you would other grasses.

Do not make a "volcano" of thick mulch around a tree.

ABOUT STAKING

Young trees are often staked when they are planted. The stakes and guy ropes should be removed after two or three years at most.

But there is some question about whether small trees should be staked at all. A tree builds girth and stabilizes roots when it's buffeted by winds. Staking a tree restricts and minimizes this movement and thus retards the creation of stabilizing roots.

There are some cases where staking for a year or two is recommended: for evergreens that have winter bulk; for trees that are in areas where gusty winds may occur (such as between houses where there can be wind tunnel effect); and in areas where winter gales may uproot a small tree.

If you decide to stake, don't make the guy ropes too tight and protect the bark from abrasion by adding padding between the rope and the trunk (strips of old carpet work well for this). Put two or three stakes equidistant around the tree and put the ropes low down on the trunk. Loosen or remove ropes in summer to allow more movement.

Protect young bark from support ropes and wires.

Help young vines attach to supports with guidelines made of string or light wires, and trim any wayward stems. For mature vines that put out bloom later in the year, keep them trimmed and on the fence, arbor, or support.

WATER

With the snow gone but summer not quite here yet, May is a good time to handle irrigation issues. Whether you have sprinkler systems for lawns and perennials or use a hose to water plants, now is the time to troubleshoot any issues such as a split in the hose or a broken connector.

ANNUALS

Keep annual seeds and young plants watered if rain isn't imminent. Use a fine spray from a hose or watering can so that you don't knock them over. Try to water early in the day so that they have moisture during the hottest part of the day. Keep annual seedlings moist this month until they are established. Usually two to three sets of true leaves indicate that the roots are established and the seedlings are doing well, but they still should not be left too long between waterings.

BULBS

Any newly planted bulbs should be kept moist until they are growing well. Bulbs are susceptible to rotting if kept too moist; outdoors, nature usually

HERE'S HOW

TO IRRIGATE A LANDSCAPE

There are several ways to irrigate a property, and some are better than others depending on where you want to water.

In-ground irrigation makes watering the whole landscape easy.

Overhead watering with oscillating or circular sprinklers: These are manually positioned and attached to a hose that is, in turn, attached to an outside faucet. Watering with these static sprinklers delivers water to a small area. You move the sprinklers to water a second area. This method is fine for small areas and is the most economical way to water. Waste occurs when the sprinkler waters the sidewalk as well as the lawn or flowerbed. Disconnect from the faucet for winter and drain the hose before storing.

Soaker or leaky hoses: These hoses allow water to seep out along the length of the hose. They're great for getting the water directly to the soil level, where it soaks into the ground. This method is good for row crops (peas, beans) and flexible enough to be wound through perennial and shrub beds. Anchor the hose in position with landscape clips and bury under mulch. The end of the soaker hose is either attached directly to the faucet or via a regular hose. Disconnect from the faucet for winter and check for leaks when you attach it in spring.

Drip irrigation: The hose in this setup, like the previous ones, can be attached directly to the faucet or via a regular hose. The pipes are solid plastic with secondary lines taking the water to a specific point. Systems can be designed to water containers, raised beds, or specific landscape shrubs. This system is good for individual items such as tomatoes, peppers, and shrubs or roses. There is no water wasted between the items, and the water is delivered at ground level. Bury the pipes under mulch if needed and disconnect from the faucet for winter.

In-ground systems: These systems are designed to deliver water from aboveground sprinkler heads. The landscape is divided into several zones so that each area can be watered individually. For instance, you might have one zone on the front lawn and plantings, one zone for the vegetable garden, one for the side or driveway plantings, and one for the back lawn. The distributor hoses are buried about 2 feet below the ground. The main line runs to the zone where secondary lines take the water to the sprinkler heads, which are placed so that the whole zone is watered. The whole system is regulated by a control box placed in the basement or garage. Remember to take the system off the auto setting if you're getting rain.

provides enough water for them to be vibrant and healthy. When new growth shows above the soil line, you can cut back on the water and treat them as you would any other perennials—about an inch of water a week if you don't get rain.

EDIBLES

The vegetable bed is one area that needs watering all summer, and it's a great idea to optimize your time with this chore. Small beds can be irrigated with a sprinkler; when attached to a timer on a faucet, this chore can be automated. Beds with row crops are best irrigated with soaker hoses that run up and down the beds. Individual plants such as peppers and squash fare better with an irrigation system that delivers the moisture just to individual plants.

LAWNS

Most years there's no need to water lawns during this month, but it's a good time to check that

HERE'S HOW

TO CALCULATE THE AMOUNT OF WATER A LANDSCAPE RECEIVES

Lawns require about an inch of water a week, while vegetables and annuals need daily watering to stay healthy in hot weather. To determine how much water your landscape is getting:

1. Set up the irrigation system in the garden. This can be oscillating sprinklers or a sprinkler system.
2. Set a measuring gauge within the area that you are watering. A rain gauge or small can marked at 1-inch marks works fine. Put several over the area to check that all areas are getting the same amount of water.
3. Start watering.
4. After 30 minutes, turn the water off and see how much water is in the collection vessel. If you have a full inch, you know that the rate of application is 1 inch per 30 minutes, or 2 inches per hour. Use this gauge to determine how long the water has to be on each day or each week.

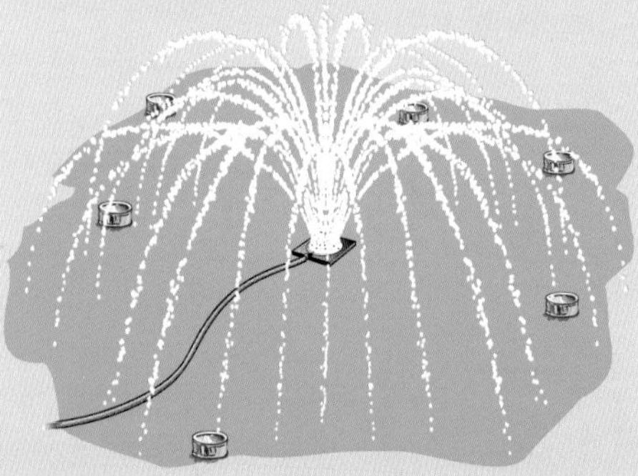

your in-ground irrigation system is working. Clear nozzles and make sure that they're delivering water where they should, and repair any damaged lines so that the system will work correctly when you need it this summer.

HOUSEPLANTS & CONTAINERS

Houseplants need their usual watering regime this month.

Containers need a little extra water on warm days. Mixed containers and hanging baskets look lovely unless they are stressed from lack of water. Hoses with extendable wands attached can help you reach high baskets. On a deck or patio, consider getting an irrigation system similar to the one in the vegetable garden. A circle of drip attachments that are connected and deliver water to each container can save time and energy.

For single, large containers, put several 1-inch perforated plastic pipes vertically into the soil before anything is planted. The pipe has ¼-inch holes drilled into it at 2-inch intervals and should reach the bottom of the container. The top should be above the soil level. Plant the container as normal and water well. But fill the tube as well, so that the roots get water. When the container is full of summer flowers, you will still be able to provide sufficient water and fertilizer through the tube.

PERENNIALS, VINES & GROUNDCOVERS

Established perennials that are in at least their second year don't need to be pampered this month. Newly planted perennials should be treated like annuals and kept hydrated for a few more weeks. If your lawn has an irrigation system, check to see if it can water your perennial beds when needed too.

TREES, SHRUBS & ROSES

These more deeply rooted parts of the landscape can be connected to an irrigation system, but they rarely need as much water as other areas of the landscape. Soaker hoses or drip irrigation that serves just the shrubs keeps them hydrated without wasting water. An infrequent but deeper watering regime is better than the frequent and shallow schedule that annuals require.

FERTILIZE

Most areas of the landscape enjoy a spring pick-me-up in the form of compost or fertilizer. An annual spring fertilization is in order for all areas of the landscape with the exception of lawns. Skip this if you fertilized your landscape beds in March or April.

ANNUALS

If the annuals are still in their seedling containers, then give them a light fertilizer in the same pattern that you established last spring—every two to four weeks depending on the fertilizer directions. They don't need any additional nutrients when you plant them into the landscape.

BULBS

Once spring bulbs are dormant, they don't need any fertilizer. Spring-planted, summer-blooming bulbs can be treated to same general fertilizer as you put on the rest of the perennial beds.

EDIBLES

Compost is the best fertilizer for early vegetables. Most cool-season peas, kale, and salad crops do not need any further fertilization. When pulling out the cool-season crop and replacing with summer tomatoes, replenish the nutrients with another dose of compost.

LAWNS

If you treated your lawn last month with a general lawn fertilizer, then you do not need to redo that. Most cool-season grasses, which are green all winter (fescues, rye grasses), don't need much in the way of spring fertilizer. Warm-season Bermuda grasses, which are brown in winter, benefit from spring fertilizer after the brown grass turns an even green.

HOUSEPLANTS & CONTAINERS

Repotted houseplants and newly planted containers have sufficient nutrients in the new potting mix to last them a month or two. Winter containers that you're transitioning to summer flowers without changing the mix should receive a general fertilizer to the soil so plenty of nutrients are available for the fast-growing and usually crowded annuals.

PERENNIALS, TREES, VINES & GROUNDCOVERS

These need to be fertilized just once in spring as part of the general spring routine. Complete annual fertilizing in perennial beds before you replenish mulch in the area.

SHRUBS & ROSES

Spring-blooming shrubs should be fertilized with a general fertilizer after they have bloomed, while summer-blooming shrubs and roses are fertilized when they start to put out new growth. A slow-release general fertilizer is a recommended for shrubs, particularly those that are coming into summer bloom. If you are fertilizing a mixed bed with perennials, shrubs, and roses, then there is no need to put a second application down. Too much fertilization is worse than too little.

PROBLEM-SOLVE

ANNUALS

Damping-off disease and cutworm are problems for newly planted seedlings—see Care in April. A tray of new petunia seedlings can disappear overnight by browsing deer. Use sprays and fences to deter rabbits and deer. Note that there's not very much help for deterring groundhogs.

BULBS

Borers in irises are a common problem and can be spotted this month by observing notches in the leaves. The eggs hatch on the leaves and the borers eat downward through the plant, eventually entering the rhizome itself where they do the damage. If you notice borer notches, dig the rhizome and check. Discard any afflicted rhizomes.

EDIBLES

Protect those in the cabbage group from the early white butterfly, which lays eggs on them. The little green caterpillars that hatch from those eggs are a major problem. Cover plants with netting to keep the butterflies off the plants.

Cabbage plants are attacked by this well-disguised caterpillar.

Use an old milk carton to protect plants from weedkillers as you spray them.

LAWNS

Cutting the lawn and letting the clippings return to the lawn, rather than bagging them, is a good practice. Mow so that the clippings fall onto the lawn rather the sidewalk and street. Mowing lawns to the height of about 3 inches and having a healthy stand of grass goes a long way toward avoiding weed problems.

HOUSEPLANTS & CONTAINERS

As you repot and put containers outdoors, perennials and small citrus trees often go through transplant shock. Drooping leaves, loss of leaves, and general malaise are not uncommon for a few days. Keep the container well watered and out of full sun for a few days until the plants are settled.

PERENNIALS

Most perennial problems don't arrive until June or July, so enjoy them now. However, check for deer or rabbit browsing and address that as soon as possible with deterrent sprays. Look for nibbles on stems (rabbits leave a ragged look, deer a straighter edge), half-eaten leaves, and scraped bark on trees plus disturbed ground or footprints. Rabbits and other small rodents can be deterred with a granular treatment whereas shrubs subject to deer damage are better guarded with a liquid deterrent. Check January for more on animal deterrents.

SHRUBS & ROSES

Scout for lacebugs on azaleas, rhododendrons, and other evergreen shrub leaves and other newly opened leaves and blooms. These little white flies with lacy wings eat soft tissue in azalea leaves, giving the leaf a bleached look. Control them by applying horticultural oil or soap onto the eggs, larvae, and insects, which are found predominantly under the leaves.

Caterpillars, leaf miners, and aphids arrive this month to eat the new growth, but they are rarely an issue. A good general guide is to take six steps backward and see if you see any problems. A little nibble here or curled leaf there is not noticeable and

HERE'S HOW

TO SPOT-TREAT LAWN WEEDS OR WEEDS AMONG FLOWERS

Weeds have a tendency to grow wherever their seed lands, under the peony or right in the lawn. Violets are a particular lawn nuisance that need an herbicide rather than a lawn weed killer, but ugly grasses are also tough to control by lawn weed killer chemicals. Spot-treating the weed is a way to target the herbicide directly onto the plant without affecting the surrounding ones. Always wear gloves to protect you from getting the chemicals onto your skin. Either:

1. Isolate the plant from the surrounding lawn by putting an old, large container over it. The container can be any milk carton, juice carton, or other container that opens at the top (so that you can get the chemical onto the plant) and is cut off at the bottom (wide enough to surround just that one plant at ground level).
2. Spray the herbicide into the container so that it covers the weed.

or

1. Wearing a pair of gloves, take a paint brush and dip it into the chemical.
2. "Paint" the plant with the brush so that it is fully covered with the herbicide.
3. Discard the gloves and brush in the trash when you have finished so that you do not contaminate anything else in the garden.

TYPES OF LAWN WEEDS

Lawn weeds are a major concern to homeowners. They can be divided into grass-type weeds and non-grass or broadleaf weeds.

WEED GRASSES

Annual weed grasses are dealt with by applying a pre-emergent treatment prior to the seeds germinating. For crabgrass, this is about the time forsythia blooms are falling or when the soil temperature is 60°F. The following is a list of common annual weed grasses that are controlled with pre-emergent.

Barnyard grass (*Echinochloa crus-galli*): Spreads from a central mass, starting along the ground, and then growing upward.

Annual bluegrass (*Poa annua*): Short upright stems grow in a clump.

Crabgrass (*Digitaria sanguinalis*): Coarse upright grass with narrow seedheads.

Goose grass or crowsfoot grass (*Eleusine indica*): Spreads from a central area putting down roots where the nodules touch the ground.

Perennial grass fescue (*Festuca arundinacea*): Is treated with non-selective herbicide.

BROADLEAF WEEDS

The following are common broadleaf weeds that are controlled with lawn weed treatments. Note that if the perennial weed sets seed, the seed will not germinate if you have applied a pre-emergent.

Dandelion (*Taxacum officinale*): Low rosette of leaves, bright yellow flowers with lots of seeds.

Ground ivy or creeping Charlie (*Glechoma hederacea*): Slightly fuzzy, rounded leaves with little blue flowers.

Clover (*Trifolium* spp.): Some clover is beneficial to a lawn, but too much is weedy. White or pink flowers, depending on variety. Some clovers are annual, some are killed by frost, and some are perennial.

Wild strawberry (*Fragaria virginiana*): Spreads by runners and produces little strawberries.

Violets (*Viola*): Are not affected by most lawn weed treatments and need a general spot herbicide. Little clumps with spring flowers.

Nutsedge (*Cyperus esculentus*): Perennial. Neither a grass nor a broadleaf plant although it looks like a pale upright grass. Look for herbicides that indicate they treat sedges, and spot-treat as needed.

is probably not worth worrying about. Monitor insect populations to ensure that they do not get out of hand, but often birds and other insects take care of the problem before it becomes critical.

TREES

Damage on new growth occurs when early spring weather comes to a screeching halt with a few days of late frosts. This is seen on trees as well as the rest of the garden when new leaves are killed. The trees may look rough for a week or two, then new growth will return. By midsummer, they will look normal again.

VINES & GROUNDCOVERS

Vines and groundcovers suffer from many of the same problems as the rest of the perennial garden—fungal and mildew problems in damp, cool weather and insect attacks. For environmental issues that cause fungus and mildew, the only remedy is to wait for dry summer weather. Spray a fungicide if you have extreme problems. Aphids, whiteflies, and leafhoppers can be dealt with using an insecticide (preferably on the eggs) such as pyrethrum-based sprays or horticultural oils and soaps.

June

The start of summer is everywhere, and with kids, vacations, and enjoying an evening with friends in the garden, time for working in the garden is scarce. Adjust your workload to match the time you have and prioritize the important tasks. Lawn mowing and weeds need attention, but much of the landscape should be low maintenance by now.

By June, it is a little too late to start new plans for this year's garden, so continue implementing those winter plans. For inspiration for projects that you can do in your own garden, the Garden Conservancy has Open Garden Days across New York and New Jersey, a great day out for gardeners. Check out its webpage to see which gardens are open near you. Public gardens are also a great place to find inspiration—take a walk through the grounds and take pictures of combinations that you like and containers that appeal to you.

There is still time to assemble some bright containers for the porch, deck, or patio. There is even time to sow some summer annual seeds. Those seeds that germinated in May had to deal with cooler soil and cooler temperatures. Seeds sown in June take advantage of warmer conditions and soon catch up to the ones you put in earlier.

In May you watched the weather report for frost warnings, but in June you will be watching for when, and if, there will be rain. Annuals and the vegetable garden need consistent water to grow and produce well, which will likely mean some supplemental watering on your part. The region rarely suffers long-term drought when water restrictions are put in place, but a rain barrel is an easy way to help out the plants without raising your water bill. A rain barrel is great for containers, shrubs, roses, and other individual items, but it is not a sufficient supply for soaker hoses delivering water to multiple plants.

Summer is for relaxing: don't forget to create a place to sit, relax, and enjoy your garden close up.

PLAN

Now that your summer garden is in bloom, you can look toward fall planning for the vegetable garden and adding fall color.

ANNUALS

Annuals are great to fill in spaces between perennials, and also add color to areas that previously had spring-blooming flowers, like creeping phloxes. Add a few annuals to the vegetable garden to attract lots of pollinators: cosmos, marigolds, and zinnias are good. Best of all, plants start to go on sale this month, so plan on picking up a few 6-packs for added color in your summer garden.

BULBS

Although summer has only just begun, start thinking about fall-flowering bulbs. Saffron, colchicums, and cyclamen bloom in late summer to fall and are planted in June and July. There is time to add to the summer bulb palette with elephant ears and even some gladiolus.

EDIBLES

In July and August, you'll start planning your fall garden. Crop rotation and succession planting are ways to get a longer harvest from the garden. Peas, beans, sweet corn, and lettuce are just a few vegetables that work well for succession planting. Most crops produce for several weeks before they peak and go into decline. Sow a few seeds every two weeks, and each sowing will come to maturity successively and overlap the previous one, giving a harvest that is extended over a longer period.

Crop rotation means that you don't plant the same thing in the same space twice in the same year or in consecutive years. So if you planted early spring cabbages, you don't follow with anything from the cabbage group in fall in the same location. Ideally, crop rotation is done on a three- or even five-year cycle, meaning tomatoes (or anything in the tomato family) have a different location for each of the next three to five years.

LAWNS

This month, you'll get to see how important a drought plan is. Make adjustments for weather conditions and the general health of the lawn. Cool-weather grasses go dormant in long stretches of hot summer days. That green grass can be kept alive by watering well and often, but unless you have just a small patch or in-ground irrigation, this is a lot of work for summer.

A cool, damp spring slows the growth of everything, including lawns. Warm springs promote more rapid growth, so use this month to reassess the condition of your lawn and adjust lawn care plans accordingly.

HOUSEPLANTS & CONTAINERS

There is still time to grab a few more containers and plants from nurseries and retail stores. Groups of different sizes of containers or sets of the same container can decorate a shady corner in the garden, line a set of steps to the house, or add color to a large gravel parking area.

PERENNIALS

Do you have any fall-blooming perennials? Decide where you'd like to see them in the garden. Fall weather can be unsettled with cool mornings. Plan fall-blooming perennials where you can see them shine from indoors on those cold mornings. Good fall perennials include grasses, asters, and black-eyed Susans.

SHRUBS & ROSES

Some shrubs have wonderful color in fall and into winter, which makes them great garden focal points. Check the overall size of the shrubs you want (to see if they'll fit) and find a reliable source for purchasing them online or check your local nurseries or home-improvement stores. Fothergilla

These containers hold a mix of annuals and trees.

and witch hazel both have winter or spring flowers as well as great fall color.

VINES & GROUNDCOVERS

Pachysandra and ground ivy are popular groundcovers for shady areas, but the species are often dark and uniform in height. Think about putting a topiary in the middle of the bed area to provide some height and interest. Use a contrasting vine or groundcover, such as vinca with its bright green leaves or an ivy with variegated leaves, for the topiary.

PLANT

June is the last month for planting much of the garden. Yet in many areas where May is cool or even frosty, June is the first real opportunity to plant tender annuals. So June is still a busy planting month for everyone. Pick cloudy days with some rain in the forecast, if possible, for planting.

ANNUALS

Tender annuals that haven't been planted should be put into the ground this month. Watch store-bought annuals; they take a day or two longer to settle into the garden than the annuals you carefully hardened off in May.

There is still time to sow sunflowers, zinnias, and other summer flowers directly into the garden. Leftover packets of flower seeds will fill in gaps in the landscape.

BULBS

Plant summer alliums, dahlias, gladiolus, and other summer-flowering bulbs this month if you didn't plant them last month. Check this planting guideline, as each plant has specific preferences. For instance, dahlias like to be well covered in the ground (a hole 3 to 6 inches deep for most), whereas cannas prefer being closer to the surface.

EDIBLES

In cool areas you can still plant a crop of snow peas. They mature in just 50 days or so. Beans are the main crop to plant everywhere. They do just as well in 60°F as they do in 80°F. Coat beans and peas with inoculant (see April). Both need some support in place before you plant.

Daffodil bulbs have bulbets coming from the side.

Crocus corms have cormels growing from the side and base.

Cannas are rhizomes that fall apart or can be cut apart.

PLANT	PLANTING DEPTH
Alliums	3–4 inches
Begonias	2–3 inches
Caladium	2–3 inches
Calla lily	2–3 inches
Canna	Surface
Cyclamen	1–2 inches
Dahlia	3–6 inches
Elephant ears	3–4 inches
Freesia	1–2 inches
Gladiolus	3–6 inches

HERE'S HOW

TO PLANT A CONTAINER

Containers can be of any size and hold one or many plants.

1. Pick the container and plants that work together.
2. Make sure that the container has a drainage hole in its base. If your container doesn't have a hole at the bottom, you can make one. First, check for one of more indentations in the base, which can easily be knocked out with a screwdriver and hammer. If the container has no indentation and is plastic, you can drive a nail into the base to make four or five holes.
3. For ceramic containers that do not have drainage holes, use the ceramic container as a cover or cache pot. Plant your plants in a container that has drainage holes and is slightly smaller than the

In the lettuce patch, transition from cool-weather to heat-tolerant or all-season lettuce varieties. Sow a few seeds a week for a long summer of lettuce.

LAWNS

Continue to reseed areas that need it.

HOUSEPLANTS & CONTAINERS

Tender annuals such as zinnias, coleus, and petunias can be added to containers outside. A general guide to container design is one tall plant in the center or back of the container (the thriller) and something to fill out the main part of the container (the filler). Finally, include one or two plants to drape over the sides of the container (the spiller). The plants can be perennial or even small shrubs that can be planted into the garden in fall or next spring. Some designers suggest containers and plants should be in a 1:3 ratio; that is, you'll have one-third container to two-thirds flowers.

ceramic pot. Place that pot inside the ceramic container. Finish with mulch at the top to disguise the inner planting pot. Periodically check that there is no water standing in the bottom of the ceramic container.

4. Position large containers where you want them to be *before* adding soil mix. The combined weight of plants, soil, and the container can be heavy.
5. For large or deep containers that are intended just for annuals, save costs by reducing the amount of potting soil by filling the lower half of the container with packing peanuts or a plant shelf.
6. Fill the container with potting mix, to about 6 to 8 inches from the top rim of the container. Potting mixes that contain added slow-release fertilizer are good choices for containers. Don't use garden soil, as that is too dense and can contain contaminants.
7. Play with the arrangement of plants until you get the right look.
8. Plant the selected plants into the soil starting with the middle first.
9. Add more potting mix around the plants and settle them into the soil.
10. Water the container when you have finished.

Repot indoor plants this month. Take a plant outdoors and give the leaf surfaces (tops and bottoms) a good spritz with water. Repot indoor plants in a potting mix suited to specific varieties and water well.

PERENNIALS

Perennials are the workhorses of the summer garden. *Echinacea*, *Gaillardia*, and *Phlox* species are just some of the great perennials to grow in a sunny garden that can be planted this month. For shady gardens, try *Tiarella* (foam flower), astilbe, or bleeding hearts, which are all deer resistant and very winter hardy (to Zone 3).

SHRUBS & ROSES

The last of the shrubs and roses should be planted this month.

CARE

June marks the end of spring and the start of summer. It's the ideal time to divide spring bulbs and prune spring-flowering shrubs.

ANNUALS

Deadhead annual flowers as they mature and die. If you want more flowers, the dying flowers have to be removed before the seed is mature. Deadheading is also a way to stop some self-seeding annuals, such as cosmos, from straying too far from where you want them to grow.

BULBS

Trim off dead flowerheads from early-blooming alliums unless you have an artistic flair, in which case you can spray-paint their lovely globes for summer color. By now all the browning, decaying leaves from late-blooming tulips and daffodils can be cut off.

June is a good time to divide spring daffodils, tulips, and even iris if they are just starting to grow.

EDIBLES

As soon as you plant anything from the cabbage family, a little white butterfly will find and lay eggs on it. These will soon become green—and hungry—caterpillars. Cover all cabbage family seedlings with light netting to prevent the butterflies from getting to the leaves.

Potatoes need darkness to grow well, so as the plant grows upward, bury its stem (mounding soil or mulch upward). Let the plants get to about 8 to 10 inches tall, then bury the lower 6 inches with compost or straw to keep the developing tubers dark. As a plant grows, you'll be burying the stems several times over summer.

HERE'S HOW

TO DIVIDE BULBS

What we call "bulbs" are actually a collection of true bulbs, corms, tubers, and rhizomes. They are all slightly different and are divided in different ways.

Trim iris leaves before dividing the plants.

True bulbs: Daffodils, hyacinths, and tulips are true bulbs. The bulbs are layered in a similar way to an onion, with scales around the outside. The mother bulb contains the flower stem in the center of the bulb; this grows in spring. Daughter bulblets grow from the base between the scales. The number of younger plants increases around the original bulb and eventually, crowding takes place. When that happens, the daffodils produce lots of green growth but very few flowers. Dig the whole bulb up and remove the daughters. Replant all of the blubs for an even better display next year.

Corms: Crocus and gladiolus are grown from corms. The growth point on corms is the top, and the base is a single, large root. As the corm ages, small cormels form under its flat base. Just dig up the corm: these pea-like cormels easily come apart and can be planted.

Tubers: Potatoes are tubers, as are caladiums and dahlias. New tubers actually grow on the roots. Over the season these enlarge and can each be planted next year. Look for sections that have "eyes," similar to potato eyes. Dahlias and caladiums are dug up at the end of the year and divided before planting in spring. See October for more on storing bulbs.

Rhizomes: Cannas and iris have rhizomes that form horizontally along the soil surface. After a few years, cannas and iris separate into smaller division when they're dug. Iris rhizomes are divided in spring as the new shoots are starting. Cannas are divided either before storing (if the rhizome falls apart into smaller sections) or in spring before planting. The rhizomes can also be cut with a clean knife to increase the number of divisions. Division by cutting with a knife should only be done in spring, not fall. Look for natural divisions where growth is already starting, and make sure that each division has one of the growth points included.

Start harvesting herbs for use in the kitchen or to store for winter use. Thyme, sage, mint, and chives all freeze or dry well for winter casseroles.

LAWNS

Continue to mow as needed and keep newly seeded areas moist until the grass is well germinated. When the new grass is about 3 inches tall, include it in regular mowing.

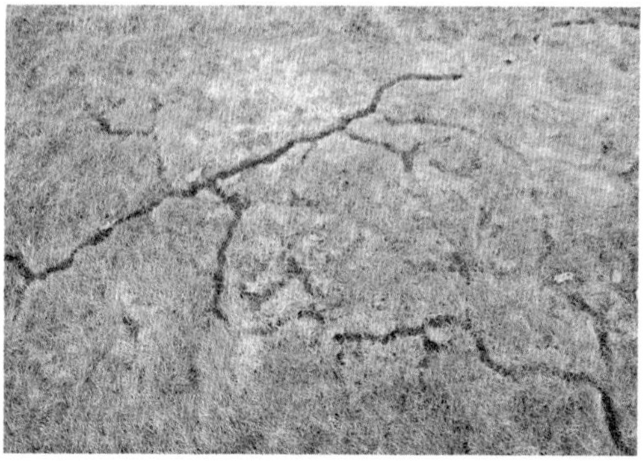

This lawn is showing the tell-tale tunnels of voles.

Both moles and voles tunnel under lawns and make ridges that disfigure the whole appearance of a lawn. Moles are after grubs, worms, and insects in the lawn (and landscape in general). Voles, on the other hand, are after tender vegetation, which could be lawn grass roots, spring bulbs, or perennial plant roots. Moles rarely appear aboveground, but they do leave little piles of dug-out earth on the surface—good diagnostic evidence. Voles do come to the surface, and vigilant neighborhood cats help control these. Havahart® traps (or similar brands) and commercial treatments are available.

HOUSEPLANTS & CONTAINERS

Keep outdoors containers looking sharp by deadheading flowering plants promptly. Move plants that are spending the summer outside, like citrus trees and patio hibiscus, into their summer locations.

PERENNIALS

Trim spent blooms on spring-blooming perennials and generally tidy up perennials. Remove dead bloom stalks from daylilies as these blooms fade too.

After some perennials flower (bee balm), the lower leaves tend to go brown and die off, leaving a rather ragged-looking plant. Trim the stalks of these perennials to about 6 inches tall and let vibrant new growth return. Often a second flush of flowers arrives in late summer on these perennials.

SHRUBS & ROSES

Prune spring-blooming shrubs after they bloom.

If needed, repeat-blooming azaleas should be pruned after the first spring flush of growth. Most don't need attention every year.

Prune boxwood, holly, and other evergreens after the first flush of new growth slows down.

Just as some bee balms suffer fungal issues in summer, so do some shrubs, specifically crape myrtles and lilacs. Planting these shrubs in full rather than part sun reduces these issues.

TREES

Trees will all be in leaf by now, so any dead areas will be noticed and can be pruned out. For young fruit trees (two years old or less), remove most of the fruit as it starts to form. This allows more energy to be put into the roots and overall growth. Prune heavily laden branches of apple, plum, and peach trees to just a few fruits per branch so that fruits can all grow to the correct size without crowding or rubbing against one another.

Netting helps protect crops from insect damage.

VINES & GROUNDCOVERS

Prune spring-blooming perennial vines such as spring clematis and wisteria. These vines bloom on the previous year's wood and need to be pruned immediately after they bloom. Roses and many other summer-blooming vines bloom on the current year's wood and would have been pruned in March or April. All vines should be pruned to keep them within the confines of your arbor/trellis or fence.

Remove pieces of groundcover or vine that are moving in the wrong direction.

WATER

All new plants, including trees, shrubs, and lawns, should be watered when rain is scarce. A good watering (about an inch) at least once a week is a good guide for the whole garden. Established shrubs and perennials can last a little longer, but when the temperatures rise into sunny 80s, even they will start to wilt without some help.

ANNUALS

Annuals are thirsty for water most of the summer. A good watering most mornings or evenings when temperatures are lower is a good way to keep them healthy and vigorous. Water with overhead sprinklers in the morning. Evening watering is best done manually, at the base of the plant. Overhead watering at night allows water to stay on leaves overnight, which creates a better environment for

HERE'S HOW

TO HARVEST & PRESERVE HERBS

Herbs can be dried, frozen, or preserved in a different medium such as vinegar or sugar/salt. For harvest, pick a time early in the day when the herbs are fresh but the dew has dried. Ideally the herb should not be in flower. Herbs can be harvested all summer. Do not take more than about one-third of the plant each time.

HOW TO DRY HERBS

1. Pick the herbs and inspect for insects.
2. Remove any dead or damaged leaves.
3. Divide the herbs into small groups and secure the stems with a band or string.
4. Label the herb.
5. Let the herbs dry for several weeks in a cool, dry, and dark place (*not* the kitchen).
6. Store in small, labeled glass jars.

Tie herbs into small bunches for drying.

If you're using a dehydrator, place the herbs on the dehydrator shelf and let them set for about an hour. Check the herbs often and remove when they're totally dry; this takes just two or three hours for mint, thyme, and oregano, which have small leaves, and longer for lemongrass or sage, which have thicker leaves.

Use dried herbs in winter recipes. For a classic mix of herbs such as Herbes de Provence or bouquet garni, dry the herbs individually and combine them when dried. Herbes de Provence includes rosemary, sage, thyme, oregano, lavender, and winter savory. A bouquet garni has thyme, parsley, and bay leaf. For use in recipes, 1 teaspoon dried herbs equals 1 tablespoon fresh herbs.

A microwave can be used, but it's not the best way to dry herbs. Even at 30-second bursts, it's easy to overdry herbs.

HOW TO FREEZE HERBS

Most herbs, with the exception of basil, can be frozen. Use straight from the freezer in winter casseroles or on baked potatoes.

1. Pick and prepare as described in how to dry herbs (steps 1 and 2).
2. Strip the leaves from the stems. Snip chives into 1-inch segments.
3. Place the herbs directly on a baking sheet into the freezer (open freeze).
4. Scoop the frozen herbs from the sheet and store in labeled freezer bags.

Herb vinegars are easy to make, and are great gifts too!

HOW TO PRESERVE IN A THIRD MEDIUM

Vinegar, salt, and sugar can be used to preserve herbs.

Classic French tarragon vinegar is popular in French cooking.

To prepare 1-quart herb vinegars:

1. Prepare the herbs as described and dry thoroughly (steps 1 and 2 in how to dry herbs).
2. Put a good handful of herbs into a clean glass jar.
3. Cover with wine vinegar.
4. Seal and place in a cool, dark, and dry cupboard for about two months.
5. Pour the now-infused vinegar into a clean jar, and discard the herbs.
6. Label the vinegar. Add a single stem of fresh herb in the bottle (optional).

Good mixes for white wine vinegar are French tarragon, red or green basil (red makes a pink vinegar), or mixed herbs. Good mixes for red wine vinegar are mint, rosemary, or mixed herbs.

Chopped mint can be preserved directly in vinegar: chop the mint, put into small jars, and cover with wine vinegar; then process in boiling water (to cover) for five minutes.

Lemon verbena or lemon balm can be layered with sugar to create a lemon sugar. Put a layer of sugar in a small jar, add a layer of herbs, and add another layer of sugar. Continue until the jar is filled. Cover and let the mixture cure for about two weeks. Remove the dried herbs and store the sugar in a clean jar. Sugar can also be infused with lavender. Herb-flavored salts are created in the same way. If you don't want remnant pieces of the herb in the sugar or salt, place the herb in a small muslin bag before layering.

Caution about herb oils: Vinegar is acidic and safe to use for preserving. Oil does *not* have the acidity needed to safely preserve herbs; to be safe, they need to be processed at very high pressure. Without sufficient pressure, there is a danger of botulism surviving. So herb and garlic oils should *not* be attempted at home.

fungal issues. Timers are a great way to water in the morning before you get up.

BULBS

Spring-blooming bulbs are dormant for summer and don't need any extra water. Summer bulbs like alliums and dahlias should be treated as newly planted annuals until they are growing well, at which point they can go on the same schedule as the rest of the perennials.

EDIBLES

For a vegetable garden to be productive, whether it's planted directly in the ground, in raised beds, or in containers, it needs to be well watered. Tomatoes that receive uneven moisture—too much water one day and far too little for several days following—grow a scar on the bottom called *blossom end rot.* Infrequent water when the fruit is developing can create cracking on the skin of the tomato called "catfacing." Sometime this is unavoidable, particularly when early season storms deliver large amounts of water in just a few hours. A good rule is to ensure that this part of the garden gets a daily watering.

LAWNS

As summer temperatures rise and rain gets less frequent, the lawn can suffer. One inch of water a week minimum is the correct goal amount. This should be delivered at one time so grass roots develop deeply below the surface. A rain gauge that measures what moisture the lawn receives at any particular time is helpful in deciding whether it needs watering or not. You can also just observe the grass; if the grass springs back when you walk on it, then it is fine. If it stays flat for a minute, it needs water. See May for information on irrigation.

HOUSEPLANTS & CONTAINERS

All outside containers need attention this month and for the rest of summer. A good watering each day is ideal, but large containers can cope with an alternating daily schedule (every other day).

For hanging baskets, consider using a water wand that extends several feet beyond the hose and can deliver water to baskets without you taking them down each time. You can also attach a hanging basket plant to its hook with a long chain, which you'd anchor on another hook that you can reach.

HERE'S HOW

TO PRUNE SPRING-BLOOMING SHRUBS

June is a great time to prune spring-blooming shrubs such as forsythia and lilacs. These shrubs produce new growth from late spring onward, and that growth develops flower buds for next year. Pruning these shrubs too late in summer doesn't give them enough time to develop flower buds, so it's important to do any pruning as soon as the shrubs finish flowering. For more on pruning, see February.

Shrubs are divided into multi-stem and single-stem shrubs.

For multi-stemmed shrubs (such as forsythia or lilac):

1. Remove peripheral stems and thin outside stems to reduce the overall girth of the shrub.
2. Reduce stems to a reasonable height. The ultimate height is dependent on the shrub, your landscape needs, and your personal preferences. For a hedge of forsythia, reduce all the stems to about 3 feet for a 4- to 5-foot yellow hedge next spring.
3. Completely remove a few stems in the center of the shrub to allow light and air flow into the middle and to encourage new growth in the center.
4. Do not trim the stems after this June pruning. The new stems that grow from the base can be removed to control the overall size of the shrub, but these too will bloom next year if left alone.

Note: For vastly overgrown shrubs, prune back all the top growth almost to the ground (to about 12 inches). Within a few weeks, new stems start to grow and will flower next year. It takes a few years for the shrub to fill back out, but with enormous shrubs that have not been pruned for many years, it is a good way to rejuvenate the shrubs.

For single-stem shrubs (such as quince or witch hazel):

Sometimes, these shrubs send up new shoots around the side. These can be removed, but overall these shrubs rarely get out of control and do not have to be pruned every year.

1. Trim back each individual stem to the desired height, clipping close to another stem or bud.
2. In dense shrubs, remove a few stems almost back to the main stem. This allows more stems to grow from the center of the shrub and yields a fuller overall look to the shrub.
3. Once pruned, do not prune again until next year.

Unhook the chain and lower the basket to water it, then raise the basket back to its normal position.

PERENNIALS

Unless your garden looks excessively dry, perennials should not need water this month. Pick an "indicator" plant in your garden that requires slightly more water than the rest of the plants. When that one starts to wilt, you'll know that you need to water soon.

SHRUBS & ROSES

Established shrubs and roses rarely need extra water in June. If they do, run a soaker hose around

SPRING-BLOOMING SHRUBS—PRUNE AFTER THEY HAVE BLOOMED

These spring-flowering shrubs are safe to prune this month.

PLANT	BLOOM	TIME OF BLOOM	HARDINESS
Azalea and rhododendron (*Rhododendron*)	Reds and whites	Late spring	Varies with variety
Daphne (*Daphne cneorum*)	Scented white flowers	Mid-spring	3–7
Forsythia (*Forsythia* × *intermedia*)	Bright yellow	Mid-spring	5–8 (some varieties 4–7)
Fothergilla (*Fothergilla gardenii*)	White	Late spring	4–8
Kerria (*Kerria japonica*)	Yellow pompons, green stems	Mid-spring	4–9
Lilac (*Syringa vulgaris*)	Purple or white	Late spring	3–7
Spirea (bridal wreath) (*Spiraea* × *vanhouttei*)	White, cascading	Mid-spring	3–8
Viburnum (*Viburnum carlesii*)	White	Late spring	4–7
Flowering quince (*Chaenomeles speciosa*)	Bright red	Early spring	4–8

the garden to water all the shrubs at one time, or water the shrubs at soil level, individually.

TREES

A tree has much deeper roots than other plants, so the best way to deliver water to the root zone is to run a hose directly to the tree. For young and newly planted trees, water with a dripping hose. Turn the water on as low as it can go so that the hose is barely dripping. Leave the hose on for about two hours to thoroughly water the tree. Move the hose to the opposite side of the tree and repeat so that the entire root zone is watered. Do not let the hose seep directly onto the tree trunk but position it an inch or two away from the trunk for saplings, to about 1 foot away for larger trees. Water does not travel in a straight line downward, so most roots get some over the four-hour period. Newly planted trees are the ones that need water most, not well-established one.

VINES & GROUNDCOVERS

Groundcovers in shady areas rarely need water this month. Those groundcovers and vines that are in sunny locations may need extra water. Stressed plants have leaves that droop or have areas that die out.

FERTILIZE

Most fertilizing is finished for the year with the exception of the vegetable garden, annuals, and containers. We expect a lot from these areas, and a boost of nutrients is one way to achieve success.

ANNUALS

Newly planted annuals that were purchased will retain much of their already-fertilized seedling soil, so they don't need any further attention. Those gardeners who were able to plant annuals in mid- to late May should add a little fertilizer to the water particularly for annuals in containers and hanging baskets (about half-strength every two weeks is sufficient). For annuals in the ground, sprinkle a little general fertilizer in that area of the garden.

EDIBLES

The early vegetable garden does well when fertilized just once at the start of the growing season. The early lettuces and kale do not need fertilizer, but a general compost or organic fertilizer should be added to the garden before you replace cool-weather crops with warm-weather ones. So before

HERE'S HOW

TO INSTALL A RAIN BARREL

Every summer there are weeks when no rain arrives, and there are some summers where almost no rain falls at all in June through August. What little rain does arrive does so in storms, which bounces off the dried ground and into the storm gutters and drains. One way to capture that much needed rainfall is to install a rain barrel to water from a home's roof. Rain barrels vary in size, but a standard barrel holds between 50 to 60 gallons.

1. Decide on the location for the barrel. They're attached to downspouts, and most people prefer that they be placed discretely at the back of a home or close to where you plan to use the water.
2. Rain barrels have a spigot that is either already in place or that you install. The spigot should be close to the bottom of the barrel but high enough up that you can fill a bucket or watering can. A concrete block or other support can elevate the barrel if it doesn't come with platform.
3. Install the spigot. If the rain barrel kit comes with a faucet and the barrel already has a hole, place the spigot into the hole and secure it by screwing it in until it is facing the correct way and is snug against the side. If the rain barrel does not have a predrilled hole for the spigot, purchase an outside faucet and place it against the side of the barrel. Trace around the pipe at the back of the faucet; this is where you will drill a pilot hole. Using a small saw, make a hole in the side to accommodate the pipe. Push the faucet into the hole and secure. Put caulking or putty around the pipe to stop any drips.
4. The top of a rain barrel needs an attachment to the downspout that will carry incoming water into the barrel. Mark a location on the top of the barrel where the diverter will go in, and a similar location on the downspout where the diverter intercepts the water coming down. Cut these two areas out with a small saw.
5. The barrel also needs an overflow attachment to cope with excess rainfall that could cause rain barrels to overflow. The overflow attachment returns excess water back to the downspout. This is sometimes part of the downspout attachment; other times you have to install a second piece of pipe to reconnect the barrel to the downspout. Place the overflow pipe close to the downspout and close to the top of the barrel. Mark and cut these areas. Insert the overflow pipe to the barrel and the downspout.
6. Run a little caulking around the joints and wait for rain.

you plant beans, peppers, squash, and tomatoes, add some nutrients to the beds. If you've been growing peas in spring and you plan to replace them with beans, add a light fertilizer to the bed.

A second fertilizer is usually applied as a boost when flowers start to appear. This can be a compost tea or side-dressed compost.

LAWNS

The only lawns that need fertilizer are those that are newly seeded or lawns in cooler geographic areas where the lawns are not yet fertilized. Check the notes on general lawn care, including some of the legal restrictions, in April and adjust for your climate.

HERE'S HOW

TO SIDE-DRESS WITH COMPOST OR FERTILIZER

Sidedressing with fertilizer is a way of spreading fertilizer alongside the growing crops rather than broadcasting over the whole area. For peas and row crops, side-dress down one side of the crop; for tomatoes and single crops, place the fertilizer in a circle around the main stem.

1. For a row crop such as peas and beans, make a furrow about 4 or 5 inches from the shoots.
2. Evenly spread the compost or fertilizer along the furrow.
3. Cover the furrow and lightly till the area to incorporate the fertilizer or compost into the soil around the plant roots. A rake is a good way to lightly till the area as that does not disturb the roots of the plants in the row.
4. For individual crops, make the furrow within the drip line of the plant. The drip line extends as far as the branches/stems extend to the side.
5. Incorporate as described in Step 3.

HOUSEPLANTS & CONTAINERS

Gardeners have high expectations that all containers will be very floriferous all season. This requires plenty of nutrients in the containers in the form of monthly fertilizer applications. Make a check mark on your calendar so that you don't over- or underfertilize your containers.

PROBLEM-SOLVE

Along with the arrival of warm temperatures, there is an increase in the insect populations. Some overwintered under the mulch and are just getting started with the next stage of their development, while others are onto their second generation already. For all bug and fungal issues, it is important to identify *what* you have before you research *how* to correct it.

Dog vomit fungus on mulch is an unsightly but common occurrence, particularly in shady areas under shrubs. This fungus is bright yellow and spreads several inches in all directions on top of the mulch, seemingly overnight. The fungus is part of the slime mold group and thrives in damp, warm weather. As soon as dry conditions arrive, it will disappear. If you don't want to wait that long, raking the mold will help it dry out so it can be scooped up and disposed of in the trash.

ANNUALS

Cool, damp weather can increase the occurrence of wilts and fungus. Tender annuals are particularly prone to these problems. The best remedy is to resist planting until the soil is warm and outdoor temperatures settle into a summer pattern. Some areas in western New York can still get frost in late May, so no one plants annuals until after Memorial Day.

BULBS

Digging animals might be unearthing your bulbs. Keep a check on the bulbs' location and promptly replant any that have been pushed out of the ground. Discard any that are chewed or rotten.

EDIBLES

Like the annuals, the biggest issue is from planting basil and pepper too soon. You may not have a frost, but without 80-degree days, these hot weather plants fail to grow. Help them along with protection from cloches or other mini-greenhouse arrangements.

LAWNS

Lawn fungus becomes apparent this month. Some of these are weather related, and others can be brought on by poor cultural practices such as faulty watering habits and fertilization issues.

Fairy ring.

Mold on mulch.

Dollar spots are circular brown patches on the lawn. Upon closer look you'll see it's the grass blades that are turning brown rather than that the patch is dying. This tends to be more common on lawns with poor fertility. Give adequate, weekly water to the lawn (at least an inch delivered at one time to ensure that the water reaches the root zone), mow only when the grass is dry, and look at your fertilizer schedule to boost nitrogen levels. The fungus likes damp weather with warm days and cool nights (typical early-season weather).

Fairy rings are green circles that appear on lawns that are due more to decomposition of something other than the lawn itself. Sometimes this is a buried tree stump that's decomposing under the lawn and adding extra nitrogen to that area. Deep thatch or underlying, decomposing roots can also cause fairy rings. They are more noticeable in lawns that are brown or a less-vibrant green.

Red threads or pink patches are noticed during cool but dry conditions. Typically, the subsoil is compacted and the lawn is stressed from poor nutrient levels. Perform a soil test (see March for directions), review your fertilizer applications to make sure that you are giving the right amount to the lawn, water weekly, and mow only when the lawn is dry.

Slime molds give a metallic gray or oily sheen to grass blades. Like dog vomit fungus, slime molds go away when drier weather arrives.

HOUSEPLANTS & CONTAINERS

Check for the ever-present aphids on houseplants. Plants spending the summer outside should be checked for aphids and scale as well as being kept well-watered. Tend to issues promptly before they get serious.

PERENNIALS

Damage from rodents and deer continue to plague unprotected gardens. Over-the-counter deer and animal deterrent sprays work well for most of these issues. Whiteflies are little flying insects that congregate on and eat the stems or leaves, disfiguring the plant. If a cloud of insects takes flight when you brush against a plant, then you likely have whiteflies or something similar. Small colonies are soon taken care of by birds, but spraying an insecticidal soap may be needed. Check the directions on the soap container to see if it's a concentrate that needs to be diluted.

Depending on the weather, watch bee balm (*Monarda*) for signs of powdery mildew. This white, powdery covering is not only disfiguring but causes leaves to fall off, compromising the health of a plant. A general fungicide can be applied to control this condition if it gets too severe. Warm, humid weather is perfect for fungal issues on this and other plants in the garden.

Hollyhocks get a disease called "rust" on leaves and stems. Rust is unsightly and damaging to a plant. Remove infected leaves, noticeable due to their orange dots, as soon as you see them, and discard in the trash (not in compost). In fall, remove and discard all leaves and stems of the hollyhock plants. A fungicide can help if rust strikes early in the season; otherwise remove the plants. Hollyhocks are biennials, and the disease is not soilborne, so

This hollyhock leaf shows rust.

Monarda often suffers from powdery mildew in humid summers.

the waiting crown should not be affected assuming you remove all debris in fall (see October for a reminder).

SHRUBS AND ROSES

Scale on woody plants is a summer issue, so be aware of its arrival. Scale is usually seen as little beige or white caps on a stem. The actual insect is protected by the cap, making it difficult to treat by a spray. An oil-based treatment is more effective—the oil cuts off oxygen to the insect. To treat just a few scale insects, scrape them off with your nail or a blunt knife (so that you do not scar the branch).

Azaleas and rhododendrons are prone to attack from lacewing bugs. These little pests eat the undersides of the leaves, which create a dappled, bleached look. The insect is named for the webbing on its back. Insecticidal soap can help at the nymph stage (you'll see dark blotches on the undersides of the leaves). Other remedies include a strong spray from a hose.

With all shrubs, check young growth for insects and treat early by picking them off.

Leaf-eating June bugs make an appearance by the end of the month; these are easy to handpick.

TREES

Look for anthracnose on dogwood trees; you'll find there is a diagnostic ring on the leaf that is a brown spot encircled with a purple rim. Most modern dogwoods varieties are now immune to the disease, which killed a lot of dogwoods a few years ago.

VINES & GROUNDCOVERS

Scout groundcovers for insect damage and small animal damage. Nibbled leaves or holes in a leaf are common indicators of animals and insects. Sprinkle a deterrent over the area if you have problems with rabbits and other animals. Horticultural oils and soaps plus neighborhood birds keep insect damage to a minimum.

Remove rodent nests from dense groundcover and bird nests from vines as soon as you see them. Field mice and chipmunks find homes under the groundcover leaves to bring the next generation into the world. They eat vegetation and roots including surrounding groundcover roots.

This lacewing insect feasts on smaller summer bugs.

July

July and August are the "dog days of summer," characterized by warm to hot temperatures and scarce rainfall. For the gardener, this requires a change in tempo and routine. Garden chores are limited to the cooler evening or what can be done before heat drives us indoors during the day.

Fortunately, there is not too much outdoors that needs attention. Annuals and summer perennials like *Echinacea* should be in full bloom by now, and the garden just needs a little weeding and deadheading to keep it tidy. Watering is the main concern; small containers dry out quickly when they are in full sun.

The fun part of summer is the harvest from the vegetable garden which, by July, should be providing the first of the green beans, tomatoes, and some summer squash. Barbecues are a part of summer every year too, and having fresh zucchini, tomatoes, and salad greens from the garden make the meal just that much more fun. Flowers from the garden make great summer arrangements for the patio table as well as for the dining table. Try adding a few flowers to your meal: squash flowers and nasturtiums look and taste great in salads.

While so much is going on outside, your sights should now be set on the fall garden crops, which are started indoors this month.

Bugs are also at their peak in July, with the Japanese beetle leading the charge in landscape destruction. Bugs are particularly troublesome in the vegetable garden, where we start to see Mexican bean beetle, squash bugs, and powdery mildew from hot humid weather. A daily trip to the garden alerts you to the problems early, which makes it easier correct before too much damage is done.

Between garden maintenance and troubleshooting to keep the garden healthy, we sometimes forget to enjoy our garden. Warm summer evenings and quiet mornings are perfect for sitting in the garden and enjoying the view. Create a couple of casual seating areas where you can appreciate what you have done this year rather than worry about what was not done.

PLAN

Summer planning is finished, so now your plans can focus on fall. Remember to take some photos of the garden, showing what is working and what is not. These will help when you start your garden plans next winter.

Make plans for vacation care of the landscape if needed. A lawn that gets overlong while you're on vacation is a sign to everyone that no one is home and brings your home to the attention of criminals.

ANNUALS

Even though it's still summer, you can take a moment to plan for some fall color with late-blooming annuals including many that are in flower in summer. Sunflowers, marigolds, and zinnias are all great annuals for a long summer and right up to the first frosts of fall. Add some sedums and asters for more late-season color along with the usual chrysanthemums.

BULBS

Fall flowers will be in retail stores next month, but online stores are promoting fall-flowering bulbs this month. A much smaller collection of bulbs bloom in fall compared to spring, and they include belladonna lily (*Amaryllis belladonna*), spider or surprise lily (*Lycoris*), and some fall-blooming crocus. All these bulbs can be used in the landscape among the fall flowers or used to decorate the porch when planted in a container.

Many summer perennials, such as these coneflowers, bloom all summer long.

Lettuce is a cool-season crop for spring or fall.

Add compost to the garden before starting fall crops.

EDIBLES

Just when your vegetable garden is planted and growing well, it's time to start planning the fall garden. Order seeds for snap peas, lettuces, radishes, and carrots to arrive in late July or early August. Plan to start the cool-weather cole crop group indoors where it's cooler, and transplant them outdoors in August. Young vegetables added to the garden in late July or August mature in September when the days are much cooler and shorter. Consequently, the number of days to reach maturity gets a little longer. Adjust by adding a week or two to the time given in spring catalogs or on the seed package label.

LAWNS

The June plan that you made last month regarding summer lawn care should be maintained.

HOUSEPLANTS & CONTAINERS

Fall containers can include more than store-purchased pumpkins and flowering cabbages! Fall-blooming perennials such as small *Rudbeckia* varieties, asters, and ornamental grasses are all happy in containers. Look for some bargains this month on the "perennials on sale" table, and design a container that celebrates fall colors. Plan the containers this month and purchase the perennials next month, then assemble the arrangements. Look for warm red- and orange-colored containers that look great with grasses and other fall flowers.

PERENNIALS

Although a perennial bed doesn't require as much water as the rest of the landscape, you'll need to irrigate in hot weather. Schedule the irrigation system to include perennial beds about once every week, particularly if you hit a stretch of hot, dry weather.

SHRUBS & ROSES

Like perennial beds, shrubs and roses don't need the same amount of water as lawns and annuals. Shrubs and roses are easily watered if you install a soaker hose or drip irrigation. This can be installed in July or anytime over the summer to ease the workload. Check Water in May for directions on how to install soaker hoses and drip irrigation.

TREES

As trees mature and spread their branches farther away, the shade created by their canopy increases. Sometimes, for various reasons, trees have to be removed and what was once a nice shady area is now in full sun. Be prepared to adjust your landscape plans to accommodate such changes.

VINES & GROUNDCOVERS

Morning glory is a fast-growing annual vine.

PLANT	WHERE TO START	WEEKS BEFORE FIRST FROST	TRANSPLANT	DAYS TO MATURITY
Cabbages/cauliflower	Start indoors	8–10 weeks	4 weeks before first frost	60–70 days
Carrots	Direct-sow outside	10 weeks		50–70 days
All-season lettuce	Direct-sow outside	6 weeks		50 days
Cool-season lettuce	Start indoors	8 weeks	Up to 4 weeks before first frost	40 days
Kale	Direct-sow outside	Up to 4 weeks before first frost		50 days
Salad greens	Direct-sow outside	4 weeks		50 days
Snap peas	Direct-sow outside	10 weeks		70 days

By now, annual summer vines such as colorful morning glories are in full bloom. Sometimes the vigorous growth of these vines extends away from the fence or support. Keep some string or wire handy to direct the vine back to where it should be.

PLANT

Anything that is planted in July (or August) needs a little extra care from the gardener. Perennials and grasses, in particular, are offered at good prices in summer and some great bargains can be had if you can keep the plants alive and revive them.

ANNUALS

A few quick-growing annuals such as calendula and zinnias can still be sown in the first few days of July for late-summer bloom. Six-packs of common annuals such as marigolds and petunias are still for sale and are great for filling in those extra little gaps from spring-blooming flowers or to fill out a container with some summer color.

BULBS

If you need to divide spring-flowering bulbs, July is a good month to do that. Assuming you marked the ones that you're dividing, dig the bulbs up. Split the bulbs (see June for how to do this) and replant. The bulbs are fully dormant in summer so they'll be ready to grow next spring. Daffodils that produce lots of green leaves but no flowers usually need dividing, as well as any bulb that's been in the same place for four or five years. Although these may not show signs of reduced flowering, you can increase the number of bulbs for next year without having the expense of buying more. Think about moving a few bulbs to places where the snow melts first, especially if those bulbs that are not thriving because they don't currently get enough sun.

Zinnias are fast-growing annuals that thrive in summer temperatures.

EDIBLES

Continue to plant beans and squash the first part of this month. They still have plenty of time to mature before the temperature turns cool in fall. Beans do well all the way up to frost.

Start cool-weather cabbages and cauliflowers for planting outdoors next month in order to harvest in late September. They can be started indoors where it's cool or outdoors where they will grow. If outdoors, shade the area to keep it cool enough for germination. Carrots can be planted outside this month for a fall crop.

LAWNS

The only repair and seeding of lawns this month should be for emergency situations. Emergencies include grass dying because a kiddie pool was left sitting on it for too long or because your dog decided to hunt for bones in the middle of the lawn.

HOUSEPLANTS & CONTAINERS

Adding a few extra annuals to a container doesn't usually increase its maintenance. Look for end-of-season sales at nurseries where you can get some great bargains, and plant them right away. If the store-bought plants are stressed from too much sun and too little water, baby them in a shady place for a few days to recover and rehydrate fully. Browning on leaf edges and general drooping of leaves are signs of poor care. Also, the container soil is often dry and shrinks away from the sides. Put these containers in a larger bucket with a water level that reaches almost to the top of the container. Leave it until the potting mix rehydrates.

ABOUT CROP ROTATION

Vegetables can be divided into groups of like families, and each family has a similar set of problems that'll remain in the soil from one year to the next. Planting the same crop in the same spot, year after year, allows viruses or bugs to increase to the extent that they compromise plant health. Rotating plant groups from one area to another lowers the risk these issues cause. In addition to avoiding or reducing problems with soilborne diseases and some soil-dwelling insects, the goal of crop rotation is to manage soil fertility. Crop rotation allows heavy-feeding tomatoes to take advantage of the enriched soil that legumes leave because the legumes fix nitrogen in the soil, which the tomatoes take advantage of.

The cabbage group: Lettuces, cabbages, kale, cauliflower, Brussels sprouts, broccoli

The tomato group: Tomatoes, eggplants, potatoes

The legume group: Peas, beans

The root crop group: Carrots, parsnips

PERENNIALS

Perennials can still be planted if you take care of them. In addition to general malaise, perennials purchased now can have potbound roots. This occurs when roots don't have enough room to grow outward, so they circle around inside the container walls. Water well and untangle the roots before you plant them.

Perennials that have been poorly tended end up on the sale racks at nurseries along with perennials that are past bloom—these can usually be picked up at great prices. Nurse these back to great health by giving them some good soil to grow in and a little extra care. Give them plenty of water and trim back old flower stems and any damaged stems. A dose of liquid fertilizer also helps to bring these plants back to full health. It is probably too late for most of them to bloom this year, but by next year they should be fine.

TREES, SHRUBS & ROSES

These should *not* be planted this month. If you have some delivered or have found a great item while you were on vacation, temporarily "plant" them in a container kept in a shady location until fall. When the real heat of summer passes, they can be planted in a permanent location.

VINES & GROUNDCOVERS

If your groundcovers have spread too far, dig up the excess and replant them in sparse areas or a new area altogether. Keep the new plants well watered.

Mandevilla vines are popular tropical annual vines that will probably be on sale this month. The vines grow rapidly in warm weather to cover porch posts or freestanding mailboxes. Either plant the vine in the ground or sink the container into the ground for easy removal in fall.

CARE

Summer is a great time to spend long, hot days by the pool and for vacationing, but these are not great conditions for plants in your landscape. Excessive heat can dehydrate a plant quickly, and a day without watering a container can indeed be the end of those plants.

Check where your mailbox and utility boxes are located. Overzealous vines and perennials can make access difficult. Trim back and corral these items before you get a "love" note in the mailbox from your carrier or a notice from a utility.

ANNUALS

To keep annuals blooming well all summer, they need to be deadheaded. For most annuals the dead flowers can be pinched off with just your thumb and finger. Many annuals such as zinnias flower more profusely when they are kept picked.

BULBS

Gladioli are in bloom in July and August. Most of the time they stand brightly upright at the back of the perennial border, but moderate rainstorms or deer walking through knock them over. If the blooms are still fresh, pick them for your vases. If blooming is over, support the stems with another

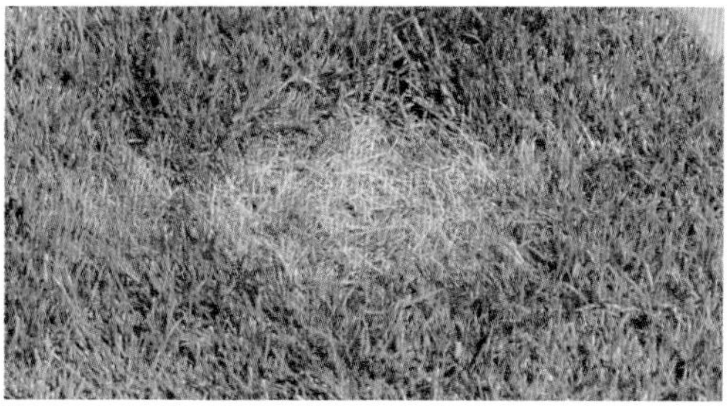

Dog spots are common on lawns.

shrub or stick for a week or two until you can cut the stems down.

EDIBLES

Pinch basil back often to keep it productive and bushy. Perennial herbs like lemon balm and French tarragon, whose growth starts early in the year, will show browning lower leaves in July. Trim the whole plant back in July to about 6 inches from the ground and wait for the new growth to return; it'll be ready to harvest again in August or September.

Summer harvest is in full swing. To keep plants producing, pick crops that mature quickly every day, because they go from underripe to overripe almost overnight. If you have too much to eat in one day, preserve or freeze the excess.

LAWNS

Move garden toys, such as kiddie paddling pools and slip-and-slide water toys, around the lawn every few days or weekly during summer. The constant jumping on the slide, the weight of the pool, and wet feet running over the surrounding grass are not things that a lawn appreciates for long. Additionally, the grass under larger toys needs light to grow.

Rinse areas where your dog relieves himself daily. Repeated high nitrogen applications from urine in the same area can cause grass to die out. A thorough rinse with a hose dilutes the chemicals and is an easy preventative measure.

HOUSEPLANTS & CONTAINERS

Houseplants are one of the easier plants to take care of during a vacation. Take them from their very sunny windowsill (where they would dry out without daily moisture) and put them on a nearby shady floor for a few days. Placing them in a pool of water such as the bathtub keeps them happy too.

Move outdoor containers to a shady location for the duration of your vacation. Keep them hydrated by connecting them to a tub of water. Create a "wick" using a strip of old towel and drape that over the container plant's soil with the opposite end of the strip in the tub of water. Anchor the wick to the bottom of the bucket, under the water. This damp wick arrangement is fine for small containers, but larger ones really need a couple of wicks to remain hydrated. Test this to make sure you can get enough moisture to the container before you leave for vacation. Self-watering containers and drip systems on a timer also cope well if you are away.

PERENNIALS

Perennials should be up and flowering now. Most perennials flower from two to six weeks, while a few flower for most of the summer (such as *Coreopsis*). Deadhead perennials and remove the dead stalks from any daylilies that have faded.

If you put last season's poinsettia in the ground, it should be growing well now. Trim all the stems back by about one-third so that the plant is compact for this season. This is the last pinching that it will get before being brought back inside in September. (I think poinsettias grow better in the ground, so I wait to pot them back up again in August or September.) Pinch back any chrysanthemums that are growing.

TREES

On conifers that produce "candles" whose length reveals its new growth each year, you can reduce the overall growth rate by pruning its candles. To reduce growth, cut the candle back to about one-third of its length in July.

Finish pruning shrubs this month. Don't prune any winter or early-spring flowering shrubs, as they are already producing the buds that produce those flowers. See February for the list of shrubs to leave alone. Boxwoods, hollies, and most conifers can still be tidied up and pruned.

HERE'S HOW

TO STAKE PERENNIALS

1. *Stake tall perennials to stop them falling over. Place stakes around the plants about an inch away from the stems.*
2. *Run twine around the stakes at 18 inches and 30 inches.*
3. *Plants will hide the string as they grow.*

Conifer "candles" are signs of new growth.

VINES & GROUNDCOVERS

Climbing roses and other climbing plants are often put next to footpaths and arbors. By midsummer, some are straying below the structure and need to be trimmed off. Even though July is not the "correct" time to prune a climbing rose, if it's impeding your ability to walk through an arbor, cut it back. Use sharp pruners and take the vine back to the next joint with a branch, which is usually about a foot or so back.

WATER

Hot summer days are sometimes sprinkled with afternoon storms, but not always. A lack of rain means more watering for your landscape, but you'll have some decisions to make regarding how much water you can afford for irrigation, particularly if you are paying high prices for city water. Wise watering can save your wallet as well as your landscape this month.

HERE'S HOW

TO LAYER SHRUBS

Some shrubs, like forsythia, willows, and roses, have long branches that grow out to reach the ground. These can be propagated by layering.

1. Select a nice, long stem and bend it down so that it reaches the ground. Ideally, the branch will reach the ground plus have about 4 to 6 inches of growth beyond that point. This will ultimately be planted in the ground. For shorter segments, you might need to put a brick or block under a container in which you could grow the cutting.
2. Strip the leaves from the branch tip; a 2- to 3-inch section is sufficient.
3. Score (scrape with a knife) the outside of the branch tip on the section that touches the ground or container soil so that you remove the tough outer bark.

   At this point you should have a stem that is still growing on the mother plant. It's bent down to the ground or container, where a segment without leaves is about to be buried.
4. Bury this section in the ground and anchor with either a rock or landscape pins. Water the segment. It takes several weeks for the section to grow roots, and summer-layered shrubs are best left until next spring to ensure that the daughter plant has sufficient roots to survive on its own.
5. When the daughter segment is growing well and has lots of roots underneath, lift the young section complete with its roots.
6. Sever the segment from the mother plant and replant the section where you want it to grow.

ANNUALS

Annuals, whether they're in the landscape or a container, are the thirstiest part of the landscape. In the landscape, group all annuals in the same area so that they can all be watered together (this is called *hydrozoning*). If you're in a long-term

Anchor soaker hoses and drip irrigation with ground stakes.

drought, install a rain barrel (see June) to collect whatever rain does fall.

BULBS

Any bulbs that you divide this month should be watered in to settle the soil around the bulbs, but as they are dormant they don't need much more than that. Summer bulbs are treated like annuals as far as watering schedules go.

EDIBLES

Like annuals, the vegetable garden is *thirsty*. Providing constant water for tomatoes and beans is important to obtain a good crop. Container-grown apple trees or blueberries need a moist soil to thrive. Using water-saving soaker hoses or drip irrigation in the edible garden to optimize water use also ensures that vegetables get sufficient water where they need it—at the soil and root level.

LAWNS

If you decided to keep the lawn green through summer this year, it needs approximately 1 inch

Proper watering encourages deep root growth on grass.

HERE'S HOW

TO TAKE SHRUB CUTTINGS

You can take cuttings from shrubs and most trees this month. Most cuttings, including those from roses and trees, are best done on new or semi-soft growth (the current year's growth that has matured for several weeks and is darker than the new growth). For propagating (taking cuttings) of conifers, look at the instructions at the end of this sidebar.

1. Pick a section of the shrub or tree that is has lots of new growth on it. The branches will look pale compared to last year's growth.
2. Cut a 6- to 10-inch section from the shrub branch (larger sections are for trees and shorter segments for smaller shrubs such as boxwood). Choose one that's close to another branch.
3. Recut the section at the cut end. The second cut should be close to the lowest set of leaves.
4. Strip the leaves from the lower one-third of the cutting.
5. If you have rooting hormone powder, dust the cut end with the powder (or dip it in the powder). Note that you do not want to contaminate the whole container of rooting powder, so pour a little powder onto a saucer or small jar and dip the cutting into that. Many shrubs will root without powder but slow-rooting trees do better with a dusting of powder. Rooting powder can be found at some nurseries and many online stores.
6. Make a hole with a pencil or your finger in a container filled with damp potting mix and put the stem into the container.
7. Refill the hole so that the soil is firmly around the branch.

Keep the container and cutting in a shady location and keep it moist. Containers can also be placed indoors and covered with a tent of plastic to keep the moisture level high. Shrubs and trees can take anywhere from a few weeks to several months to put out roots, so be patient. New growth on a cutting is a good sign that roots are forming.

TAKING CUTTINGS OF CONIFERS

Taking cuttings of conifers is similar to that of shrubs in that a section of the conifer is cut off and planted in new potting mix.

1. Take cuttings from this year's wood; that's usually a piece that is radiating out from last year's growth.
2. Trim a piece of the conifer down to the brown part at the next branch.
3. Trim lower green needles so that about one-third of the branch is without any needles and you have a piece about 3 to 6 inches with needles above the potting mix.
4. Dip the cut ends into hormone rooting powder (found at nurseries or online and meant to promote growth of new roots).
5. Make a hole in the potting mix and put the stripped and powdered cutting into the hole.
6. Fill the hole and put the pot in a shady location for the plant to root. **Note:** Conifers can take months to root, so be patient. Leave the container so that it gets natural rain but don't let it dry out.

Taking cuttings is not difficult and increases your stock of shrubs, roses, and trees. Check your local Extension office for more information on the best times to take cuttings from specific woody materials. Some cuttings work better with mature wood, while some need fresh new growth.

of water per week, preferably in just one or two sessions. (Check how to gauge this in Lawns in May.) A weekly 1-inch watering is much better for a lawn than daily sprinkling with the hose or irrigation system. Longer, less frequent watering forces grass roots to grow deeper so they can withstand short-term droughts better.

It takes about six weeks of hot weather and drought to kill a well-established lawn, but in hot weather they will go dormant (brown). When rain and temperatures moderate slightly, they'll perk right back up.

HOUSEPLANTS & CONTAINERS

Indoor plants should be watered on a steady schedule. Outdoor containers need water at least once daily and sometimes twice a day. Let the plants tell you what they need. Hanging baskets are generally quite shallow and often full of pretty, thirsty annuals, so need plenty of water to stay healthy.

PERENNIALS

Check perennials in the evening to ensure they are not drying out. Most perennials do well until temperatures go past the mid-80s for an extended period. Compound this with a lack of rain, and even the most drought-tolerant perennial bed will droop a little. A rain shower or an occasional watering is all that's needed to help perennials survive the whole summer. Water early in the day or in the evening so that plants get water at the root level rather than having it quickly evaporate from the soil level.

SHRUBS & ROSES

Large-leaved hydrangeas take on a drooping look on hot days. By evening, the shrubs return to normal appearances. If, however, the hydrangea still looks dehydrated in the evening or first thing in the morning, then that is a sign you need to provide water.

Large-leaved hydrangeas often show wilt in the middle of the day.

TREES

Trees that are over five years old rarely need watering, but young trees sometimes need a little help. Run the hose at a very slow output level (literally a trickle) and place it close to, but not onto, the tree's trunk. (Most young trees don't have roots going very far out yet, so that's why they're watered closer to the trunk.) Let the water thoroughly seep into the ground around the tree.

VINES & GROUNDCOVERS

Vines and groundcovers can be treated like annuals and perennials. Groundcovers in shade, such as pachysandra, tend to do better than those in full sun, like clematis, so prioritize those that need the water.

FERTILIZE

During the stress of summer is not a good time to fertilize with granular materials that need moisture to activate them. Compost teas and liquid fertilizers can augment the watering schedule to add a boost to containers and annuals, but most plants in the landscape still have plenty of nutrients from spring fertilizing. Never apply fertilizer when the temperatures are above 85°F.

ANNUALS

Annuals benefit from a light application of liquid fertilizer to keep them going through summer. Water the fertilizer in well so that the nutrients get to the roots where it is needed.

BULBS

Bulbs don't need fertilizer this month.

EDIBLES

All vegetables benefit from a dose of compost tea or fertilizer this month, particularly beans and squash. Tomatoes can be fertilized with a slightly different tomato fertilizer or a generic compost tea if preferred. Tomatoes and eggplants are heavy feeders and need regular boosts from a side-dressed organic fertilizer or compost tea.

HERE'S HOW

TO SIDE-DRESS COMPOST

1. Remove any weeds or twigs from the row of the growing crop.
2. Put compost into a bucket that is easy to carry.
3. With a cup or scoop, evenly distribute the compost along the side of the crops.
4. Lightly rake the line of compost to incorporate it into the ground.

Sidedressing allows nutrients to reach the root level of the plants and is a convenient way to fertilize row crops such as beans and peas. Rows of tomatoes and peppers can also be side-dressed or fertilized on a plant-by-plant base.

Add fertilizer directly to the watering can for easy application.

HOUSEPLANTS & CONTAINERS

Annuals in containers benefit from a liquid fertilizer this month. Use one-quarter-strength fertilizer every other day when you water or normal strength every month.

PROBLEM-SOLVE

Pests are the major problem this month. Look for damage from Japanese beetles on ornamentals as well as in the vegetable garden. Leaf curlers and aphids are common on perennials, as is powdery mildew in humid weather. Before you head to your favorite chemical aisle of the local store, find out what's causing the problem, which is part of Integrated Pest Management (IPM).

Be alert for signs of animal damage on stems and leaves. Nibbles on leaves and truncated stems are typical signs that something is feasting on your plants.

ANNUALS

Annuals that put out lots of green growth but no flowers are probably getting too much nitrogen. Back off on the fertilizer and let the plant flower. Check for aphids and whiteflies on annuals. A spray with the water hose or some horticultural soap usually sorts them out quickly.

BULBS

Summer-blooming and dormant spring bulbs are in danger of being dug up by rodents. If there's just the odd uprooted bulb here and there, rebury the bulbs. If you find that whole areas are being disrupted, try a general animal deterrent.

Leaf curlers on cannas can be an issue, but this is primarily cosmetic and won't be noticed unless you are viewing the plant close up. It rarely needs treatment.

EDIBLES

Be vigilant for bugs in the vegetable garden this month. Japanese beetles, squash bugs, Mexican bean beetles, and caterpillars are just some of the insects that would like to share your harvest. Tomatoes, summer squash, and beans are all ready for harvest this month, and constant picking keeps the plants putting out more flowers and fruit.

Cover berry crops before berries ripen to stop birds from stealing. Watch for bean beetles and other leaf-eating bugs on all vegetables. Some bugs such as bean beetles or squash bugs are common on the specific plant they target, but they also land and nibble on other vegetables, too, so don't ignore them on eggplants or other vegetables. Remove eggs when you find them and encourage predators such as birds to visit the area to reduce damage. Egg clusters are a variety of colors, from white, to black, to bright orange. Picking off pests like the Japanese beetle is more successful in the morning

USING IPM TO PROBLEM-SOLVE

Integrated Pest Management (IPM) is a way to assess damage to a plant and determine how best to treat the cause of that damage. Critical to IPM is that the gardener first *identify* the insect or animal that is eating the landscape shrubs or plants. Here's how to do it:

A Japanese beetle.

1. Determine what is causing the damage—fungal, animal, insect, or a virus. For damage from common animals, check notes in January.
2. For insects, identify the insect.
3. Get to know the life cycle of the insect; many common pests lay eggs in spring and several other times during the summer.
4. Insect eggs and insects that crawl require much less pesticide to control than full-sized flying pests, so they should be the first things to find and treat. Crawlers are slower than flying insects, which make targeting them for treatment much easier.
5. Establish your tolerance level for the problem—not everything is worth treating. Honestly.
6. Always start with the lowest toxic treatment: start with a stream of water from a hose, then move on to horticultural oils and sprays, pyrethrum sprays, then to chemical pesticides and so forth, only *if needed*. If you need a chemical treatment, always read the label to check that it treats the insect effectively and is safe to use on your plant or shrub.

You can also use nature to help you win the insect war. Just as there are things that eat your landscape, there are bugs that eat the insects. These are termed "predator insects." Inviting them to visit the garden by offering a variety of plants goes a long way to controlling insect damage.

Some common predator insects are ladybugs, praying mantis, lacewings, parasitic wasps, and some nematodes. Birds are also predators and deal with a variety of slugs, caterpillars, and flying insects. Spraying insect repellant to rid a plant of a pest insect also kills the good guys, so identification of whether you have the good insects or the demons is important.

FUNGAL ISSUES

1. Identify the fungus, if possible; many fungal issues are generic and cannot be identified further than a mildew or fungus, but there are some common ones such as blackspot on roses, hollyhock rust, or downy mildew on squash leaves.
2. Learn what causes the fungus; often it's environmental (weather), which cannot be changed. For a fungus or mold to grow there have to be three points: think of a triangle. One point is the right environment, one is the fungal pathogen, and the third is the host plant. Some issues are very plant-specific and without that plant, the pathogen will not move to the next plant.

Using this triangle image, each point can be in existence without the others. So we can have a damp spring, but if nothing is planted, the pathogen (fungus) can exist without anything to infect. Likewise, in hot, dry weather, your plant might be fine because the fungus cannot exist in high temperatures. So for a problem to occur, all three points have to be in existence at the same time. For fungus and molds, the best environment is usually related to humidity or temperature. We cannot change the weather, but as soon as a weather front comes through that drops the humidity, the fungus that relies on moist air struggles. Some mold/fungal issues are pH sensitive, which is why a treatment of diluted milk is considered a low-toxicity remedy for common problems such as downy mildew or sooty molds. Some fungi only exist on one host plant such as hollyhock rust. Gardens that have phlox and monarda but don't have hollyhocks cannot be infected with hollyhock rust.

when temperatures are cool and they are less active. Using the IPM guides discussed, here are some remedies for some of the more common insects in the summer vegetable garden:

Asparagus beetle: This is a small black or orange flying beetle. They are found primarily on asparagus stalks and spears. Handpicking these fast movers is tough, so finding the egg stage is helpful. Look for little green or light brown elongated eggs hanging on the stalks.

Colorado potato beetle: This beetle is more elongated than a ladybug and has black stripes on a yellow back. It is found on potatoes, eggplants, tomatoes, peppers, and other vegetables.

Cucumber beetle: This is an elongated yellow beetle with stripes or spots. Its eggs are brown and laid on the ground rather than on a leaf. This is a more serious pest that pierces the leaves and stems, but it also transmits a virus that kills a whole plant. When it visits several plants, they all become infected. *Do not* compost infected leaves or plant debris.

Flea beetle: This little guy eats tiny holes in leaves. The holes are perfectly round and look like the leaf was attacked by a miniature army.

Tomato hornworm: This is a really large caterpillar. It can defoliate a tomato plant overnight. Remove tomato hornworms when you see them *unless* they have little white spines sticking out of their backs. The white spines indicate that the hornworm has already been attacked by a parasitic wasp and is already going to die (as the wasp's larvae eat it from the inside out).

Colorado beetles

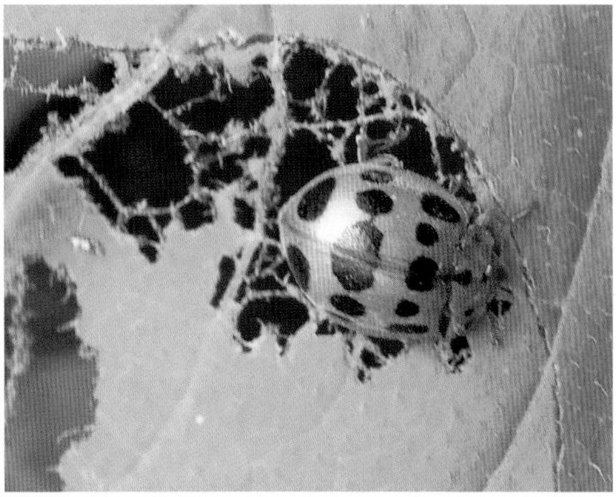

A Mexican bean beetle.

Japanese beetle: Japanese beetles are pests throughout the landscape. Pick off the beetles, which have a metallic sheen to them, whenever you see them.

Mexican bean beetle: These look like yellow ladybugs, and they can fly to find food. Their young stage is a crawling insect with spines along the back; they are easy to pick off your plants. The eggs are bright yellow.

Squash vine borers: Check the stems of squash plants close to the ground where the borer enters. Look for a mass of yellow mess close to the end of the stem. Pick out the borer if you can see it. Borers that arrive later in the season do not do as much damage as there is plenty of growth to sustain the plant. For young plants, planting the seedlings inside a cardboard collar helps stop this problem.

Squash bug: A squash bug is a dull brown/gray-colored insect. Its bronze eggs are seen under leaves. In its immature stage, it's a small white crawler. This is a beetle that eats the leaves of squash plants. Remove squash bugs by hand and apply a horticultural oil or soap on any eggs that are noticed, or squash them with your fingers.

LAWNS

Spot check lawns for summer fungus (fairy ring) and germinating weeds. Address these issues as you see them. See Lawns in June for more on molds.

HOUSEPLANTS & CONTAINERS

Keep checking for aphids, whiteflies, and other small insects that affect container plants that have lots of flowers growing closely together. Remove them as you see them.

PERENNIALS

Animal damage is more easily noticed in summer, as flowers are eaten off the stems or stems are truncated (eaten). Applying deer and other animal deterrents will help to stop

ABOUT INVASIVE PLANTS

You may have heard about invasive plants and how some laws around the country ban certain plants. The problem is that many invasive plants were originally brought into the country as ornamentals. Many have wonderfully attractive features like fall color (burning bushes) or berries (porcelain berry), but they have escaped cultivation and are growing wild. Birds and other animals carry the seeds, and the invasive plants are strong enough that they'll outcompete native plants. In waterways they clog the currents and impede flow, which disrupt the activities of wildlife. In woodlands and prairies, they happily spread, causing both environmental as well as economic problems. Unfortunately, many invasives are still for sale in nurseries and even more are in our friends' and neighbors' gardens. Once established, some invasive plants, like Japanese knotweed, are almost impossible to control, let alone eradicate. Some plants on the invasives list will not be a problem across all of New York or New Jersey. Some cannot deal with salt water or shade; others cannot survive in cold temperatures, so double-check with your county Extension Service before you rip out a valuable plant.

If you have an invasive plant in your garden:

1. Identify the plant and find out how it traveled to your location; seed is the most common.
2. Remove as many of the flowers or berries as you can before they ripen.
3. Dig up what you can and dispose of the plant waste.
4. Remove any seedlings promptly.
5. Replant something just as beautiful that is not on the invasive list.

Some of the more common invasive plants in New York and New Jersey follow. A full list can be found at your state's invasive flora webpage.

INVASIVE TREES

Tree of heaven (*Ailanthus altissima*)

Norway maple (*Acer platanoides*)

Russian olive (*Elaeagnus angustifolia*)

Smooth buckthorn (*Rhamnus cathartica*)

Black locust (*Robinia pseudoacacia*)

INVASIVE SHRUBS

Butterfly bush (*Buddleja davidii*)

Burning bush (*Euonymus alatus*)

Japanese barberry (*Berberis thunbergii*)

Multiflora rose (*Rosa multiflora*)

Privet (*Ligustrum vulgare*)

Sacred bamboo (*Nandina domestica*)

Scotch broom (*Cytisus scoparius*)

INVASIVE PERENNIALS

Japanese knotweed (*Fallopia japonica*)

Purple loosestrife (*Lythrum salicaria*)

Spotted knapweed (*Centaurea maculosa*)

INVASIVE VINES

Asian bittersweet (*Celastrus orbiculatus*)

Japanese honeysuckle (*Lonicera japonica*)

Porcelain berry (*Ampelopsis brevipedunculata*)

this. Many brands are available, including many that are made from herbal oils/essences that are safe to use on food crops as well as ornamentals.

Powdery mildew is common on bergamot and summer phlox all season; it can cause leaves to fall and trigger a general decline in the perennial. An application of sulfur during the season has traditionally been used to reduce mildew and can help save a plant. A mix of 1½ tablespoons baking soda in a gallon of water is recommended by the University of Vermont as a helpful solution as well. Other organic-based fungus solutions are available. Most of these treatments are sprayed onto the leaves and plant at the first sign of problems. Plant resistant varieties if you can find them. 'Marshall's Delight' and 'Blue Stocking' are some mildew-resistant *Monarda* cultivars while 'David' and 'Starfire' are recommended as mildew-resistant garden phlox.

Identify plants in the garden that you did *not* plant. Sometimes an attractive native finds its way into the garden, but just as often an invasive plant will take hold. Getting these nuisances out of the garden as soon as possible is worth the effort.

SHRUBS & ROSES

Blackspot is always an issue with roses and will likely afflict those that are not resistant to it. Remove any diseased leaves and spray with fungicide to protect any new leaves. Blackspot and other fungal issues are more prevalent in humid weather; application of preventative fungicide can help avoid problems altogether.

Shrubs are primarily affected by Japanese beetles, which can defoliate a shrub if their numbers are serious. Cover the bushes if needed to stop the attacks.

Shrubs in particular get minor infestations of many bugs, but not everything is worth treating. Birds and predator insects control problems very effectively before populations get too large. See the advice under IPM for some common predator insects.

TREES

Many trees like sycamores and dogwoods are affected by anthracnose, a fungal disease. When a tree is infected early, the fungus causes the leaves to drop before midsummer. Some trees put out a second batch of leaves and no harm is done. Look for small holes surrounded by concentric rings of orange, then brown. Deformed leaves and buds are also noticeable. Smaller landscape trees can be treated with a fungicide if needed. Modern ornamental dogwood varieties are resistant to anthracnose. Spring Grove® and 'Cherokee Sunset' are reported to be less susceptible, as is Kousa dogwood.

Check apple trees and cedar trees for rust. Cedar apple rust is seen on cedar branches as an orange mass and also on apple trees as circular yellow discoloration around holes on the leaf. Cedars show signs of the disease in mid- to late spring while apples show signs in July and August. Usually the rust is not an issue for cedars, but it can defoliate apple trees. Treatment (if needed) should be a systemic in spring.

VINES & GROUNDCOVERS

Invasive vines can be found climbing up and throttling trees across the area. Poison ivy, Japanese honeysuckle, and mile-a-minute vines are just a few of the varieties that can weaken and even kill trees over time. Once established, they are very difficult to eradicate. If you suspect you have a wild vine climbing up your trees:

1. Identify the vine. Not all vines are invasive and harmful in the landscape.
2. Determine where the root is for the individual vine.
3. Sever the vine about 3 feet up the tree.
4. Dig out the root and discard in the trash.

Poison ivy and some other vines can cause rashes; wear protective clothing and wash all tools and clothing after clearing the vines. Mature vines may take several seasons to totally eradicate and sometimes chemicals are needed.

August

August is our second month of heat and infrequent rainfall. When both July and August are hot and dry, the accumulated stress on trees and the landscape becomes noticeable as some leaves start to turn to their fall colors. This is not something to worry about for most landscape trees—winter moisture restores normal leaf canopy right on schedule next spring. Perennials start to look "tired" too; as the flowering stage of perennials passes and seeds are formed, the lower leaves drop off, leaving a rather ragged-looking plant. Cannas are terrific at creating focal points of summer color to draw the eye away from those spent, early-summer blooming plants.

The stars of the fall landscape are late-blooming flowers. Rudbeckia, sedum, chrysanthemums, Shasta daisies, and asters are starting to flower, and the magnificent berries of the *Callicarpa* start to turn from white to iridescent purple. Grasses, too, are putting up plumes, which catch the late summer breezes and shine in the sunset. The flowers of our native ironweed and milkweeds brighten the August perennial garden.

Gardening in August's heat and humidity is tough, so keep chores to the essentials and aim for just a few minutes weeding/deadheading each day. Watering is likely to be the biggest issue unless storms roll across your area. Check plants regularly and water before they start wilting. Remember to check the plants in the morning or evening for signs of water stress, not the middle of a 90°F day when the leaves curl down to save moisture.

As plants flower, particularly annuals, we promptly deadhead the flowers to prevent seed from being formed and to stimulate production of more flowers. However, both flower and vegetable seeds can be saved, and leaving a few flowers to set seed is a great way to save on seed costs for next year.

The vegetable garden is in full swing, giving you a chance to preserve some of the produce for winter use. Drying or freezing herbs, peppers, and tomatoes for sauce are all great ways to enjoy everything you grew—into next year.

PLAN

Hot, humid evenings are as good as cold winter days for planning, but now you're planning fall and spring gardens.

ANNUALS
Many annuals that flower early in the year are best planted in fall, right along with spring bulbs. Summer annuals will be replaced with fall-blooming pansies and kale next month. Letting a few seeds mature on those annuals that sow seeds is worth trying. Groups of colorful annuals look attractive in the landscape and if the plants self-sow their seed, you really don't have to do anything.

BULBS
It's time to think about the spring garden and to order bulbs. Daffodils are the most popular but there are a number of little irises that bloom alongside crocuses in late winter/early spring, when we really need a pick me up. Spring bulbs, whether outside or forced indoors, are a great remedy. Pick a few varieties for forcing next year, too. Keep these in the back of the refrigerator until January when you'll plant them in containers.

Salvias are a standard in many gardens for their easy care and long bloom.

EDIBLES
Fall gardens are moving from the planning to the action stage this month. Decide what to take out of the vegetable garden so that you'll have room to plant fall seedlings. August is still very warm everywhere, so figure out how to give seedlings some shade too. Shade cloth or dark netting keeps some heat away from the young plants.

Outdoor herbs that are not winter hardy, like lemongrass, rosemary, and marjoram, can be potted up next month for winter use. They'll be brought indoors in September or October. Decide which herbs you'll want to take cuttings of to flavor winter meals. Chives, sage, thyme, and lemon thyme are popular herbs for this.

August is a good time to order cover crops for the vegetable plot. These beneficial plants grow where the vegetables were in summer. The idea is that the plants protect the soil from erosion and add nutrients to the soil as well when they're tilled under in spring. Clovers, alfalfa, and vetch are some cover crops that add nitrogen to the soil.

LAWNS
Plan to replant or repair your lawn at the end of August. Areas for major lawn reseeding or planting sod need to be cleared of weeds and stones and any chemicals, such as lime, should be incorporated into the soil before grass seed is sown. If you didn't get a soil test earlier, early August is a good time to do that—see February for instructions.

HOUSEPLANTS & CONTAINERS
Houseplants that have spent the summer outside need to head back inside in September or October. Just like they took a few days to get used to outdoor conditions earlier, they need to be slowly transitioned for indoor conditions before the big move. First take the plants to a shadier location to get them used to lower sun conditions. Plants that have spent the summer on a bright sunny patio should be brought closer to the home where they get more shade until late afternoon.

PERENNIALS
By the end of August, local nurseries start selling their remaining perennial stock. As you visit the nurseries this month, take a look at what's there

and research to see if the plants will work for you. When they go on sale, you'll be ready to take advantage of the great new prices.

SHRUBS & ROSES

Like perennials, shrubs and roses go on sale in fall. Check your landscape to see where you can add a few. Look for shrubs that add interest to the landscape for more than one season. Oak leaf hydrangeas, for instance, bloom midsummer with great white flowers, and the bark peels to make the whole shrub attractive even in a midwinter snow.

If they're on sale, start picking up a few more shrubs and roses. Keep them on the deck or in a semi-shady location for a week or two and water regularly. Plant these next month when more water is available and temperatures are lower, offering a much higher success rate.

TREES

Small landscape trees work for many places in the landscape, and some will be on sale in September. Research what could enhance your landscape; for instance, star magnolias have lovely late-winter flowers and only reach about 20 feet in height. They are hardy down to Zone 4.

VINES & GROUNDCOVERS

Perennial vines and groundcovers go on sale next month, and with a little planning this month, you'll have a support in place and ready for the vine to clamber onto next year. Vines can be used to cover a trellis or create a topiary. Dense vines such as ivy are great for topiary, while climbing roses, clematis, and morning glories work well on obelisks and arches. Heavier vines like wisteria or trumpet vines are good on arbors. Think about brightening up the spring-blooming perennial vines by planting an annual one that will grow up and through it for color.

Wisteria vines need sturdy support.

PLANT

BULBS

Fall-blooming spider lilies and colchicums can be planted early to mid-August. These little bulbs come up in just a few weeks. Plant them in the garden as you do the fall-planted spring bulbs and summer-flowering bulbs. Water the bulbs in.

EDIBLES

If you want to have basil or cilantro past October, plant more seeds now. Plant them in a container that you can accommodate in the kitchen; just one or two seeds is sufficient. Transplant root cuttings of chives and thyme into containers too.

Saffron crocus bulbs are planted at the end of August for late September bloom when you can harvest the bright yellow strands of spice.

LAWNS

The end of August is a good time to start lawn repair and renovation. Plant the seed on well-prepared soil and cover with a layer of compost or straw. See Care in September for more on preparing the ground for seed or sod.

HOUSEPLANTS & CONTAINERS

Containers don't have to be empty for winter—try adding a small conifer to a container. Little arborvitae and spruces are still likely to be in the nursery. Plant them in August, keep them moist, and add some pansies next month for color. When spring bulbs come in next month, add a few to the container so you have a cheerful early-spring container.

Late summer is a good time to pick up miniature plants to start a terrarium or fairy garden, a great winter project. While you are still busy outside, keep these plants indoors. A tray covered with a layer of gravel is a good way to be able to keep them all together in one place for watering and care.

HERE'S HOW

TO ATTRACT POLLINATORS

There is a crisis in the pollinator world that affects not just your landscape but ones across the nation. Helping pollinators move from one location to another is important to their survival, and you can help by including some plants in the garden that are a food source for pollinators. Colorful plants usually attract a wide variety of pollinators, a win/win. Many pollinators ensure that summer squash and green beans are pollinated, too, not to mention that many pollinators consume some bugs that infect our landscapes each year.

Pollinators include bees, butterflies, flies, beetles, bats, and birds. They come in various sizes and have differently shaped mouthparts for retrieving food, so a variety of plant types will attract the maximum number possible.

Flat, daisy-shaped heads: For pollinators that land on a plant to feed, such as bees and beetles, the flat heads of daisy-type plants are best. These include zinnias, chrysanthemums, sunflowers, and asters.

Tube-shaped flowers: Salvias, catmint, goldenrod, thyme, and others with tube-like flowers attract bees, beetles, and small insects.

Perennial flowers: Yarrows, butterfly weed, coreopsis, monarda, lavender, phlox, and milkweed are great perennial flowers for pollinators.

Annual flowers: Dill, cleome, cosmos, nasturtium, and snapdragons are all great for small insects, bees, and butterflies.

A long flower season is healthy for pollinators, too, so aim for something to be in bloom from spring through fall.

Late winter/spring flowers: These include anemone, lupines, and creeping phlox. Strawberries and chives bloom early too.

Summer-blooming flowers: Consider gaillardia, coneflowers, sunflowers, and sedums.

Late-season flowers: Obedient flower, asters, and goldenrod are great choices.

Some plants are useful as food sources for the larval stage of butterflies, so allowing some plants to be eaten by hungry caterpillars is important too. Milkweeds, parsley, dill, and violets are all important sources of food for the larvae of a variety of attractive, and important, butterflies.

A water source is a good addition to the pollinator garden as is some cover or shelter. Shrubs are great places to give birds shelter, and mulch is used by beetles and small insects as cover. You want all types of pollinators to stick around as much and as long as possible. Restrict the use of pesticides both in the pollinator garden and in the landscape as a whole—pesticides are indiscriminate and will kill the beautiful visitors as well as the pests.

More information on pollinator gardens and a full list of suggested plants can be found at www.pollinator.org.

PERENNIALS

Any perennials planted this month will need lots of care (particularly watering). Check the new additions daily but do not overwater (see Shrubs in July for watering tips). Fall grasses and the first chrysanthemums are arriving in the stores. Hold off buying chrysanthemums until next month when the temperatures are lower. Grasses, goldenrods, and asters are all fine to plant this month.

VINES AND GROUNDCOVERS

Fall vines can be found at nurseries or online. Native Virginia creeper (*Parthenocissus quinquefolia*) and American bittersweet (*Celastrus scandens*) both have wonderful color.

CARE

ANNUALS

Tall stands of annuals such as delightful purple heliotrope or taller marigolds often fall over in summer storms. Place a few bamboo or metal stakes discreetly around the stand to support the flowers when necessary. Individual stems can be tied to the support or whole groups can be encircled with a rope or string, which is then tied to the support.

Annuals sometimes slow down in high temperatures and, apart from maintaining their watering schedule, there is not much you can do. When the temperature drops next month, they'll revive and put out more flowers.

Tender annuals peak and slow down as the day length shortens. Keep blooms on petunias and zinnias picked so that the plants continue to flower right up to frost.

BULBS

Summer bulbs that have not bloomed are likely in a site that is too shady. Make a note to change the location of the bulbs next year.

EDIBLES

Sometimes the vegetable garden produces more than we can use, so preserving some of the produce for winter use is worth trying. Herbs are generally dried or frozen. Vegetables are more often canned or frozen; tomatoes and peppers also both dry well.

Let onions dry, then trim their roots and top growth before storing.

LAWNS

If you plan on reseeding a large area of lawn at the end of August or in September, clear the area first. Both old grass and weeds can be removed with an herbicide. Check the manufacturer's notes regarding how soon after an application you can sow new grass seed. Smaller areas or areas that are going to be overseeded are prepared this month, too. Lightly till the area, rake smooth, and apply any chemicals needed before seeding next month.

HOUSEPLANTS & CONTAINERS

Winter-blooming cactus, poinsettias, amaryllis, and lilies that have been planted in the ground should be dug this month. If you want flowers between Thanksgiving and New Year's, these plants need to be conditioned and brought indoors in September. Dig the plants a week or two before transitioning them for indoor light conditions. Rinse as much soil off the roots as possible, and repot in a good potting mix. Keep the plant outside in the shade for a week or two before finally bringing them indoors in early September.

PERENNIALS

Deadhead and generally tidy perennials and, if they have gone ragged at their base, trim them down to about one-third. New growth will soon fill in and although it won't rebloom, the plants will be fine for next year.

SHRUBS & ROSES

All pruning should have been completed last month and the equipment put away this month.

HERE'S HOW

TO SAVE SEEDS

Each year, annuals in the garden grow, produce flowers, set seed, and die. By removing the flower prior to the seed formation, annuals are prompted to put out even more flowers. You can prevent many plants from becoming invasive, like mint and lemon balm, by deadheading. But sometimes you might actually *want* to save seed so you don't have to buy any next year. Tomatoes, peppers, and many vegetable seeds can be saved, as can those of some of your favorite flowering annuals. Before you decide to save seeds, there factors you need to be aware of:

- Some seeds need specific treatment over winter (stratification) to be able to germinate the next year. Most catalog-based and online companies take care of this for you.
- Many commonly grown flower seeds are hybrids. The parents of the seed had different traits that were combined (crossed) to obtain the specific flower and plant that you grew. Saving hybrid seed is the same process as it is for any other seed, but the resulting plants will often revert; that is, the seed will contain traits of both parent plants as well as the plant you grew this year. You'll have a wild card in terms of planting. However, if a plant is described as "open pollinated," then you know that it's not a hybrid. Many vegetables and flowers are heirloom and are open pollinated, but vegetable hybrids are still available.

1. Allow the plant to flower, and let the flower remain on the plant until it drops off naturally.
2. Check the seeds or seedpods to see if they are ripe; often the seed still needs to mature after the flower has dropped.
3. When the seed is mature, pluck the whole seedhead and put it into a baggie to dry.
4. When completely dry, rub the seedheads to release the seeds.
5. Put the dry seeds in a labeled envelope or small jar, and store in a cool dry, location.

Some seeds have lots of chaff, which is easily removed by spreading the seed and chaff on a piece of paper and blowing lightly on it (or use a fan). The chaff is lighter than the seed and should separate easily.

Tomatoes have a gelatinous coating that is removed by soaking the seeds for a little while until it dissolves. Dry tomato seeds before storing.

Some annuals like self-sow (produce their own seed) and although they may sow a few too many, you, the gardener, do not have to worry about collecting and saving the seed at all.

The new growth that starts after pruning does not have time to harden, which makes it more susceptible to winter damage. The only exception to the no-prune rule is to clip stray branches of climbing roses that encroach a walkway or dangle down too low from an arbor.

VINES & GROUNDCOVERS

As with shrubs, all pruning of perennial vines should have been completed last month. The only exception is for vines that impede access to areas, such as under an arch or through your doorway.

New wood on annual vines does not have to mature and harden before winter, so annual vines can continue to be clipped back this month.

Summer storms can knock over supports for vines. If this happens, resurrect the support, reattach the vine, and clear any leaves that have been ripped off. Where groundcovers start to show some areas of sparse or dying growth, remove the dead areas but wait until next month to replant.

WATER

The weather dictates how much water plants are going to need. As with last month, annuals and containers need more moisture; water containers daily. The rest of the garden takes less, but still needs moisture. When nature doesn't provide at least an inch per week, supplement that.

ANNUALS

Water established annuals every few days to keep them looking great in the landscape. Remember to water the flower beds—not the pavement.

EDIBLES

Edibles are primarily annuals and need daily watering if possible. Some vegetables like celery need to have extra water each day to keep them healthy. I've had to water my celery with an extra 2 quarts per day at times.

LAWNS

Keep to your resolve regarding whether to let the grass go dormant or not. Switching back/forth because the lawn is going brown is detrimental to the lawn in the long run, and it will take a week or two of watering for the lawn to come out of dormancy. By September, the temperatures come down and you get more frequent rain, so the lawn will come out of dormancy by then anyway.

HERE'S HOW

TO FREEZE VEGETABLES

1. Pick ripe, unblemished vegetables.
2. Rinse and prepare as you would for fresh consumption: slice carrots, split broccoli into florets, and so on.
3. Blanch the vegetables. Blanching is a term for partly cooking the vegetables. The vegetables should be hot enough inside to kill bacteria, but not enough to make the vegetables soft:
   - Put prepared vegetables into a can of boiling water.
   - Time the vegetables from when the water returns to the boil—small batches are better than large one. Cook in boiling water for about one-third the normal cooking time.* Sliced carrots take about 2 to 4 minutes; shelled peas, about 90 seconds; snow peas, about 2 to 3 minutes; beans, about 3 minutes.
4. Remove the vegetables from the water (having them in a strainer helps with this step).
5. Dunk the vegetables into a sink filled with ice cubes and cold water to stop the cooking.
6. Drain and dry the vegetables.
7. Pack in freezer containers or bags.
8. Label with contents and date.

***Note:** For accurate blanching and processing times, consult your Extension office or check the resources at the back of this book. You'll find the latest recommendations for canning fruit and vegetables at the local Extension office.

HOUSEPLANTS & CONTAINERS

Keep to your watering schedule and make sure that containers, particularly smaller containers and hanging baskets, are watered twice a day if needed. Look for stressed plants with wilting leaves in the evening, even when you have watered in the morning.

FERTILIZE

Hot, dry conditions are not a good time to add fertilizer to a landscape. If you feel the need to fertilize, take particular note of the directions regarding whether the product needs watering in and temperature guidelines. Do not apply fertilizers above 85°F.

ANNUALS

Annuals flowers do a lot of work for us, and a dose of fertilizer to keep them going through to fall is beneficial. Use a liquid fertilizer and incorporate it with your regular watering. Or scratch the granular fertilizer into the soil gently around the root area but do not get it on the leaves where it can burn. Water well to get the fertilizer into the soil.

EDIBLES

The vegetable garden is the one area of the landscape that could use a boost in August. Beans, tomatoes, and all the summer vegetables will still be producing (hopefully) at the end of September, so a sidedressing of compost or fertilizer this month is a good idea to ensure that.

If you cleared out the early bean crop and are putting in a fall crop of peas or lettuce, fertilize to ensure the new crop will have plenty of nutrients for fast, productive growth.

Water containers often during hot summers.

LAWNS

The only lawns that need fertilizer this month are those in cooler areas where frosts occur in the middle or at the end of September (Zone 4). Here, you still have to wait until the weather has cooled before applying fertilizer, which usually happens in mid- to late August. For most of us in Zones 5, 6, or 7 gardens, we have October frosts, so the fall fertilizer should not be applied until September.

HOUSEPLANTS & CONTAINERS

Next month, tender plants will be transitioned to indoor life. This transitioning includes some repotting or general nutrient application so those plants don't need anything this month. Likewise, seasonal containers are fertilized before you replant with fall pansies and grasses.

Tender houseplants that stay indoors all summer welcome a monthly dose of fertilizer and that should continue this month unless you're repotting them.

PROBLEM-SOLVE

Most of the issues in August are heat and drought related. Bugs never seem to be bothered by summer heat and humidity, and some positively thrive in it. Caterpillars emerge year-round and affect both flower beds as well as the vegetable plot. Well-watered plants also seem more attractive to deer and rodent damage in August as the surrounding landscape dries out.

ANNUALS

Humid conditions lead to a variety of fungal conditions including downy mildew, which occurs on petunias as well as other annuals. If the problem is severe, remove the plants out but *do not* add them to the compost. Minor cases can be dealt with by removing affected leaves.

BULBS

Watch for leaf curlers on cannas and remove the offending bugs by hand before they curl a whole leaf. Look for leaves, particularly young leaves, curling under. On inspection you'll see a webbing of sticky strands drawing the edge of the leaf over itself. The worm is hiding under the webbing and can be removed.

Canna leaf roller disfigures the whole plant.

EDIBLES

It's bonus time for insect problems in August. Beetles and caterpillars are still very active. As a vegetable winds down production, such as the early-planted beans and squash, take the vines out rather than increase the likelihood of attracting more insects by leaving them in place. It also permits more room and better airflow around the remaining plants.

Very warm weather (upper 80s to 90s plus) has an effect on the blossoms on several edibles. There are fewer flowers produced on summer vegetables like beans and tomatoes and often pollination is incomplete, leading to aborted fruit or no fruit at all. When temperatures moderate, plants resume their summer production. Scarlet runner beans always do better with more moderate temperatures in the lower 80s to set fruit.

LAWNS

Dry and crisp is the description of many August lawns. This is temporary: the normal springy green will return when temperatures cool and rainfall increases. Fungal problems are more from humidity and resolve themselves when the humidity decreases. See June for more on lawn fungus. Moles and voles create tunnels (or runs) under the lawn's surface, usually in fall or early spring, but they sometimes arrive earlier. Moles are after grubs and other insects whereas voles are more interested in vegetation, including the roots of your lawn. Traps are available for both problems.

PERENNIALS

Powdery mildew still affects phlox and bergamots, but as soon as the weather changes this should ease. In the rest of the garden, fungus issues also persist in humid weather. This will continue until the humidity decreases. Treat any problems with organic or commercial fungicides.

SHRUBS & ROSES

Blackspot is a fungus specific to many roses and is prevalent this month. Keep fallen leaves off the ground, and pick off affected leaves promptly. Treat with fungicide for blackspot if it's severe; remove all infected leaves and apply fungicide to work on new leaves as they are produced.

Some roses and most shrubs are single-blooming varieties. There are some roses, though, that bloom sporadically through summer. These put out a second flush of flowers in fall. Watch out for insects attacking the new buds as they form.

TREES

Cedar apple rust appears around this time of year and occurs on the leaves of the apple tree, the alternate host for the disease. You'll see little holes surrounded by a yellow ring. Eventually a whole leaf yellows as the rust takes over. This late in the season, it is not usually worth treating the problem. Severe problems can occur in areas where cedars get the disease; treat apple trees early in the year with systemic treatments (see March).

Some areas may see some signs of fall webworms starting; see September for more about these unsightly pests.

VINES & GROUNDCOVERS

Most annual as well as perennial vines are subject to the normal insects that affect the rest of the garden. Japanese beetles nibble leaves and skeletonize them, and aphids, whiteflies, leafhoppers, and beetles are sometimes noticed. Most of these can be removed with a spray from the hose or simple horticultural oils and soaps.

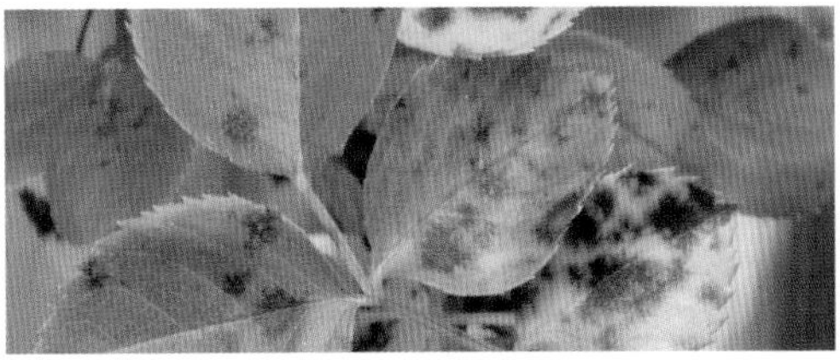

Blackspot is common on rose leaves in humid weather.

September

September is an action month with lots to do in the garden. Temperatures moderate, allowing gardeners to work all day and still be comfortable, and rain arrives more often. Most of the garden is still going strong, and colors are transitioning from the hot reds and pinks of summer to the subtle oranges and browns of fall.

Farmers' markets, full of fall apples, corn, and pumpkins, make a great morning out with the family, including the dog. Fall craft fairs are also common, and they're filled with wreaths and decorations for the season. For your own wreathmaking, consider the mature blooms of many hydrangeas, which dry to an attractive dusty pink, and the berries of the beautyberry (*Callicarpa*), which are now turning purple. Both of these can be used successfully in outdoor wreaths for several weeks and are not damaged by frosts.

Fall reds and yellows fill landscape trees this month and continue through October. Blueberries and andromeda (*Pieris japonica*; Zones 5 and up) are also turning color. In the perennial beds, ornamental grasses are at their peak, and the tall plumes sway in fall sunshine. Contrast the grasses with fall-blooming asters in blues or pinks as well as the usual chrysanthemums.

Check out fall education days in nurseries and public gardens that are held this month and which sometimes are combined with perennial sales. Fall is a great time to plant perennials, shrubs, and trees; in many ways it's preferred to spring planting. The ground is warm from summer, allowing new roots to form quickly, and fall rains keep the plants healthy. Plants will have a full four to six weeks to settle into the ground before frost hits, but even then the subsoil is still warm enough to keep the shrub roots from freezing.

Fall is great for taking advantage of end of season sales in garden shops everywhere. The nurseries do not want to keep the perennials and shrubs over winter because they have to start the year repotting and selling them before the spring items arrive. Look for great deals on everything this month (and next).

PLAN

September is the countdown to the first frost date and that includes lots of plans. What needs to be brought indoors, what can stay outdoors for a little longer, and where are you going to put them? Spring plans also need to get started this month.

BULBS

Spring-flowering bulbs are the focus of this month's planning. For a great display of spring bulbs that will greet you next year, order now. Check images you shot this past spring to see where the snow melted first; this is a great place to plant very early-blooming bulbs. Design landscape areas using groups of bulbs rather than single bulbs in a row. Check for early-, mid-, and late-season bloom times and for how tall the plants get. If you want to plant tulips, make sure that it's in an area where deer cannot enjoy them. If rodents dug up last year's bulbs, plan steps to prevent that from happening this year; one way is to encase the bulbs in chicken wire.

EDIBLES

Get some protection ready for early frosts, which start in October. A light horticultural blanket or old sheet over lettuce and fall crops keeps light frosts off the plants. A simple raised bed can be easily turned into a small cold frame that protects late crops from frost and snow, as well as warms the soil up quickly for a jumpstart on spring planting. Add a sheet of Lexan or other rigid plastic to the top of the raised bed, or use old window frames. It is important that the whole bed is covered with the cover. Hay bales around the outside of the bed give some added protection from cold temperatures.

Covering fall beds with cloth extends the season by a few weeks.

Grubs from beetles are best treated in fall while they are still small.

LAWNS

Many beetles lay eggs in fall, which turn into grubs in spring. If this was a problem last year, look for treatments that kill the eggs while they're small. Milky spore is one treatment that has to be done on a neighborhood-wide base, and lawn treatments that include pesticide/grub control can be applied.

HOUSEPLANTS & CONTAINERS

Tender houseplants that spent the summer outdoors need to be rehoused indoors by the end of September. Decide where you are going to put them and clear that area. Oftentimes, vacant windowsills or corners become occupied with other things in summer and need to be cleared again to make way for plants.

Amaryllis and poinsettias that spent summer outside in the garden now come inside to be conditioned for the holidays. Winter-blooming cacti also need to come inside so that they'll be ready to start blooming at the end of November.

Some winter interest from a small conifer or evergreen such as small holly complete with berries could be planned, and you could add spring bulbs to the containers for spring.

PERENNIALS

Pack a tarp to protect the back of your vehicle and hit the sales at nurseries! Many perennials won't be in bloom, but a little research to check color and height will provide that information.

SHRUBS & ROSES

As with perennials, trees, shrubs, and roses are all on sale too. Check out early- and late-blooming shrubs, and aim for four-season color or interest in the garden. Oak leaf hydrangeas have wonderful winter bark, and berries on *Callicarpa* and hollies are always welcome. *Viburnum carlesii* has fragrant spring blooms as well as vibrant fall color, and fothergillas also have spring blooms and great fall color. See January for a list of other shrubs that give year-round interest.

VINES & GROUNDCOVERS

Perennial vines put out their fall color and berries this month, adding to the color in the garden. Hops, American bittersweet, and Virginia creeper have wonderful fall color. Plant against a wall to admire them. Birds enjoy nesting in some of the vines as well as eating the berries on plants that produce them, like American bittersweet.

PLANT

Warm soil, mild weather, and fewer bugs are all conducive to great conditions for plants. Whether it is reseeding the lawn, taking advantage of sales to buy new plants, or planting bulbs for spring, there is plenty to plant in September.

ANNUALS

Chrysanthemums are in the stores and can be planted now. Chrysanthemums are really perennial but most of the ones sold in stores this month are produced in very controlled conditions so that they are just coming into bloom when you buy them. If they are planted early enough, they *may* return next year, but for the most part they are treated as annuals. They will, however, still bloom after light frosts and come in a delightful range of all colors.

BULBS

Plant spring bulbs when the ground cools to about 50°F (this feels cool to the hand). There are many web pages that tell you how deep to plant the bulbs, and the packages will have instructions also. Check Plant in October for a general guide to planting all spring bulbs.

EDIBLES

September is a quiet month in the vegetable garden. In cooler areas, after you have had a frost, you can start planting garlic. This is usually toward the end of the month for Zones 3 and 4 gardeners. Continue to plant fast-growing radishes and salad crops; you'll be able to harvest before winter. Planning the fall vegetable garden is past, but for next year think about how to nourish the soil. One way is to plant cover crops over the beds for winter. Look for fast-growing cover crops that are killed by frost. Alfalfa, for instance, is full of nutrients which, when the crop decomposes, are incorporated into the soil. Clovers add nitrogen compounds, and all cover crops keep the soil surface from eroding.

HERE'S HOW

TO SOW A COVER CROP

1. Measure garden space and calculate how much seed you need to cover the garden.
2. Clear the garden bed of all debris from the current crop of vegetables.
3. Lightly till or rake the area.
4. Broadcast the appropriate amount of cover crop seeds over the garden bed.
5. Rake to incorporate the seed into the garden bed.
6. Water well.
7. Early next spring you will turn over the cover crop into the ground so that it decomposes in time to plant vegetables; see March.

LAWNS

Any lawn areas that need patching or replacing are addressed this month.

HOUSEPLANTS & CONTAINERS

Plant fall containers with perennial grasses and fall chrysanthemums.

September is the time to bring poinsettia, amaryllis, and other tender bulbs inside to condition for winter color. See later in this month for how to condition them.

Christmas cactus generally puts out buds in October without any conditioning. Keep it lightly watered during the production of the blooms.

HERE'S HOW

TO SOD AND SEED A NEW LAWN

Prepare the ground. Remove all existing grass and weeds.

1. If using a herbicide, check how soon you can seed after application.
2. Remove all stones and rocks. Add any amendments such as lime or compost. Your soil test will indicate if you need to apply lime or phosphorus.
3. Check the grade; most homes have property grades that move water to a back corner or ditch. All grades should go away from your home and should not be toward someone else's property. Check and remedy any low and high spots: add extra topsoil if needed. Rake the area smooth.

If you plan to use seed:

1. Divide the seed into two parts and load the hopper or distribution vehicle with half of the seed.
2. Walk slowly up and down the area distributing seed along the way. At the end, refill the hopper with the other half of the seed and walk at right angles to the first pass.
3. Add a layer of straw over the seed to protect it.

If you plan to use sod:

1. The sod should be fresh and not left outside to dry out; lay it as soon as you can after delivery.
2. For ease of laying the sod, make the area with straight edges and start at one corner of the bed. Lay the first piece of sod along the edge of the lawn, pressing firmly to seat it on the prepared soil bed.
3. Take the second piece of sod and lay it end to end with the first one. You will make a line along the edge of the lawn area. When you place the second and subsequent pieces, overlap by about an inch with the next piece. This knits the lawn together evenly.

On watering:

- Water the new lawn thoroughly.
- For seeded lawns, water twice a day.
- For sod, once per day is sufficient.

On mowing:

- Seed lawns should be about 4 inches tall before you try mowing.
- Sod lawns need to grow and set roots before the grass starts growing again, so wait until it is growing well before mowing.

PERENNIALS

Plant perennials this month. There are bargains to be found, and they'll have plenty of time to settle in before winter. Fall-blooming asters and true perennial chrysanthemums are on sale along with lovely hibiscus plants too. Fall-flowering perennials are easy to put into the landscape and replace summer plants; for example, *Sedum* replaces summer salvias, and asters will bloom alongside the last dahlia blooms.

Rake and level the ground before sowing grass seed or laying sod.

A drop spreader puts seed right under the hopper.

Lay sod carefully and press the edges together firmly.

To stand a chance of chrysanthemums returning again next year, plant complete with their container; then, after a few good frosts send it into dormancy, bring it into a cool to cold location for winter. You want to keep mums dormant until spring. Plant it out early next year, so that it gets used to being a perennial again. Trim it next summer to keep it compact and delay blooms (see May and July).

SHRUBS & ROSES

Shrubs, particularly smaller shrubs in 5-gallon-sized containers or smaller, are good to plant this month. The ground is easy to dig into to make a good-sized hole for the shrub, and plants settle in quickly. When planting containerized shrubs (see April), there's a good chance that it's rootbound by fall. Take the shrub out of its container and break apart its roots so that they are not all tightly bound. In some instances, a knife may be necessary to split the rootball.

TREES

The only sort of trees that seem to be better planted in spring are some conifers. Everything else is perfectly happy when planted in fall when it is much easier to dig the size of hole required for the tree.

VINES & GROUNDCOVERS

Plant new groundcovers this month. Remove plants that are growing too far out from the allocated area, and transplant the sections in areas that have sparser coverage.

Plant perennial vines. They won't start growing until spring, but have the support structure in place before you plant.

CARE

The garden is enjoying the last few weeks of summer before the first frosts hit. Harvest vegetables and save seeds before cold weather.

HERE'S HOW

TO MAKE A NEW GARDEN BED

Almost every gardener runs out of space at some point and needs a new garden bed. Start by determining approximately where you want the new bed and how large you want the bed to be. Most often a new bed will be within what is now lawn or grassy area.

- **The build-it-as-you-go way:** Decide approximately where you want the new bed and what its shape will be. Assuming the new bed will include shrubs and perennials, start with shrubs and plant them directly into the lawn. After you have enough shrubs (this is strictly a personal decision, but make sure to leave room for the shrubs to grow), start removing the grass between them. After the grass and all weeds and roots are removed, lightly turn over the subsoil and enrich it with compost. If you're planting perennials immediately, prepare an area by removing grass and till in any needed amendments. Mulch all the areas that you've planted. Eventually all the shrubs and perennials are connected with no grass between them.
- **For immediate use:** Prepare a whole bed at one time. Mark the shape of a soon-to-be bed area with a hose or landscape paint, then remove the grass and weeds. Add a layer of peat moss and compost

ANNUALS

Commercial landscapers rip out annuals and replace them with chrysanthemums this month. But if your annuals are still doing well, leave them and plant fall flowers around them. When frost kills the annuals, take them out.

BULBS

October is the best time for most of us to plant bulbs, but irises can also be divided this month. They can also be divided in spring.

EDIBLES

Keep vegetables picked. As squash or bean vines start to die, remove them to the compost pile. Pick up any spoiled vegetables that have landed on the ground, such as cherry tomatoes. These are messy and can attract animals/insects, so are best composted when you find them. Watch fall crops such as Brussels sprouts and kale, which relish a hard frost. Other crops need the protection of a cold frame to survive anything more than a light touch of frost. For low-growing lettuce, placing a cloth to a depth of about 2 inches above the subsoil. Till the amendments in and cover with mulch. Water the new garden. Let the garden sit for a week or two before planting.

- **Making a new bed from an area covered with gravel:** This is harder work. Gravel usually has landscape fabric beneath and, in a poorly maintained area. Remove the gravel and any landscape fabric plus any underlying rocks and roots. If the area is tillable, do that; otherwise, add about 6 inches of compost on top of the area. Tillable areas can probably manage with just 3 or 4 inches of compost. Plant the area, then mulch.
- **The no-till method of making a new garden bed:** This takes longer, but is easier. As fall leaves are used, this method is best started when the leaves are falling. Start by marking the new garden space. Cover the space either with a layer of flattened cardboard boxes or a thick layer of newspaper (about 8 to 12 sheets). Weigh the paper down by sprinkling it with water. Cover with a thick layer of leaves (about 6 inches deep) and a 3- to 6-inch layer of mulch. Leave the bed over winter. In spring, add a 3-inch layer of compost, a new layer of mulch, and your new garden is ready to plant. This particular way of making a new garden space is great around trees as you won't disturb any roots. Aim to keep less than 4 inches of leaves and mulch beneath the tree canopy.

over the top of their bed can help them through those first one or two nights of frost. Typically these first frosty nights are followed by several more weeks of great fall weather with no frost at all.

Frost-tender herbs such a lemongrass, lemon verbena, pineapple sage, and marjoram need to be potted up and brought indoors for winter. Trim lemongrass and lemon verbena down to about a foot from the crown, and divide the root mass of lemongrass for easier handling. Pineapple sage is large and likely to be in bloom this month. After it flowers, trim this back too. Marjoram, oregano, and thyme cuttings are rarely overly large and fit conveniently into a windowsill-sized container.

Chives can be potted up, but let them go dormant outside before bringing plants inside. They will resprout with new chives in just a few weeks.

LAWNS

Lawns that went dormant this summer should revive in cooler September temperatures. Watering helps get a lawn back into condition and ready for winter. Any areas that don't revive need attention. Look for bugs eating grass roots under lawns or insects destroying the blades. See Problem-Solve this month to identify and treat these issues.

HOUSEPLANTS & CONTAINERS

Bring all tender potted plants inside. Patio hibiscus and other tropicals really don't like temperatures below 60°F, let alone a frost. Leave rosemary until the weather is cooler.

SHRUBS & ROSES

September is too late to prune any shrubs or roses. Rooted side shoots you layered in spring can be dug up and moved to another area. You can still layer roses this month, and by spring you should have a viable cutting with roots. (See July.)

Burlap helps keep wind chill from shrubs as well as browsing from deer. To wrap a shrub, take a long length of burlap and start at the shrub's base. Start wrapping the burlap around the base, and continue wrapping as you go up the shrub until the entire plant is covered. Secure the burlap with rope to stop it unraveling in winter winds.

To protect from winter browsing (mainly deer), surround a shrub with four or five stakes about 2 feet away. Affix burlap or chicken wire to the stakes to make a perimeter fence around the shrub.

In cold Zone 4, lay climbing rose stems onto the ground and protect with mulch. For roses that can be removed from their trellises, do so and bury them in mulch. For roses that cannot be removed from trellises, protect the roots by surrounding the base of the rose with burlap and covering the rose

ABOUT HEDGES

Hedges are a great way to divide your property from your neighbor's, as well as to define specific areas. They can shield a home from chilling winter winds and provide a habitat for birds. Hedges are made from a variety of plant types, from lavender to yew, and vary in height from less than 1-foot borders that surround a flowerbed to several feet tall for bordering a property.

Informal hedges are not clipped to a neat and even form; they are simply a line of shrubs that form a visible barrier. Forsythia, azalea, bridal wreath spirea, and abelia are just a few spring-flowering shrubs that make excellent hedges. Stems between the original planting are restricted to those that help increase the density along the length of the hedge rather than width of it.

Formal hedges are clipped all season to keep both the width and height even. Boxwood is the most common hedge shrub, and it takes clipping very well. Holly, yew, and arborvitae are other conifers and evergreens that make excellent hedges.

The most important decision is the height. Planting a boxwood species that grows to 4 or 5 feet high is not a good choice when you want a 2-foot border hedge. Conversely, a pigmy barberry is not a good candidate when you want a 6-foot hedge for privacy or screening. How fast a plant grows is another consideration. Evergreens or conifers are a good choice for a year-round hedge. Always pick something that is confirmed hardy in your area and where possible pick varieties that are resistant to common diseases.

A uniform hedge of one material is, by default, a collection of the same plants growing together. If one gets a disease, it's quickly transmitted to the rest; so hardiness and disease resistance is important.

TO PLANT A HEDGE

1. Measure the length of the intended hedgerow.
2. Mark the length with a string between two stakes—this establishes a straight line for the hedge. Most hedges are linear, but they can also curve.
3. Mark a second length parallel to this string, but 2 to 6 feet away. This is to account for the spacing between the shrubs. Very small shrubs are planted 24 inches apart whereas larger ones might require a 4-foot spacing. Large yews and arborvitae planted for windbreaks need even more distance to maintain healthy growth.

with chopped leaves or with mulch. The upper stems may not survive but the root should, and that will produce new stems next year.

TREES

Trees, particularly conifers and small trees, are apt to have branches snap under the weight of snow. They are also a delicious snack for deer in winter. Protecting them by wrapping helps minimize these problems.

VINES & GROUNDCOVERS

Mulch the base of climbing vines and make them secure against their support. Winter storms easily topple obelisks or other temporary structures. Perennial vines using these supports should be removed, if possible, and laid on the ground for protection. Store obelisks in a garden shed or garage until next year.

WATER

Very little needs watering in September with the exception of anything that is newly planted. Water Christmas cactus lightly this month as the blooms are setting. These "cacti" are really succulents so don't need a lot of water most of the year.

4. Using flags or sticks, start at one end of the line and mark locations for the specific shrubs. Small shrubs surrounding a garden bed are placed in a single line, the correct distance apart. Larger border shrubs are offset from one another (one at the front, the second at the back) making two rows for planting.
5. Either dig a trench the whole length of the hedge line that is deep enough for the shrubs or dig individual holes for them. For long hedge lines, a trench is usually the most efficient way to keep the depth and line even.
6. Plant, water, and mulch the shrubs as you would for planting other shrubs.
7. Prune the shrubs lightly the first year, then establish regular pruning to keep the hedges neat.

Boxwood is a common shrub to use as a border hedge.

HERE'S HOW

TO DIVIDE IRIS

1. Using a garden fork or spade, dig up the iris clump. Put rhizome sections that fall off the clump to one side. Tease apart the other rhizomes into smaller sections.
2. Check the rhizomes for rotted areas and borers. Discard these sections. Rhizomes with borers have holes in the side where the worm (borer) entered.
3. Replant the rhizomes. Iris like to be planted close to the surface, so prepare the area before dividing. Lightly till the area, add compost, then nestle the new rhizomes into the loose soil. They should be just an inch or two below the surface. Mulch to protect over winter and water to settle them.
4. Trim the leaves to about 6 inches, to a fan shape.

BULBS

Water amaryllis when it's brought indoors but only sparsely for the next few weeks as the plant goes dormant.

EDIBLES

Any herb seeds that you sowed need water. Basil and cilantro both sprout easily from seed and make great additions to winter meals. The rosemary that you'll bring inside for winter doesn't need a lot of water but it does like a cool, sunny location. Other herbs growing on a windowsill need to be on a regular watering schedule to thrive.

LAWNS

Newly seeded lawn areas need water this month, but established lawns should not. The exception is if the temperatures at the start of the month are very warm for more than a week, in which case some water will be needed. Lawns that were dormant in August are helped by a weekly 1-inch waterings in September to speed their recovery from summer drought.

HOUSEPLANTS & CONTAINERS

Containers are getting used to drier conditions indoors, but they'll still need a little extra water

HERE'S HOW

TO CONDITION AMARYLLIS FOR BLOOM FOR THE HOLIDAYS

Dig up the plant and repot it in a small container that's not much larger than the bulb; you want a snug fit. Bury just the lower *half* of the bulb so that the shoulders and leaves are above the soil. Water, then set it into a cool, dark room and forget it for a few weeks—basements work well for this. The leaves will turn brown when the bulb goes dormant. Keep the bulb dormant until early November for late December blooms. After breaking dormancy, an amaryllis blooms in about six to eight weeks.

to keep them from drying out too much. Indoor conditions are less humid than outside, so plants will take a week or two to adjust. Aim for just-damp soil that stays damp for about two to four days before drying out.

PERENNIALS

Newly planted divisions and plants from friends and the store need a little water this month to get them settled. Hold off watering during cool, damp spells.

SHRUBS & ROSES

New additions that you planted this fall need a little more attention than established shrubs and roses. Water them if you don't have rain for a week to keep them hydrated.

FERTILIZE

Fall is a good time to add a dose of fertilizer to the lawn and areas where bulbs are going to be planted. Most of the garden is winding down for winter, so skip fertilizing perennial beds, shrubs, and trees.

ANNUALS

Annuals don't need fertilizing this month.

BULBS

Incorporate a little bone meal to the areas that have dormant bulbs or where you plan to plant bulbs next month. Some dogs and rodents have been known to dig where they smell bone meal, so if that's a problem, use a regular garden fertilizer or general bulb fertilizer instead. One cup of garden fertilizer per 50 square feet is sufficient. For specific bulb formulations that incorporate slow-release

HERE'S HOW

TO MAKE A COLD FRAME

Cold frames have been used for years to protect plants from cold winter winds and as a place to winter over some vegetables such as carrots and lettuces. More recently, a less-formal design of cold frame has become popular, and now almost everyone can build a simple design.

Traditional Cold Frame: Redwood or cedar is best as they're weather resistant. Angle the side of the frame so the lid captures as much winter sun as possible; about 15 percent is normal or a 3-inch slope over a 4-foot length. Cold frame lids were traditionally glass, but modern Lexan plastic is more common today. For maximum venting options, construct the lid in two parts that slide under each other, or a hinged lid that props open for ventilation. Other options include a center hinge between lid sections that allow the lid to bend from the center as it is withdrawn. An upside V is created as the lid is raised from the center.

Material list for a traditional cold frame (use weather-resistant wood for the frame):

1 2×6 plank of wood for the front.

1 2×10 plank of wood for the back.

2 pieces of wood for the sides. Each is 4-foot long, 10 inches at one end, and 6 inches at the other end.

1 4×4 clear, rigid plastic or glass window affixed to a frame (or two 2×4 pieces).

ASSEMBLE THE WOOD PIECES

1. To make the base frame, use metal angled corner ends, or 1×1 wood blocks, to secure

each end of the side pieces to the back and front of the cold frame. Use screws rather than nails.

2. Attach the glass (or plastic) to the lid of the cold frame.
3. Attach hinges to the lid so that it can be lifted up and closed. For sliding lids, the lid is permanently fixed to the base and the glass sections move past one under the other.
4. Locate the cold frame so that the sun is on the glass most of the day. Usually, facing the slope of the frame to the south is best.

Informal Cold Frame (photo, right, top): You can use a 4×4-foot raised bed as a cold frame for winter protection.

1. Create a lid. This can be made from a variety of materials such as old windows or doors or rigid plastic roofing material.
2. Place the lid over the raised bed frame—a snug fit is ideal, but since windows/doors/roofing material rarely match the bed size, some added protection around the sides may be needed. Use old towels to plug any gaps.
3. Venting is important. With these simple beds, that means manually propping the lid open on warm days.

Rigid plastic covers help protect winter crops from excess cold.

It is important, even in winter, to vent the cold frame.

Using Hay/Straw Bales: Rather than using a 4×4-foot raised bed, hay or straw bales can be used as the base for the cold frame. The bales add insulation from the sides.

1. Arrange the bales in a square or rectangle; just one or two bales long is more convenient.
2. Make a lid from similar material as described above. Clear plastic sheeting can be used for the lid, which protects from winds, but does not have a lot of thermal protection at night. It can also increase the interior temperature of the cold frame very quickly on sunny winter days.

phosphorus, check the product recommendations. All bulb areas should receive a dose of compost yearly.

EDIBLES

Seedlings of cilantro and basil should be ready for a light fertilizer this month. As they're small, a one-quarter-strength formula is sufficient or apply diluted compost tea.

LAWNS

September and October are the main lawn fertilization months. One application this month

HERE'S HOW

TO CONDITION A POINSETTIA FOR THE HOLIDAYS

1. Bring the poinsettia inside and place it in an out-of-the-way location.
2. The trick is to force the poinsettia into thinking the day length is very short. Do this by putting a large box over the plant every evening and removing it the next morning. A total of 14 to 16 hours of darkness is optimal for flower formation, and more important, the colorful bracts.
3. When the box is off, place the plant in a sunny window and keep lightly watered.
4. When the flowers and bracts are fully formed and colorful, bring the plant into the main living areas to enjoy.

and a second dose next month is typical. For those gardeners in colder regions, where snow is possible in October, just make a single application early this month. See Fertilize in March to learn how to evenly distribute lawn chemicals.

HOUSEPLANTS & CONTAINERS

Outdoor containers that were replanted with fall flowers in September were planted with some new potting mix that already contains fertilizer, so no more is needed.

Indoor containers and those that were brought inside earlier this month are still adjusting to interior conditions; a light dose of fertilizer is fine for these. This is the last fertilizer for these plants as they are going into dormancy soon, so a slow-release fertilizer is best.

PROBLEM-SOLVE

As the garden slowly goes dormant, green leaves drop off, so deer and other animals may start to nibble stems and anything aboveground. Monitor shrubs, in particular, and apply a deer repellant to the garden. Most hardware stores sell a range of natural deer and rabbit deterrents that are safe for pets.

ANNUALS

Annuals that are getting leggy and past their prime can be ripped out this month and composted. Replace them with vibrant, hardy fall plants.

BULBS

Squirrels bury their nuts in the garden *and* dig up bulbs. If this is an issue, cover bulbs with a layer of chicken wire that a squirrel cannot breach.

HERE'S HOW

TO WRAP A SMALL TREE FOR PROTECTION

1. Get a long piece of strong string; a clothesline type works well.
2. Starting at the lower limbs, gently bend the limbs upward.
3. Start wrapping the rope around the lower limbs as you bend them upward.
4. Secure the whole tree with rope.
5. For added protection, wrap the tree with burlap and secure.

Wrapping limbs close to the main trunk stops snow landing on them and causing them to break. Burlap helps stop wind damage as well as reduces wind chill on a tree.

Aerating helps compacted lawns by taking out cores to allow water and nutrients get down to the root zone of the lawn.

EDIBLES

Enjoy harvesting late-season beans and other late-summer crops. Any insects that share the harvest are going away soon, so they're not worth worrying about.

LAWNS

In spring, root-eating grubs were an issue. Though they're much smaller now, they're eating *ravenously*, so use the same method described in March under Care, Lawns to identify if you have an issue worth treating. Milky spore is a biological control that works well on grubs.

Chinch bugs are a surface insect that's more active in fall than spring. To identify the bugs, sink a bottomless can into the soil and fill it with water. Chinch bugs will rise to the surface. They like to feast on the sap in the green blades of grass. A tolerance for a light population in a well-tended lawn is acceptable, and the bugs will do very little damage. If you have issues with yellowing grass due to a major infestation, treat just the affected areas with a pesticide.

As leaves fall from trees onto the lawn, rake them up or mow to mulch them. Leaving lots of leaves on the lawn isn't healthy for the grass, but mowing them breaks them into smaller pieces, perfect for mulching perennials. Don't throw leaves away.

HOUSEPLANTS & CONTAINERS

Before you bring outdoor plants inside, check them for bugs. Look for eggs under leaves, scale on the bark (little buff-colored scabs), and small holes in leaves. Keep these plants away from your other houseplants for a week or two so that any eggs or insects that have hidden in the soil can make themselves known and be treated before infecting other plants.

PERENNIALS

Do not apply mulch to perennial beds until the first hard frost. If applied too early, rodents will find homes in the mulch and nibble perennial roots and crowns. After the first frost they'll have already found other places to nest.

SHRUBS & ROSES

Shrubs are going dormant and don't have many problems. Gardeners in cold areas need to protect borderline-hardy shrubs and roses, particularly climbing roses.

DEALING WITH THATCH

Lawns that are just surface-watered or overfertilized accrue a layer of dead matter at the soil's surface called "thatch." Thatch includes grass clippings that have not fully decomposed as well as other debris. As this matter collects, it impedes nutrients and water from entering the soil where the lawn can use it, leading to a poor lawn overall.

To dethatch the lawn, drag this matter away from the surface, and scratch the soil surface so that it loosens. Most people rent a dethatching machine, which does this hard work for you, but the machine itself is heavy. The tines on a dethatcher pick up tufts of thatch and deposit them on the surface of the lawn for you to rake up.

Poor lawn conditions can also result from compacted soil, which leads to thatch. Aerating is often recommended after dethatching is completed. An aerator takes soil plugs (cores) out of a lawn so that water and nutrients can penetrate to the root zone of turfgrass. The cores are deposited on the surface of the lawn and are raked up and composted.

After aerating and dethatching, you are ready to reseed and/or apply fertilizer.

Good practice in lawn care (fertilizing and watering) goes a long way toward avoiding thatch buildup.

October

The summer growing season officially ends in October with most of us getting a frost this month. All tender plants should be indoors by now and, for many, the garden will be left alone until next spring. That, however, means missing some great planting weather, because even though the annuals are composted after the first fall frost, there are bulbs to plant for spring and there is still time to add a few perennials and shrubs. Shrubs, trees, and perennials are on final sale alongside chrysanthemums, and the stores are motivated to sell them before the Christmas trees arrive. So don't put the garden tools away too early in October.

Harvest all the tender vegetables and pick a final bunch of colorful annuals for the table before the first frost hits. Cooler nights bring brilliant color to trees in and outside of our landscapes. Take advantage of the comfortable weather to visit parks that have trails through the trees. Kids and dogs particularly love running through piles of crisp fallen leaves.

In the garden, many shrubs are also getting color in their leaves, while others are putting on color with their berries. Fothergilla, blueberries, and viburnums are just some of the shrubs that put on a splendid fall display to contrast with fall chrysanthemums and late-flowering grasses.

Look for fall festivals, pumpkin-picking farms for kids, and apple farms serving spicy hot apple cider. For older kids, corn mazes and haunted hayrides are wonderful fun. These are great for family entertainment and lasting memories.

Get out your camera to take some images of the great fall color in the garden, and note what worked and what is missing. A garden should have something in flower or something of interest even after the first frost arrives. Berries, bark, and leaf color as well as fall flowers give you something to admire all the way through fall and into winter. Take pictures and make some notes about how to beef up the fall views that you see from inside the home.

PLAN

The first fall frosts arrive for most of us this month, which is the end of the active gardening season. You'll hear the term "putting your garden to bed," which is really just basic garden cleanup. Clearing leaves from the lawn and removing dead annuals from the garden need to be done this month.

Anything below 29°F produces a moderate or hard frost that kills tender foliage on annuals and summer vegetables. A frost cloth, sheet, or cold frame is usually able to protect plants when the air temperature is above 30°F. A killing frost, with temperatures below 25°F, damages most plants' leaves: it definitely puts an end to annuals and most vegetables.

Between 30 and 32°F, frost is less severe and frequently spotty. Cold air is dense and rolls downhill, so the coldest air settles in valleys or at the bottom of a slope. Garden plants at the lower end of a slope can be killed while plants higher up are fine. The areas directly around walls benefit from a few extra degrees of heat which keeps them warmer a few days longer. These very site-specific areas of warmer/cooler air are called "microclimates." Winds that move the air around help keep frost from settling, and cloud cover keeps some of the warm fall heat from escaping.

ANNUALS

Some annuals will survive the first 32°F night, but when temperatures dip below 28°F, most wither and die. Add removing dead annuals to your to-do list before temperatures get too cold. Wait until the ground is free of frost before you try to pull the annuals out, so you get the roots as well.

BULBS

October is the first big "bulb month." Spring bulbs can be purchased and planted. If you have a soil thermometer, wait until it reaches 50°F before planting: most soil will be cool enough by the end of October. Plan to have early-, mid-, and late-season spring bulbs, as well as some for forcing indoors.

After the first killing frost, the leaves of tender bulbs, like cannas and dahlias, go brown; these should be removed and prepped for storage.

Dig cannas when the top growth has been killed by frost.

EDIBLES

Beans, tomatoes, and peppers all need attention this month. Clear dead vines and be ready for last-minute harvests. After you clear the plants, find somewhere to store trellises and other supports. Decide what you are going to do with borderline plants such as rosemary (hardy to about Zone 6) and fig trees, which are root hardy to about Zone 5.

LAWNS

Lawn renovation and seeding should be finished this month, but plan to keep young grass moist until it's established.

HOUSEPLANTS & CONTAINERS

Outdoor containers have been changed to fall plants and decorations. Layering spring bulbs is a good way to reuse the summer containers.

PERENNIALS

If you have a deck or porch filled with perennials that you have not found homes for in the garden yet, then it is time to do that.

SHRUBS & ROSES

This is the last chance for a while to find a few extra shrubs for the garden. Plan to secure climbing roses against winter storms. Check home-improvement stores for more great prices on shrubs, as they are motivated to move summer and fall stock out to make room for Christmas trees.

TREES

As the leaves turn color and fall, decide how to deal with them—you can bag them and put out for garbage collection or drag them onto the curb for the annual collection by your township, but that wastes the leaves when they would be great for mulch in your garden. Run the mower over the leaves to chop them up and use them as mulch on flowerbeds and the vegetable garden.

PLANT

The focus for October planting is spring bulbs, but you can still plant perennials and shrubs in most places. The ground should be cool but not frozen yet.

ANNUALS

Annuals outside die with the frost so no new annuals will be planted this month.

BULBS

Plant spring bulbs this month; many are on sale at retail stores. Daffodils have many different varieties and colors ranging from rich buttercup yellow to pure white. Sizes range from just a few inches to over a foot in height. Clumps of early small daffodils or little grape hyacinths can be planted in the lawn. They'll flower before the lawn really needs mowing next spring.

Do not plant tulips in areas where deer browse. Tulips are on a deer's favorite meal list, right along with petunias. Miniature tulips such as 'Emperor' are not damaged so much by deer browsing, but even they can disappear overnight

EDIBLES

Plant garlic bulbs this month and in November. The bright green sprout comes up from the bulb,

Dig a hole for planting individual bulbs that is about four times as deep as the bulb. Place the bulb with the narrow, pointed end facing upward.

GENERAL PLANTING FOR SPRING-FLOWERING BULBS

Small crocus bulbs are planted just an inch or two below the surface whereas large tulip and daffodil bulbs are planted much deeper, closer to 6 or 7 inches deep. For a pleasing group of larger bulbs, dig a circular hole about 6 inches and about 2 feet across. Loosen the underlying soil and space bulbs about 3 inches apart (with the tuft of roots down and the pointed end up). Carefully refill the hole and, if you planted a group of bulbs in the lawn, replace the grass on top. Small crocus bulbs can be treated the same way, but they're just as easy to plant using a dibble or trowel. Stab the soil surface, drop the bulb into the hole, cover, and move a few inches away to plant the next one. Crocus look fine in small clumps, or try making a curved line and mix in some little blue hyacinth or dwarf iris. Early crocus also look great when planted in small groups in the lawn. They go dormant before the lawn needs its first spring mowing and, because the foliage is disguised in the lawn, they don't go through that messy, post-flowering stage that you see in the garden beds.

PLANT	PLANTING DEPTH (IN INCHES)
Snowdrops	3–4
Crocus	3–4
Muscari hyacinth	3–4
Early miniature tulips	4–5
Hyacinth	5–6
Daffodils	3–8
Tulips	6–8

then remains green through winter. Next spring they'll continue to grow and produce a garlic head in early summer.

Any basil and cilantro plants remaining in the herb garden are killed by frost, but you can sow a few seeds indoors to have a winter supply. Cilantro grows and bolts quickly, so sow a few seeds each month for a constant supply.

Pot up rosemary before cold temperatures arrive, and keep it in a cool room for winter, watering sparsely. The plant can tolerate frosts so is usually one of the last to come inside.

Outdoors, plant some cover crops to nourish beds for spring. Legumes are popular for cover crops—peas, clover, and vetch along with grain crops such as annual ryegrass, oats, and wheat. All germinate quickly and grow to cover a garden bed.

HERE'S HOW

TO LAYER BULBS IN A CONTAINER

A container whose plants take care of themselves and bloom for several weeks will be a bonus next spring. So take time to plant bulbs in a container now. More (or fewer) than three layers can be made as long as the deepest bulbs are not below about 8 inches.

1. Pick a deep container that can hold three or four layers of bulbs.
2. Fill the bottom one-third with potting mix.
3. Divide the bulbs into early crocus and iris, mid-season daffodils, and larger late-season bulbs.
4. Start with the larger, late season bulbs and layer them on the base of the container.
5. Cover the bulbs with a layer of potting mix.
6. Add a layer of mid-season daffodils and hyacinths.
7. Cover these bulbs with more potting mix.
8. Add the top layer of early-blooming daffodils, crocus, and iris.
9. Cover these bulbs.
10. Place the whole container where it will get spring sunshine.

LAWNS

Lawns can still be patched in mild winter areas, but new grass needs a few weeks to establish and seed should not be sown in areas where the frost date is early- or mid-October.

HOUSEPLANTS & CONTAINERS

Dig and replant divisions of chives and thyme for a windowsill herb garden.

PERENNIALS

Perennials can still be planted. Most will lose their upper growth with the first killing frost, but the roots will continue to settle in the still-warm soil.

HERE'S HOW

TO PLANT GARLIC

1. Prepare the planting bed with lots of compost and rake smooth.
2. Divide the garlic bulbs into cloves.
3. Plant each clove about 2 to 3 inches below the surface—elephant garlic (*Allium ampeloprasum*) is planted deeper than most kitchen garlic—and about 4 inches apart.
4. Cover the bulbs and label the row.
5. Water and wait for them to show above the ground. Garlic starts to grow the year it's planted, and it's happy even when covered in snow.

Plant individual garlic cloves about 6 inches apart.

If you want to divide a perennial this month, trim the top growth then follow the general perennial division notes in April.

SHRUBS & ROSES

Shrubs can still be planted but delay planting roses and shrub conifers until next year. Mulch newly planted shrubs well.

TREES

Small trees from the nursery (in 5-gallon containers) can be planted *early* in the month. Most trees will be heading into dormancy this month, so give the tree a few weeks to settle into your landscape before that happens.

VINES & GROUNDCOVERS

Perennial vines and groundcovers can still be planted early in the month.

Trim perennial stalks and clear dead leaves away from the garden bed.

CARE

Fall cleanup should include clearing all dead plant material, plus roots, from vegetable and flower beds. Fallen leaves from perennials and roses as well as trees should be picked up to avoid possible spread of viruses caused by the leaf litter.

Rake leaves from lawns: either mow over the pile and use the chopped leaves as mulch on perennial beds or bag them for county pick up. Keep driveways and footpaths clear of leaf litter where it can be a hazard. Clearing leaves is best done on a dry, calm day.

ANNUALS

Compost dead annuals. Leaving the growth on the ground until next year is not a good idea particularly if you plan on using the same annuals in the same place. Some nasty pathogens that cause issues such as rust on hollyhocks can remain in the soil to attack plants next year.

BULBS

Summer cannas, dahlias, and any other tender bulbs should be lifted this month. Wait until the top growth has gone brown and the plants are dormant, which happens about a week after the first killing frost. Dig the rhizomes and let them dry for a few days. Remove dead foliage, then inspect the bulbs to make sure they're not soft or chewed before storing in a container for winter. Large plastic storage boxes work well. Layer the bulbs on peat moss or sand, and store in a cool, but frost-free place until next spring.

If your daffodils had lots of green leaves but few flowers, they are likely overcrowded. Dig the bulbs up and pull the smaller side bulblets off. Replant these elsewhere. (See April for more on dividing bulbs. Replant any bulbs that squirrels unearth.)

EDIBLES

Cool-weather crops such as kale and chard can tolerate frost very well. Salad crops and cabbages don't do so well, so cover these when a light frost is forecast. If they're in a cold frame, keep the lid down on frosty nights but lift it again in the morning, as even in October the sun can burn crops if they're enclosed in a cold frame.

Trim back all annual vines from beans and peas, but leave the roots in the soil to decompose over winter. Legume roots fix nitrogen in the soil for next year. Remove potatoes, tomatoes, and peppers, including all roots, and compost the plants.

LAWNS

Keep watering newly seeded or sodded lawns. Cut the new grass when it is growing well. Correct any areas where seed didn't germinate. Early in the month, you could try reseeding these areas, particularly in Zones 7 and above, which have late frosts.

HERE'S HOW

TO CLEAN AND STORE GARDEN TOOLS PROPERLY

Basic garden tools: Brush off any debris and rinse with water to get mud and soil off the spade or forks.

Dry them, then clean the blades with rubbing alcohol (do not use bleach as that has been shown to cause pitting in the blades of spades and pruning equipment). Lightly sharpen the blade with a file or stone to smooth out pits and give a clean edge for cutting. Wooden handles are traditionally treated with linseed oil to prevent them from drying out. Most oils do the same thing, but avoid motor oil (you don't really want traces of motor oil in the garden). When completely dry, hang tools in the garage or shed until next spring. Don't forget to add a little oil to your garden clippers and pruners. WD-40® or something similar keeps moveable joints lubricated.

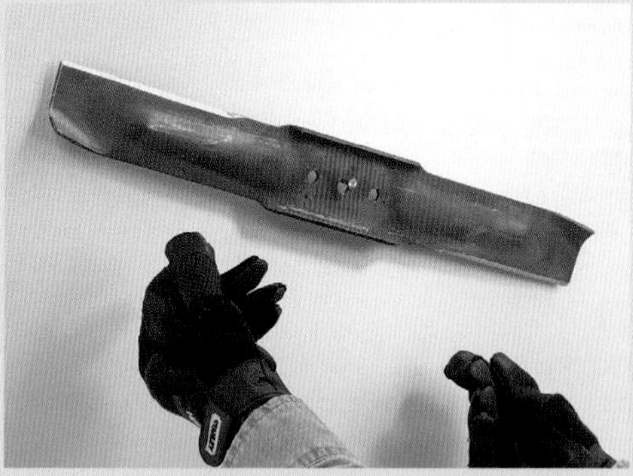

Powered hand lawn mower (photos, right): After the final mowing, let the mower run until out of fuel. Remove spark plugs. Clean and sharpen the blades. Rinse all grass from the mower and underneath in the blade cavity. Let the mower dry before storing.

Reel mower: These low-tech mowers are perfect for small gardens, and they never run out of fuel (unless you do). After the last mowing, clean and sharpen the blades. Clean the handle and rinse off any grass clippings left on the mower. Dry and store for winter.

Riding mowers: After the last mowing, let the mower run to empty the fuel tank. Disconnect and check/clean spark plugs. Replace the oil filter and empty the oil if possible. Clean and sharpen the blades (you'll have to remove the blades to do this). Clean the blade housing and remove all caked on grass clippings.

Most mower retailers offer professional mower cleaning and are usually have a calendar that is much clearer in October or November than it will be next March. Do maintenance now; next March your mower will just need to be filled with fuel and it'll be ready to go.

Garden chemicals: Store all garden chemicals in a frost-free garage. All liquid chemicals should be tightly covered; granular chemicals should be tightly covered, preferably sealed, and stored in a dry location.

HOUSEPLANTS & CONTAINERS

Winter-blooming cactus should be putting out buds now and can be placed somewhere light so that the blooms can grow well.

Poinsettias should still be given the light/dark routine from September. These too should be showing signs of bloom and coloration of the leaves around the flower. Keep conditioning the plant until November when the coloration is complete.

PERENNIALS

Trim back perennials after frost kills the top growth and compost the remains. Wait until the top of the ground is cold before adding extra mulch to the area. Mice and other little creatures like to bed down under warm mulch and are apt to snack on the perennial roots nearby.

Pick up and discard all hollyhock stems and leaves. Hollyhock rust is a virus that stays on the parts of the plant that are aboveground. Don't compost hollyhock debris.

SHRUBS & ROSES

Climbing rose stems can be laid horizontal and buried for winter protection in cold areas (see September for notes on protecting shrubs and roses). In mild winter areas, this is not necessary, but the stems should be secured for winter protection. As soon as the roses are dormant, they can be pruned or this can be left until late winter. Early winter pruning in areas subject to strong winds has the advantage of reducing the canes yourself before nature snaps them off.

TREES

If guy ropes are supporting young trees, check that they are tight enough to withstand winter storms.

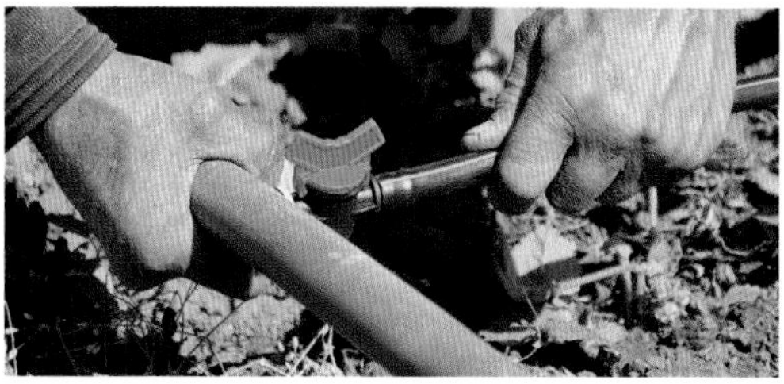

Disconnect drip hose lines now.

Also check that they are not cutting into the tree trunk. A small carpet remnant is useful to cushion the trunk. Cut a piece about 4 inches wide and long enough to go round the trunk. Put the ropes around the tree but on the carpet. Don't tighten too much. The tree needs to be able to sway in storms. (See notes on staking in May.)

WATER

Remove all hoses from outside faucets. Drain hoses and store in a shed or garage. Unhook and disconnect drip irrigation systems for outdoor containers, drain, and store for next year. Disconnect drip irrigation in raised beds and the vegetable plot. Drain and store. Disconnect distributor lines in the garden; these systems use rigid pipe and may not be convenient to take up for winter storage. Remove or disconnect them where you can. Drain in-ground irrigation systems; each line that has a sprinkler head assembly or line should have a drain; these vary with installation and by manufacturer. Take up soaker hoses and store them in a shed for next year. Turn off faucets from inside the house before cold weather settles and you have no further need for outdoor water. Empty water barrels and bird baths, and store them for next year.

BULBS

Bulbs that are being conditioned for winter blooming should be kept just moist while they're dormant. To bring a bulb out of dormancy, increase the water.

EDIBLES

Any seedlings that you started indoors need to be kept watered along with anything that you brought inside for winter.

LAWNS

Water new lawns as needed. Fall rains should provide sufficient water for new lawns, but some falls are dry. After a frost, the weather can turn mild for several more weeks so the grass will continue to grow and put down roots. Don't water if there's frost on the lawn.

HOUSEPLANTS & CONTAINERS

Water indoor plants normally. Toward the end of the month, reduce watering as plants go dormant in lower light conditions. For plants that are coming into bloom, like winter-blooming cactus, increase the watering just a little to keep them moist. Watch all containers that are on windowsills or tables by a bright window to ensure that they don't wilt in the still-warm sun.

As the weather cools, put drapes behind plants on a windowsill so that they do not get cold overnight.

FERTILIZE

There is very little to fertilize as plants go into winter dormancy.

BULBS

After bulbs are planted, a light dose of bulb fertilizer is usually applied to the soil surface.

EDIBLES

Compost can be added to the beds when the vegetables have been cleared out. Don't forget to add some chopped leaves from the lawn. They're free!

LAWNS

Late October is the last chance for the second and final fertilization of the lawn. A general guide is to apply 1 pound of nitrogen per 1,000 square feet in fall. Eastern New York and southern New Jersey can apply the second fertilizer as late as early November. (See March for general lawn fertilization and how much to apply.)

HOUSEPLANTS & CONTAINERS

A light fertilizer (half-strength) added to the water once per month for plants that either do not go dormant (African violets) or those coming out of forced dormancy like the cactus is fine. Always check the product's label, particularly for plant-specific fertilizer, such as a formulation made for orchids, as these may recommend different strengths.

PERENNIALS

After perennials have gone dormant, an application of compost over the whole bed is a good idea. This breaks down over winter to enrich the soil for next year. But wait to mulch until after you have had a killing frost so that small animals find homes somewhere else.

PROBLEM-SOLVE

Leaves are *everywhere* in October—on garden beds, lawns, and sidewalks. Remove them when they are dry and easy to collect. A few leaves on the lawn or flower bed are fine as they'll break down; you just don't want a mass of sticky, slick leaves on them.

BULBS

Bulbs you have just planted are often immediate targets for rodents. Now's the time to take protective measures. (See Here's How, at right.)

LAWNS

Leaves on lawns aren't just messy and unsightly, they damage a lawn. The leaves lie flat and when they're wet, they adhere to one another, making a slick shield that prevents water and air getting to the lawn beneath them. Damp cool days also create a great environment for fungal issues.

HOUSEPLANTS & CONTAINERS

Before you bring outdoor plants back inside for winter, check them carefully for bugs—aphids, scale, and whiteflies. Treat these outdoor if possible with horticultural oils or soaps. When you bring a plant indoors, particularly if you are bringing

Compost the leaves you rake up from your lawn rather than burning them or throwing them away.

HERE'S HOW

TO PROTECT BULBS FROM RODENTS

Sometimes rodents such as groundhogs and squirrels dig up spring bulbs as soon as you have planted them. Daffodil bulbs are the most resistant as most animals find them toxic. But you'll have to protect others, and it is worth doing so right from the planting stage.

1. Dig the area for bulbs—a squarish hole that is just a little deeper than the recommended depth for bulbs (see chart earlier in this chapter).
2. Lay chicken wire at the base of the hole and curve the wire upward to cover all sides of the hole.
3. Add a little soil from the pile you took out and lay it on the chicken wire.
4. Plant the bulbs and cover with more waiting soil.
5. Put another layer of chicken wire over the bulbs in the hole.
6. Finish the hole with waiting soil.
7. Mulch the area.

The chicken wire stops anything reaching the bulbs, and they remain protected all winter. Aboveground protection is done by applying deer or rabbit sprays to the emerging leaves if needed. Daffodils do not need any aboveground protection but tulips nearly always do. Use one of the many natural sprays or granules to protect the growth.

in the container that it grew in this past summer, isolate the plant for a week to make sure there aren't any unseen eggs waiting to hatch. Treat appropriately with horticultural oils/soaps or with a pesticide approved for indoor plants.

TREES

When hardwood landscape trees turn bright red and orange, it's a sign the leaves are going to drop. Conifers do a similar thing; their inner needles turn yellow and drop just like leaves. Unfortunately, this gives a yellow tinge to the whole tree, which makes some homeowners think that the tree is dying. But if you look closely, you'll see that the outer needles are still firmly in place and only the inner ones are dropping.

Some conifers, namely dawn redwoods, larches, and bald cypress, turn brown in fall and drop all their needles. These unusual but beautiful conifers are deciduous just like most hardwood trees. If your tree is turning brown all over, before you get concerned, check with the local Extension Service to find out if it is behaving normally.

Continue to watch for fall webworms to arrive. The bags are similar to spring tent worms, but fall webworms prefer the end of the branch to form their web and so are more noticeable. These are unsightly, but as most trees drop their leaves soon, it's rarely worth spending much time removing them.

Conifers take on a yellow hue in fall as the old needles turn brown and fall off.

November

November marks the start of the holiday season, which runs from Thanksgiving through New Year, and the garden is temporarily forgotten by many. Some areas will see snow in November, and most areas see frosts and consistently cool-to-cold weather. Nurseries and garden centers are full of seasonal plants like rosemary topiaries, poinsettias, dormant amaryllis bulbs, and Christmas trees.

When shopping for tender seasonal plants such as poinsettias and rosemary, take great care on cold days to protect them between the store and your vehicle. Brisk winter winds and crisp temperatures on the trip between can kill these plants before you even get them home! Wrap them in a bag and your jacket to keep them safe.

Branches and berries from shrubs make great seasonal wreaths for your door as well as your fireplace. The white fruit of andromeda (*Pieris japonica*) and iridescent purple berries of beautyberry (*Callicarpa*) join the more common but vibrant red berries on holly bushes. Make a simple wreath using a base of boxwood or branches from one of the many conifers. Decorate with lots of berries and pine cones, add a strand or two of ivy and a bow, and your outdoor wreath is ready to display on the door.

Look for fall and winter craft shows, which often include decorative fall- or winter-themed wreaths for sale. There are also workshops to help you create great table centerpieces as well as your own wreaths. Although November is not considered the best time to prune boxwood or conifers, you can safely cut enough for your winter crafts.

In the vegetable patch, there are Brussels sprouts to harvest, and much of the kale will still be edible. In a cold frame, lettuce, carrots, and parsnips are not actually still growing in winter, but if they are protected enough, you can continue to harvest them. Wait until frost is off the leaves before harvesting. Remember that even winter sun can heat up a cold frame very quickly, so vent it on sunny days or leave a small stick under the lid so that it cannot close completely.

PLAN

The garden is put to bed now, but that means you'll be able to review the past year and start planning for next year. Gather all your images and notes so that you have plenty of inspiration.

If you burn wood, prepare for a cold winter with a supply of good quality logs. Check the wood if possible before purchase to make sure no insects are hitching a ride onto your property.

Halloween is over, the holiday season is close, and gift-giving is part of the season of goodwill. Think about what you would like to put on your wish list, and keep an eye open for gifts for your garden friends and family. Even non-gardeners enjoy amaryllis and other seasonal plants.

ANNUALS

Catalogs start arriving again just after Thanksgiving, but you probably won't have much time to look at them over the holidays, so file them for later. Come January, you can get them out and start serious planning.

BULBS

Can you have too many amaryllis bulbs? They come in a variety of colors that complement many seasonal displays. The amaryllis that you stored from last year should be in a cool room or basement in order for it to go dormant. By now the leaves have turned brown and should fall off; cut off any brown leaves that don't fall off. Water sparsely at this stage, and give the plant about eight weeks of dormancy. It will be then be ready to come out of dormancy and start growing again. Amaryllis takes six to eight weeks to go from dormancy to flowering. Depending on when you started the process (hopefully September), amaryllis should come out of dormancy the beginning of this month. If you delayed bringing it in, or forgot that it's in the basement, when you reach the eight-week mark, bring it out to have blooms in January.

EDIBLES

Many supermarkets sell not just packets of fresh-picked herbs but also small plants. If there's an herb that you particularly like or use often in winter recipes, check the produce section to see if it has plants. You can still grow your own fresh herbs (even if you didn't pot them up yourself).

Order dormant fruit trees this month. They'll be delivered early next year. Most apples and pears do well everywhere, so your choice is plentiful. Get a matching tree for pollination (see February for more on pollination and fruit trees). For peaches, pick a cold-hardy variety such as 'Intrepid', 'Reliance', or 'Blushing Star', which are all hardy from Zone 4 through Zone 8.

LAWNS

Most lawns are still green, and you can see the results of your efforts. November is too late to do anything, but you can make notes as to what you'll need to do to address any problems you had this year.

HOUSEPLANTS & CONTAINERS

Indoor gardening can be done all year-round; think about some new indoor plants to enjoy this winter. African violets are part of a large group of tropical plants called *gesneriads*, which, along with begonias and orchids, are just a few of the more attractive indoor plants.

SHRUBS & ROSES

Order dormant roses and shrubs this month and schedule delivery for next February or March.

Colorful berries on shrubs are an asset for holiday decorations, as winter interest, and as food for birds. Winterberry (*Ilex verticillata*), holly, andromeda (*Pieris japonica*), and beautyberry (*Callicarpa dichotoma*) are some of the most colorful shrubs you can grow in order to have berries that last through fall and well into winter.

TREES

Dig a hole now for trees that are due for delivery early next year. Once you've dug the hole, fill it with mulch and then place a thick board over the top. This way, if the ground is frozen, you can still plant the dormant tree—loose mulch is much easier to dig out than frozen clay.

Buying a Christmas tree is traditional for many families. Check out the Christmas tree farms that allow you to pick a live, growing tree. Most farms provide netting, string, and helpers to get the tree onto, or into, the car. Check your room's dimensions to determine the size of tree that you need before you head out; trees in the field tend to look smaller than when they're put up in your family room. Christmas trees come in many varieties and finding the right one for you is important. Color and needle retention are perhaps the most important things to look for, but overall shape is important too. Squat, pyramidal trees take up more width than tall, upright ones. Homes with double-story hallways or informal rooms can accommodate wider and taller trees than small family rooms. Taller trees are also more difficult to secure (keep upright) and decorate.

Callicarpa *berries are stunning in fall.*

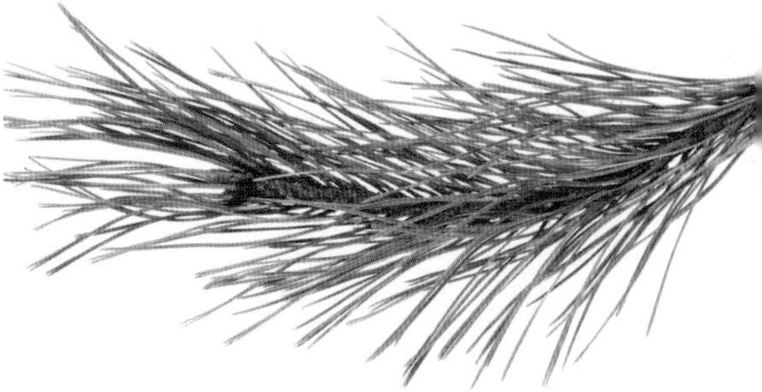

Pine.

Spruce.

Fir.

Texture is another consideration. Soft white pine needles don't poke you as you walk by or decorate the tree, but neither do they hold ornaments quite as well as the stiffer branches of spruce trees.

CHRISTMAS TREE OVERVIEW				
	NEEDLE LENGTH	*OVERALL SHAPE*	*NEEDLE RETENTION*	*SCENT*
Spruce trees				
Blue spruce	1–3 inches	Loose pyramid	Medium	Medium
Norway spruce	1 inch	Conical	Poor	Poor
White spruce	Short, ½–1 inch	Loose pyramid	Medium	Low
Pine trees				
Scotch pine	Short, soft	Dense pyramid	Good	Medium
White pine	Medium, soft	Tapered	Good	No scent, great for allergies
Virginia pine	1–3 inches	Wide base	Medium	Strong
Fir trees				
Balsam fir	1 inch	Tapered	Good	Good scent
Douglas fir	1–1½ inches, soft	Wide, tapered	Good	Medium
Frazer fir	1 inch	Pyramid	Good	Scented
Cedar trees				
Eastern cedar	1-2 inch	Narrow, tapered	Poor	Medium

VINES & GROUNDCOVERS

American bittersweet is a wonderful addition for seasonal color in the garden and for decorations. The bright red-orange berries on this attractive vine are used for seasonal decorations and to attract birds.

PLANT

Very little can be planted outdoors, but indoor miniature gardens can be planted! These fun and unique gardens definitely create a talking point in the home.

ANNUALS

Hardy annual seeds of poppies, bachelor buttons, and cosmos can be sprinkled around this month. They wait until spring before they germinate and aren't bothered by cold, wet conditions. In fact, seeds of many early-flowering annuals actually benefit from a fall sowing.

BULBS

As long as the ground is workable, you can plant any leftover spring-flowering bulbs this month, including any that you are growing in a container. Layer the bulbs for a long season of bloom in spring, and plant a few pansies on top for added color.

Plant bulbs for forcing this month by planting a container as you would any other, using a good potting mix. Place the container on the deck or porch or in the refrigerator until January when

Continue to plant bulbs as the weather allows. Or store them in paper bags, rather than plastic.

you'll bring it out to grow. Bulbs can be placed in a paper bag or left in the netting that they came in, stored in the refrigerator to chill, and then planted late December or early January.

EDIBLES

Along with flower bulbs, garlic can still be planted this month. The cloves generally send a shoot up quickly, and the shoot remains green all winter, even though snow and cold temperatures. Plant garlic bulbs about 2 to 3 inches belowground.

If you have a sunny windowsill you can plant a winter pot of lettuce or herbs. Divisions of chives should be dormant by now and can be brought indoors to grow again.

LAWNS

It's too late to start new grass this month. Wait until spring to correct any sparse areas.

HOUSEPLANTS & CONTAINERS

Purchase dormant amaryllis bulbs this month. Plant in containers that aren't much bigger than the bulb and keep the top one-third of the bulb above the soil level. Moisten the growing mix and leave in a sunny place until the flower stalk grows.

Terrariums are another form of miniature garden that are discussed in January.

PERENNIALS

By now all perennials should be in the ground. Any that are left are best kept in their nursery container until spring. Keep perennials protected on a deck by covering with mulch and burlap or sink the whole container into the ground until spring.

TREES

In warmer parts—Zone 6 and higher—if the ground is still warm and workable, dormant fruit trees can be planted or moved. Wait until all the leaves drop from the tree and consistently cooler weather has settled in. Don't move or plant if the soil is frozen or temperatures are below freezing. A better plan is to dig the hole for the tree now, fill with mulch, and then plant early next year.

CARE

The focus of care in November is winter protection. Most plants are dormant or close to that stage, and many areas are already getting snow.

BULBS

Store bulbs you're going to use for forcing this winter in a cold place. The bottom of a garage refrigerator and a shelf in the garage are ideal. Remember where you put them.

By the end of November, amaryllis bulbs should be showing lots of green leaves and hopefully a flower stalk. If your bulb was purchased, this occurs about two to four weeks after you plant it. For bulbs that were held over from last year and placed in the garden for summer, you may have a still-dormant bulb. Bring it into a warm and bright location and increase water to break the dormancy.

Look for the first Amaryllis sprouts of the season.

HERE'S HOW

TO CREATE A MINIATURE GARDEN

Miniature gardens are a version of classic terrariums that aren't contained in a covered container. Gardeners who have long winters especially love creating these little gardens and decorating them with a theme. Holiday themes are popular, as are fairy gardens, but tropical or conifer gardens are just as much fun. All miniature gardens create a welcome talking point in winter and can even be used as a hostess gift.

Fun miniature gardens are more of a miniature landscape and can depict anything you choose, from a tropical beach to a wooded hillside or a cottage garden. Keep plants in scale to fit the overall container. Accessories make the scene as individual as the creator. Add "snow" and a Santa to a woodland scene for seasonal interest.

For fairy gardens, add some natural wood furniture; fairies might use twigs and leaves for furniture. Though plants can be larger than a fairy figures, the furniture, doors, and accessories should be in scale with any figures. The plants should be in scale with the container overall. With a little imagination, your fairy garden will entertain all ages.

1. Pick a bowl, tray, or container to house the garden. Pick something that has a drainage hole at the base (or make one yourself), and that isn't too deep—3 to 6 inches is a good depth. The container can be any size but if you want to be able to move it around or give it as a gift, you should be able to lift it easily (and remember you will be adding soil and plant material).
2. Add a mesh screen to the bottom of the container so that potting material does not find its way onto your cabinet or tables. Set the container on a saucer or pan of gravel to catch water.
3. For most miniature gardens, fill the dish with a good potting mix—complete with slow-release fertilizer. Fill to 1 to 2 inches below the rim. For alpine gardens with conifers, use a slightly more acidic soil and gravel mix. A ratio of one-third each of peat moss, gravel, and sand is a standard recommendation. For succulents, a very dry mix is preferred. Use two-thirds dry pumice and vermiculite and one-third peat moss. Commercial mixes for succulents are available at most stores and can be used if you prefer.
4. Pick the plants for the garden:
   - For fairy gardens, the plants should be the sort that fairies might use: small creeping thyme or moss for lawns, tiny ferns, and miniature perennials like dwarf hostas or dwarf grasses.
   - For conifer gardens, junipers, Alberta spruce, arborvitae, as well as other trees have miniature varieties that work well.
   - For alpine gardens, a mix of small succulents like ice plants (*Delosperma floribundum*) or hens-and-chickens (*Sempervivum* varieties) plus some small grasses for height all work well.
5. Design the garden. Decide on an overall design, then plant. Include any dry "river" features you'll make from gravel and other non-plant elements like houses or arbors.
6. Plant. Carefully remove the plants from their containers and make a hole in the potting mix with your finger. Plant the miniature plant in the hole. Refill the hole.
7. Finish the garden. When all the plants and other elements such as pathways or cottages are in the garden, finish with some mulch or gravel.
8. Water lightly. Tiny plants are easy to drown and these gardens, particularly alpine and succulent gardens, don't like much water. Keep the plants in the garden in good light and enjoy your new garden.

Depending on when you brought the bulb inside, you may find the bulb does not have sufficient dormancy or that conditions are not warm enough for it to break dormancy. If things are delayed, your bulb might not be ready by Thanksgiving. Some may be delayed and don't bloom until even late January.

EDIBLES

With protection, some winter-hardy vegetables can be harvested all winter. Carrots and lettuces, as well as kale and chard, can be harvested if they're in a cold frame. Wait for the cold frame to warm up and melt any frost on the leaves before harvesting.

Pumpkins and winter squash vines wither when they're hit by frost, but many of the fruits can tolerate a little frost without damage. Harvest winter squash and store in a cool place; they keep for several weeks.

Indoor herbs on a kitchen windowsill are subject to splashes and humidity, so check for fungus and open a window on mild days to improve air circulation.

Low light conditions of midwinter are not sufficient to promote rapid growth of indoor herbs even if they're on a sunny window. Adding fertilizer will not improve this. Put your kitchen herb garden under a light for a few hours a day to increase the light levels and compensate for shorter days.

HOUSEPLANTS & CONTAINERS

Seasonal plants are in nurseries and home-improvement centers this month. Topiary rosemary, poinsettias, and colorful blooming cacti add color to the mantel or countertops. But taking plants from the store to the car to your kitchen is sometimes tricky. They don't like cold, and many November days are cold and windy. Buy them on a sunny day, if possible, and protect with bags and by hugging them against your body. Park as close to your house's door as you can to take the plants inside. Any damage will be seen in the first 24 hours but most will survive. Rosemary and cacti need a sunny location while the poinsettia can tolerate shadier interiors for a week or two. Locate the plants in a bright room away from drying air vents.

SHRUBS & ROSES

Shrubs that are borderline hardy for our area, such as crape myrtles in New Jersey and rosemary in Zone 6, as well as those in areas subject to heavy ice and wet snowstorms, should be protected for winter. Even if there's snow on the ground, you should still be able to get out and do this. Wrapping a shrub with burlap prevents cold winds from drying the shrub too much, and wrapping the branches protects them from heavy snow loads, which can snap branches. Evergreen and conifer shrubs can also be wrapped to protect them through winter storms. (See Care, Trees, in September for more on wrapping trees.)

Burlap and wrapping also helps stop deer browsing. Other options for deer include placing a fence of chicken wire around the shrub at a height sufficient to prevent deer from leaning over to munch. A 4-foot fence placed 2 to 3 feet away from the shrub should be sufficient.

TREES

You can buy a Christmas tree as a container tree, complete with roots, or as a cut tree. The first is for those who'd like to plant the tree when the season finishes. Containerized trees prefer to be kept in a cooler location than the typical tree and if you do purchase this type, let it transition slowly to your warm home. A few days in the garage help to get it ready to spend a week or two inside without dropping its needles. Rinse the tree with a hose to dislodge any insects and water well before bringing it indoors. After the season ends, transition the tree to the outside and plant in spring.

Small conifers are available for decorating outdoors. These trees aren't intended to come inside, but after the season make sure it's in a location that gets rain/snow rather than on a protected porch, where it will dry out quickly.

Traditional trees (fresh-cut, without roots) do better with a good rinse and few days in the garage before they are brought indoors. When you bring the tree indoors, keep it well watered to avoid the tree losing needles. If possible, locate holiday trees away from air vents that add to their dehydration problem.

Test all trees before you buy them by pulling at their needles. If you can pull the needles off, choose a different tree.

As heavy snow arrives, the boughs of young trees bend. After the snow event, shake the bough to remove snow before more arrives. Small trees can be helped by wrapping the boughs and securing with rope. (See Care, Trees, in September.)

WATER

All gardening is done indoors by now, and everything needs water to see it through winter.

Keep a fresh-cut Christmas tree reservoir filled with water. A long spout on a watering can directs water *into* the container rather than onto your floor.

EDIBLES

Rosemary is the most common herb to overwinter inside. Very few areas in our region have mild enough winters for rosemary to survive outside, but all too often, indoor care kills a plant too. Pay attention to water, light, and temperature. A bright but cool room is preferred, combined with sparse watering. The plant should not dry out, but daily watering is too much. A good watering every two weeks is sufficient. Unheated sunrooms and unused bedrooms are good places for rosemary to spend winter. Although rosemary is dormant and not growing, you can trim small bits off for cooking.

Water windowsill herbs as they grow. This is easier when they're on the kitchen windowsill.

HOUSEPLANTS & CONTAINERS

Seasonal rosemary topiaries that have been purchased for decoration are tightly packed and have higher water needs than others; they are best soaked weekly until after the holidays. Fill a sink about halfway up the rosemary's container and let it stand in water for about an hour. After the New Year, repot the rosemary into something more convenient to water, place it in a cool location, and

Long spouts on a watering can make it easier to water Christmas trees.

reduce watering. **Note:** These plants have usually been treated with chemicals and *are not* meant to be consumed. Give them until spring and only use new growth for recipes.

Poinsettias aren't quite as difficult and can be treated as any other houseplant. Water every other day unless a plants looks like it's drying out. Plants used to decorate working fireplaces dry out quicker than those in a central hallway. The decorative aluminum sleeve that comes with the plant prevents water from dripping onto the floor, but it also stops water from draining away from the roots. Be sure the sleeve is always free of any standing water. Or find a colorful container in which to place the poinsettia, complete with pot, for the season.

Seasonal cacti (which are really succulents rather than cacti) in bloom are watered enough to keep the soil moist. When their blooming ends, reduce water. These delightful succulents bloom profusely for many weeks and last for many years too.

Outdoor containers that have live conifers or other plant material in them need to be kept moist unless they receive rain or snowfall. Containers located in sheltered doorways won't get water from storms, so check them weekly for moisture. Already-decorated arborvitae in colorful containers are found at most hardware stores as well as nurseries. Next spring, plant these in the ground.

FERTILIZE

Very few plants need fertilizing this late in the season. Even indoor plants are getting used to long nights and short days, so many are heading into dormancy.

EDIBLES

Continue feeding windowsill herbs with weak compost tea every week. Use a compost tea bag and let it soak for five or six hours in a gallon of water. Full-strength compost tea requires a full day to steep.

HOUSEPLANTS & CONTAINERS

Tropical plants that were moved inside after summer should be given just half-strength fertilizer this month as they adjust to shorter days. Water houseplants that aren't dormant. Add a fertilizer to the water about once a month. Dormant plants, or those going dormant, don't need fertilizer (dormant plants don't produce new growth or flowers).

PROBLEM-SOLVE

Indoor conditions stress many plants, including seasonal ones. Check indoor plants for insects (now and all winter) and give them as much light as you can. Damp soil is a favorable condition to allow insects to develop around indoor plants. Reduce watering if you find little flying insects.

EDIBLES

Check windowsill herbs for aphids and insects that take advantage of weak plants. If you treat them, use a product intended for edible plants.

If you are growing mushrooms this winter, keep the box dark and moist but watch for fungus gnats that also enjoy those conditions. (See Problem-Solve, Edibles, in December for suggestions to keep this irritating insect at bay.)

Brush excess heavy snow from conifer branches.

HOUSEPLANTS & CONTAINERS

Allergies to Christmas trees are not uncommon, but some relief can be found by giving the tree a good rinse before bringing it into the house. Between dust and bugs from the field where they grew to the dusty container that they were transported in, there were lots of opportunities for debris to land on the tree branches, but most are removed by rinsing with the hose or letting rain fall on the tree. Let the tree thoroughly dry before bringing it inside.

Fertilize African violets by adding the fertilizer directly to the water in the self-watering container.

December

December is a seemingly endless round of visiting friends, gift buying, and entertaining, and decorating the home is part of the season's fun. Natural decorations for indoors and outdoors are easy to assemble from conifer branches and berries picked from the garden. If you don't have enough conifer branches, head down to the local home-improvement stores and nurseries, where they trim the bottom branches off Christmas trees. The discarded branches are often free for those who want them.

Gather a group of friends together and have a wreath-making party! Assemble a large pile of green branches from holly, conifers, and boxwood and set the pile on a tarp in the center of a room—an easy-to-sweep floor is better for this project than carpet. Get everyone to bring a 24- or 30-inch wire wreath base. You will also need some decorative items plus a ribbon for the bow and some floral wire to attach the boughs and berries to the base. Put some seasonal music on, add a seasonal drink, and spend a couple of hours chatting while putting together attractive wreaths for your doors. Door swags are easy to make too, and look great on lampposts, fence posts, and under lights as well as the front door.

This season is time to enjoy family and friends. The garden can be temporarily forgotten, but you might want to help out those who need suggestions for gifts. Gift cards to your favorite nursery (online or local), garden tools, and books all come in a range of prices to fit any budget. Gifts from your garden are always appreciated by others. Attractively packaged herbal vinegars or dried herb bundles are popular for the chef, a selection of seeds for a specific garden like a pizza garden is popular, particularly if you created the gift with seed saved from this year's peppers and oregano. Create a little terrarium or miniature garden as a gift for people who cannot get outside in winter. Add a fairy or two for young gardeners to enjoy as well—see page 170 for more about these gardens.

PLAN

With the holiday season in full swing, plan to keep indoor plants and your landscape safe from the activity. Keep plants in places where excited children and party crowds cannot bump them, and mark areas where visitors can safely park rather than having them mistake your flowerbed as a driveway.

BULBS

Check amaryllis and paperwhite bulbs frequently to see how close to blooming they are. When the bloom is just breaking, it's a good time to bring the bulb to the main living areas to display.

EDIBLES

How much turkey stuffing and general cooking will you be doing? Plan on getting fresh herbs from the store if your indoor plants aren't producing much right now. Note how much extra you use this year so you can increase your kitchen garden to accommodate that amount next year.

Poinsettias add color to fall containers indoors.

LAWNS

Do your party guests need to park on the grass? If you prefer them to park on the road or a specific place, put flags or rope out to protect the lawn. Markers showing where paths and lawns are located will be important when snow arrives.

HOUSEPLANTS & CONTAINERS

Welcome guests with a container incorporating colorful dogwood stems and conifer branches. Add a few berries and your winter container will give color for the whole season.

Along with poinsettias, Norwegian pines and miniature roses are popular seasonal plants. These aren't hardy plants and need to be treated as houseplants at least for winter. If you receive a miniature rose, find a place on a bright windowsill so it will continue to bloom.

Poinsettias don't need a lot of light for the few weeks that they are indoors, but you should keep them away from children and animals. Their sap contains an irritating substance similar to latex, and people with allergies should avoid contact with cut stems. If you're hosting a party with lots of activity, place them out of the general flow of traffic.

SHRUBS & ROSES

Birds are a bonus to gardening, and shrubs with berries attract colorful varieties. Next year, plan on getting roses that produce colorful hips in fall. Rugosa and Knock Out® roses both produce colorful rose hips. Native viburnums and *Callicarpa* have berries that the birds enjoy too.

Holly, with its bright red berries, is the most common winter attraction. Hollies are *dioecious*, meaning they need a male and a female plant to produce berries; there are varieties that are hardy to Zone 4 or colder.

TREES

If you plan on decorating outdoor shrubs and conifers with lights and baubles, find your outdoor electrical source and know how to run the lines. You'll need cords that are safe to use outdoors.

HERE'S HOW

TO ATTRACT BIRDS TO THE GARDEN

Having a garden that attracts birds gives indoor gardeners something interesting to watch all winter. A simple bird feeder attracts birds, but many other factors bring birds in too:

Grasses: Leave tall ornamental grasses uncut until spring so that the birds can sit on them awaiting their turn at the bird feeder.

Shrubs with Winter Berries: Holly, beautyberry, viburnums, coralberry, winterberry, cotoneaster, pyracantha, and yews attract birds with their berries but they also shelter birds from hawks and storms.

Conifers and Evergreen Shrubs: The dense cover from conifers is a perfect shelter for birds.

Perennial and Annual Flower Stalks: Many tall perennials make good landing places for birds. Anise hyssop, sedums, coneflowers, and black-eyed Susans are some of the more common perennials that birds can sit on. Sunflower heads are another attraction, and if left on the plants at the end of summer, finches and other birds enjoy the seeds as well as just sitting on them.

Water: Add a source for water, and you will see the birds drink and sometimes bathe in the water. Look for birdbaths that have an electrical coil to keep the water from freezing. The coil may not be sufficient to keep water free of ice in really cold weather, so check the instructions before you leave it out all winter.

Water is scarce for birds in winter, so add a heater to the bird bath to keep the water from freezing.

Decorate trees outdoors as well as indoors.

Look up into your trees to see if they have bunches of mistletoe. If not, you can try growing it. It takes several years to produce berries, but saving them this year is a good start. Remove the white berries and squeeze the sticky seeds out. Keep them on a saucer in a light place for sowing in late winter. (See Plant in February for how to plant seeds.)

VINES & GROUNDCOVERS

Holly and ivy are the traditional midwinter combination for decorations. English ivy is evergreen to Zone 4 and produces a lush groundcover in shady areas. Grow your own ivy next year for a good supply for decorations.

PLANT

Very little is planted this month, particularly outside.

ANNUALS

Small 4-inch containers of poinsettias can be repotted with other small poinsettias into a larger container. Incorporating different leaf and bract colors make attractive combinations.

BULBS

Continue planting dormant amaryllis this month. If purchased, use the container it came in and plant so that about two-thirds of the bulb is under the soil level.

EDIBLES

There is still time to plant an indoor herb garden as well as a container of lettuce. If you have a hydroponic system that is in a sunny location, you can start growing lettuce and herbs year-round. Some systems have the light source included, making it easy to grow edibles anywhere.

TREES

Live Christmas trees should be planted in a large container with drainage. Use good potting mix for the tree and cover the roots with the mix. Or leave the tree in its container and put the whole thing in a bucket that you decorate. Balled-and-burlapped trees can be put into a bucket and covered with mulch for the season. Stabilize trees in buckets with bricks. Keep all live trees watered and move them out of the warm family room as soon as the season is past. In January, transition the tree to be outside until you can plant it.

CARE

For those with children on winter vacation, there is lots of activity this month around the house. Keeping kids and pets away from indoor plants is a challenge, but some plants are poisonous, so be vigilant.

BULBS

Keep amaryllis and other forced bulbs in good light while their flower stalks are growing. Move to a sunny location when the flowers arrive.

EDIBLES

The biggest issue herbs face indoors is the light. If plants are looking stressed, leggy, and pale, move them into a sunnier location or provide a strong light source.

HOUSEPLANTS & CONTAINERS

Keep container plants away from drafts and drying vents. Windows that open to vent a kitchen allow cold drafts onto the plants, and forced air vents dry out plants quickly.

By the time poinsettias go on sale, their flower and colorful bracts have already been produced by being subjected to restricted daylight. Once the flower is produced, controlled sunlight is no longer needed. Poinsettia plants can tolerate shady locations for a few weeks, but give them a place them on a sunny windowsill for a few hours a week if possible.

TREES

Before installing a fresh-cut Christmas tree, recut the base of the trunk. Some sellers do this for you. The fresh cut allows water to be taken up by the tree, which keeps the needles fresher and on the tree, not the floor. After the trunk has been cut, get the tree home and into a water-filled container within two hours if possible. If you need to wait a day or two before bringing the tree inside, recut the trunk again.

WATER

Everything spending the winter indoors, from seasonal plants to trees to patio plants, needs watering.

BULBS

Water all bulbs that are actively growing. After the flower fades, reduce watering as the bulbs go into dormancy.

Water all indoor herbs and salad (lettuce) container plantings. Small containers need more water than larger ones, and kitchens tend to be warmer than many other rooms.

If rosemary is kept cool, it needs little water. If kept on the kitchen windowsill, it needs a little more.

HOUSEPLANTS & CONTAINERS

Check water levels on all indoor containers and plants at least every day. Moist but not wet soil is good for most plants.

Seasonal rosemary topiaries need a good soak in a sink about every two weeks to keep them alive through the season.

Outdoor containers that include live plants, such as little conifers, look great on the porch steps but they need to be watered if they are under a roof overhang. Check that they're getting sufficient moisture. After the holidays, remove all the trimmings from the tree and move it farther out from the house so that it can take advantage of rain and snow.

Keep a poinsettia moist for the season. The amount of moisture depends on temperature and humidity; adjust daily. Empty water that drains out of the container promptly.

TREES
Keep the water container under the Christmas tree full.

FERTILIZE

Midwinter day length is not conducive to active plant growth. Cloudy, snowy days when no sun arrives doesn't help either. During these conditions, fertilizer is not needed.

BULBS
Bulbs that are actively putting up flower stalks need a half-strength general fertilizer application.

EDIBLES
Feed plants that have been indoors for more than a month with a compost tea to add a few nutrients to the soil.

HOUSEPLANTS & CONTAINERS
Unless containers have actively growing or flowering plants in them, they don't need fertilizing. If flowers are still being produced, a half-strength general fertilizer is beneficial.

A purchased poinsettia has enough fertilizer in its mix to last into next year, so no fertilizer is needed.

PROBLEM-SOLVE

Low light levels and indoor heating stress plants, which makes them a perfect target for insects. Outside, animal damage starts because when snow covers the ground, there is less for animals to eat and your landscape is a target. Check tracks in snow, or put a night camera out to see who is browsing and where.

ANNUALS
Watch for toys in poinsettias and other containers left by children visiting over the holiday. Regular watering keeps the plants from dropping leaves too soon.

BULBS
Watch for animal damage to planted outdoor bulbs and those sitting on the surface of a flowerbed. Rebury anything that is dug up as soon as possible. Squirrels like to bury nuts in the same areas that you plant. Their work unearths bulbs, which are left on the surface of a flowerbed.

EDIBLES
Check under the leaves of basil and other indoor edibles for aphids or whiteflies. Indoor mushroom kits are fun to grow, but the material causes fruit flies and gnats to arrive as well. A thin coating of vegetable oil around the plastic bag that contains the mushroom mix can help trap the flies. Other suggestions are a cup of cider vinegar plus a drop of detergent to drown them. The cup of vinegar is placed next to the mushroom box and attracts the flies.

HOUSEPLANTS & CONTAINERS
Keep cats from using large containers as a convenient litter tray. Sprays to deter them work with some cats, gravel mulch helps, and covering the potting mix with a cloth also helps.

SHRUBS & ROSES
Heavy snow and winds damage shrubs and roses, so protect them by wrapping with burlap.

TREES
Large, decorated Christmas trees have been known to topple over, particularly if you have cats around. Anchor the tree upright with wires fixed to the ceiling or to a sturdy picture hook in the wall.

Squirrels continue to bury their hoard until the ground is frozen.

Glossary

Acclimate: To become gradually accustomed to a different environment.

Acidic soil: Soil that has a pH reading of 6.0 and lower. Mildly acidic is 6.0 to 7.0. Lime counteracts overly acidic soil to make it more alkaline.

Aerate (aeration): To introduce oxygen into the soil. In lawns, it's commonly done with equipment that pulls cores of soil out of the ground, depositing them on the surface.

Alkaline soil: Soil that has a pH greater than 7.0. Sulfur counteracts overly alkaline soil to make it more acidic.

Annual: A plant that lives its entire life in one season and dies at the end of that year.

Anti-transpirant/anti-desiccant: A product that reduces a plant's moisture loss by coating the foliage with a thin film—usually a type of oil, resin, or wax.

Arborist: A person trained to care for trees. Certified arborists have met the qualifications of professional organizations.

***Bacillus thuringiensis* (Bt):** A bacterium that kills caterpillars by attacking the digestive system. Available as a dust or powder that's mixed in water and sprayed on plant foliage when caterpillars are feeding.

Balanced fertilizer: A granular or liquid fertilizer with approximately equal proportions of the three key nutrients listed on product labels—nitrogen (the first number), phosphorus (the second number), and potassium (the third number).

Balled and burlapped: Describes trees and shrubs grown in the field, then dug with roots wrapped with protective burlap and twine for transport and sale.

Bare root: Plants that are shipped dormant, without being planted in soil or having soil around their roots.

Basal: Refers to growth emerging from around the base, trunk, or main origin of a plant.

Beneficial insects: Insects or their larvae that prey on pest organisms and their eggs. Examples: ladybugs, parasitic wasps, soldier bugs, predatory nematodes, and spiders.

Biennial: A plant that grows over two seasons, usually growing foliage only in the first year, and then flowering, setting seed, and dying in the second.

Bract: A petal-like modified leaf structure of a plant stem, growing near its flower. Often, it is more colorful and visible than the actual flower, as in dogwood or poinsettia.

Broadleaf evergreen: A plant that holds its leaves all season and has wider leaves, as opposed to needles. Examples: boxwood, holly, rhododendron and cherry laurel.

Bud union (graft): The point on the stem of a plant where a desirable branch or stem (scion) is attached to a plant growing in the ground (rootstock). Roses are commonly grafted.

Canopy: The overhead branching area or "reach" of a tree, including foliage.

Cell packs: Multi-compartment containers, usually made out of thin plastic and used to sell small plants, most often annual flowers and vegetables.

Chlorosis: A nutritional deficiency in plants, usually indicated by yellowed foliage with green veins. Most common in plants that require acidic soil, it's a sign that plants are unable to take up sufficient iron from the soil.

Climber: A plant that grows vertically by means of elongating stems. It may twist or cling to surfaces to pull itself up, or it may need ties to help guide it upward.

Cold hardiness: The ability of a perennial plant to survive the winter cold in a particular area. The U.S. Department of Agriculture assigns cold-hardiness ratings by zone based on winter's average lows in a given area.

Compost: Organic matter that has decomposed into a spongy, fluffy texture. It adds nutrition to soil and aids its ability to hold air and water and to drain well.

Corm: A fat, flat, scaly underground stem that's planted underground similar to a bulb. Leaves and flowers emerge from nodes on the corm. Examples: crocus, gladiolus, freesia.

Crown: The part of a plant at or near the soil surface from which the stems emerge. Sometimes referred to as the "growth point" of a plant.

Cultivar: A CULTIvated VARiety. A plant that has been bred or selected for having one or more distinct traits from the species and then given a name to set it apart. 'Pardon Me,' for example, is a cultivar of daylily.

Damping off: A fungal disease that targets young seedlings. Spores in the soil cause seedling stems to blacken and collapse. Using sterile potting medium helps prevent this problem.

Deadhead: To remove dead flowers in order to encourage further bloom, neaten the plant, and/or prevent the plant from self-sowing.

Deciduous: A plant that loses its leaves seasonally, typically in fall or early winter.

Direct-seed: To sow seeds directly into the garden rather than starting them in small pots ahead of time.

Division: Splitting apart plants to create two or more smaller, rooted sections. Useful for controlling a plant's size and for acquiring more plants.

Dormancy (dormant): The period, usually winter, when perennial plants temporarily cease active growth, and rest. Some plants, such as spring-blooming bulbs, go dormant in the summer.

Drip irrigation: A water-delivery system that uses supply lines (usually plastic) and emitters that slowly deliver water directly to the soil around plants or pots.

Drip line: Can refer both to the outer reaches of a tree's branching canopy where rainfall drips from branch tips or to a line that's part of a drip-irrigation system.

Establishment: The time needed for a newly planted or transplanted tree, shrub, or flower to produce enough growth (especially roots) so that it's adapted to its new environment. An "established" plant no longer requires the additional care needed immediately following planting or transplanting.

Evergreen: A plant that keeps its leaves year-round, instead of dropping them seasonally. These can be needled plants as well as broadleaf ones.

Fertilizer: Any material that, when added to the soil, contributes one or more nutrients required by plants. These include nitrogen, phosphorus, potassium, sulfur, magnesium, calcium, iron, manganese, boron, chlorine, zinc, copper, molybdenum, and nickel.

Floating row cover: A lightweight blanket, often made out of spun-bounded polyester or similar woven fabric, that's draped over plants to protect them from light frost or bug damage. The covers are porous enough to let in light and rain.

Foliage: The leafy tissue of a plant, including needles as well as wider leaves.

Forcing bulbs: The process of potting dormant bulbs, then giving them the necessary chilling time before taking them into warmth to encourage earlier-than-usual bloom.

Frost: Ice crystals that form when the temperature falls below freezing. Tender plants die when frost kills their leaf cells.

Fungicide: A product that acts to prevent, control, or eradicate plant diseases caused by fungi.

Germinate: To sprout. Usually refers to the initial growth of seeds.

Girdling roots: Roots that circle around the base of a tree or shrub rather than growing outward into the soil.

GMO: Refers to genetically modified organisms, which involves altering a plant or animal's genetic makeup by inserting or removing genes.

Grubs: Fat, off-white, worm-like larval stage of an insect, most often beetles and especially Japanese beetles. They hatch in the soil and feed on plant (especially grass) roots until transforming into adults.

Habitat: The living environment of a plant or animal. A native habitat of a plant or bug refers to the setting in which it's found naturally.

Handpick: To eliminate pest insects, slugs, or caterpillars by plucking or knocking them from plant foliage into a container or jar of soapy water.

Hardening off: The process of gradually acclimating seedlings and young plants grown in an indoor environment to the outdoors.

Hardscape: The permanent, structural, non-plant parts of a landscape, such as walls, sheds, pools, patios, arbors, benches, and walkways.

Hardware cloth: A stiff, metal fencing with small openings, usually used to protect trees and shrubs from rodent damage.

Herbaceous: Describes plants that have fleshy or soft stems that die back with frost.

Herbicide: A product designed to kill plants, typically weeds. Some act on foliage and stem tissues, some act on seeds.

Hybrid: A plant produced by crossing two genetically different plants, usually to achieve a desired trait, new color, or some other perceived improvement.

Hydrogel crystals: Also known as polymer crystals or water-absorbing crystals, these are clear or white dry granules about the size of coarse salt grains that can absorb and hold up to 600 times their weight in water. They're typically sold as watering aids, especially for use in potted plants.

Insecticide: A product designed to kill insects.

Integrated Pest Management (IPM): A method of controlling garden pests and diseases aimed at having minimal envionmental impact.

Larva(e): An insect in its immature stage after it hatches from an egg. Typically either a worm or caterpillar form of a butterfly, moth, or beetle.

Leader: The term for the center or main trunk of a tree.

Lime: Limestone processed as granules, pellets, or powder for use in adding calcium to soils, thereby making it less acidic and more alkaline (increasing the pH reading). Dolomite limestone also contributes magnesium.

Microclimate: Small sections of a property that deviate slightly from the prevailing, surrounding climate. A courtyard with stone walls, for example, likely will have warmer, less-windy conditions than the rest of a yard.

Mulch: A layer of material placed over bare soil to protect it from erosion, to slow evaporation loss, and/or to suppress weeds. It can be inorganic (gravel, plastic, fabric) or organic (wood chips, bark, pine needles, chopped leaves).

Native: Indigenous. Native plants are those determined to have been growing in a particular region before the arrival of European settlers.

Naturalize: (a) To plant seeds, bulbs, or plants in a random, informal pattern as they would appear in their natural habitat. (b) The tendency of some non-native plants to adapt to and spread throughout their adopted habitats.

New wood: The current year's growth. Usually used in reference to a plant "flowering or fruiting on new wood," meaning the flower buds form on the new growth.

Node: A swollen joint or ridged scar on a plant stem from which a leaf or smaller stem will (or could) emerge.

Old wood: Growth that's more than one season old. Some plants produce fruits or flowers only on older growth, not the current season's growth.

Organic matter: Gardening-wise, it's material or debris derived from plants. Technically, it's carbon-based material that's capable of undergoing decomposition and decay.

Perennial: A flowering plant that lives three or more seasons. Some die back with frost and generate new shoots in spring; others hold their stems and leaves throughout winter.

Pesticide: A product designed to kill pests, including bugs, disease pathogens, pest animals, or weeds.

pH: A figure designating the acidity or the alkalinity of soil as measured on a scale of 0 to 14, with 7.0 being neutral.

Pinch: To remove tender stems and/or leaves by pressing them between thumb and forefinger. It's a pruning technique used to encourage branching, compactness, and flowering or to remove bugs or diseased leaves.

Photosynthesis: The process by which plants, collecting energy from the sun by means of the chlorophyll in their foliage, transform carbon dioxide in the air and water from the soil into carbohydrates that fuel their growth.

Pollen: The yellow, powdery grains in the center of a flower. A plant's male sex cells, they are transferred to the female plant parts by means of wind or animal pollinators to fertilize them and create seeds.

Pollination: The transfer of pollen for fertilization from the male pollen-bearing organ (stamen) to the female organ (pistil), usually by wind, bees, butterflies, moths, or hummingbirds.

Pre-emergent: Acting prior to the germination of a seed. Describes a product that inhibits the sprouting of a seed (as in pre-emergent herbicide).

Rhizome: An underground horizontal stem that grows side shoots. Examples: canna, ginger, most iris.

Rootball: The network of roots and soil clinging to a plant when it is lifted out of the ground or pot.

Rootbound (or potbound): The condition of a plant that has been confined to a container too long, its roots having been forced to wrap around themselves and even swell out of the container.

Root flare: The point at the base of a tree where the trunk transitions into the roots. This point starts to widen and should be visible just above grade if a tree is planted at the correct depth.

Rootstock: The part of a grafted plant that's growing in the ground and providing the root system. A desirable stem or branch (scion) is attached to the rootstock.

Root zone: The area that the roots of a plant occupy or can be expected to spread to when mature.

Scion: The ornamental or desirable part of a grafted plant. Usually refers to a cutting, shoot, stem, branch, or bud that is attached to a rootstock, the in-ground plant that's supplying the root system.

Self-seeding (self-sowing): Describes the tendency of some plants to drop or distribute their seeds freely, which then sprout on their own. Can be a wanted or unwanted trait.

Shearing: A pruning technique in which plant stems and branches are cut uniformly with long-bladed pruning shears (hedge shears) or powered hedge trimmers. Used in creating and maintaining hedges and topiary.

Slow-acting fertilizer: Also sometimes called slow-release or gradual-release fertilizer, this is a product that's water-insoluble, releasing its nutrients gradually as it breaks down. Typically granular, it may be either organic or synthetic.

Sod: Sections of soil in which turfgrass plants are already growing.

Soil test: Chemical analysis of soil to determine its fertility, pH, and nutrients. This is usually done by private laboratories or state university facilities. Less-sophisticated tests can be done by gardeners using kits available at garden centers.

Spores: Microscopic particles that allow fungi to reproduce themselves, similar to the function of seeds in a flowering plant.

Sucker: A new growing shoot. Underground plant roots produce suckers to form new stems and spread by means of these suckering roots to form colonies. Some plants produce root suckers or branch suckers as a result of pruning or wounding.

Sulfur: An element that's both a plant nutrient and a key product in making soil more acidic (i.e., lowering the soil pH). Mixed with water, it's also used as a fungicide.

Stippling: A description of plant damage to leaves. Stippled leaves are discolored due to loss of chlorophyll removed by tiny insects that insert small feeding holes throughout the leaf.

Thinning: The process of removing selected sprouts from a crowded planting, or removing excess branches from a woody plant.

Transplant: The process of digging and relocating a plant. In noun form, it's a young plant that is mature enough to be planted outdoors in a garden bed or pot.

Transplant shock: The stress or damage a plant undergoes after it's been moved from one setting or location to another.

Tropical plant: A plant that's native to a tropical region of the world and typically not able to survive frost.

Tuber: Enlarged roots that send out shoots and roots from nodes along their surface. Examples: dahlia, cyclamen, perennial (tuberous) begonias.

Turfgrass: Short grasses that are mowed and used in lawns as opposed to ornamental grasses, which are left to grow as landscape plants.

Variegated: The appearance of differently colored areas on plant leaves, usually white, yellow, or a brighter green.

Water sprout: A vertical shoot that emerges from tree branches. These should usually be pruned off.

Weed preventer: A product distributed in advance of a weed outbreak that either stops weeds from sprouting or kills them before they develop. Also known as a pre-emergent herbicide.

Index

Photo Credits

Heather Claus: 14 (left), 60, 84 (left)

Kate Copsey: 20 (right), 24 (left), 25 (left), 26, 28, 34 (right), 35 (both), 38, 46, 51, 52, 53 (bottom), 67 (both), 71 (top), 81, 84 (right), 95, 98, 100, 101 (all), 106 (bottom), 113 (top, both), 116 (left, top right), 124, 132, 133, 134, 139 (top), 149 (left), 151 (both), 152, 156, 163

Katie Elzer-Peters: 27, 36-37, 58 (all), 71 (middle, bottom), 77 (both), 90 (both), 108, 111, 112 (left), 116 (right, bottom), 118, 120, 121 (top three), 122 (top), 125, 126, 127 (both), 138, 139 (bottom), 143, 153, 157, 158 (left), 159, 173 (bottom)

Tom Eltzroth: 63 (right)

Bill Kersey: 10, 17, 39, 42 (all), 44 (both), 50, 56 (both), 61, 80, 92 (left), 94, 96, 122 (bottom)

Shutterstock: 6, 9 (left), 11, 12 (both), 14 (right), 15 (both), 18, 20 (left), 24 (right), 25 (right), 29, 31, 32, 34 (left), 40, 47, 48, 53 (top), 59, 64, 66, 82, 92 (right), 104 (bottom), 106 (top), 112 (right), 113 (bottom), 114, 117, 121 (bottom left), 130, 135, 140, 142 (both), 154, 158 (right), 161, 164, 167 (all), 168, 169, 172, 173 (top), 174, 176, 177 (both), 179

Neil Soderstrom: 41, 57, 91, 104 (top), 136, 149 (right)

Bibliography

Ballister-Howells, Pegi. *New Jersey Gardener's Guide*. Minneapolis, MN: Cool Springs Press, 2004.

Bigss, Steven. *Grow Figs Where You Think You Can't*. Canada: No Guff Press, 2012.

Dirr, Michael A. *Manual of Woody Landscape Plants*. Champaign, IL: Stipes Publishing LLC, 2009.

Elzer-Peters, Katie. *Beginner's Illustrated Guide to Gardening*. Minneapolis, MN: Cool Springs Press, 2012.

Frutig-Bales, Suzanne. *Burpee American Gardening Series: Vines*. New York, NY: Macmillan, 1995.

Gasteiger, Daniel. *Yes, You Can! And Freeze and Dry It, Too*. Minneapolis, MN: Cool Springs Press, 2011.

Hill, Lewis and Leonard Perry. *The Fruit Gardener's Bible*. North Adams, MA: Storey Publishing LLC, 2011.

Jabbour, Nikki. *The Year-Round Vegetable Gardener*. North Adams, MA: Storey Publishing LLC, 2011.

Myers, Melinda. *Minnesota & Wisconsin Getting Started Garden Guide*. Minneapolis, MN: Cool Spring Press, 2013.

Viette, Andre and Mark Viette. *Month-By-Month Gardening in New York*. Minneapolis, MN: Cool Springs Press, 2005.

Walliser, Jessica. *Good Bug Bad Bug*. Pittsburgh, PA: St. Lynn's Press, 2008.

Wolk, Art. *Bulb Forcing for Beginners and the Seriously Smitten*. Voorhees, NJ: Aab Book Publishing LLC, 2012.

Zachos, Ellen. *Tempting Tropicals*. Portland, OR: Timber Press, 2005

Ziegler, Lisa Mason. *Cool Flowers*. Pittsburgh, PA: St. Lynn's Press, 2014.

Meet Kate Copsey

Kate grew up in England, where vegetables were always part of the garden.

Kate was the first host of the popular *America's Home Grown Veggie Show* and continued as host for over six years with the program. She was a national board member for The Herb Society of America, and is currently on the board of the Garden Writers Association.

As a writer, Kate has written for local, regional, and international newspapers, as well as a variety of magazines.

Kate also enjoys giving presentations to the public and has always been a popular regional speaker wherever she has lived. Her talks range from basic gardening to herbs and vegetables, including growing vegetables in containers.

She was certified as a Master Gardener in Virginia in 2000 and has kept that certification through several states. Over the past years, she has lived in Buffalo and Albany, New York, and currently gardens in central New Jersey, where she lives with her husband and two cats.